YEARNING

YEARNING
race, gender, and cultural politics

bell hooks

South End Press   Boston, MA

Publication Acknowledgments:
Grateful acknowledgment is made to the following publications for permission to use previously published material: *Zeta Magazine, Inscriptions, Art Forum, Sojourner, Framework, Emerge.*

Special thanks to Katherine Wendy Hanna for her work on the bibliography.

Cover design by Tanya Mckinnon and Cynthia Peters
Typesetting and design by the South End Press collective
Printed in the United States on acid-free paper

Library of Congress Catalog Card Number: 90-10196
Library of Congress Cataloging-in-Publication Data
hooks, bell
    Yearning.
    1. Afro-Americans—Social Conditions. 2. Feminism—United States. 3. Sex Role—United States. I. Title.

E185.86.H742 1990   305.896'073—dc20   90-10196

ISBN 0-89608-385-3 (pbk.)
ISBN 0-89608-386-1 (cloth)

South End Press, 116 Saint Botolph Street, Boston, MA 02115

99 98 97 96 95 94 93 92 91   3 4 5 6 7 8 9

for you to whom i surrender
to you for whom i wait

ACKNOWLEDGMENTS

Many of these essays were born in the heat of passionate dialogues, sometimes even at moments of intense emotional pain. Deeply grateful for the loosely constructed "community" of progressive black intellectuals who have been "on my bone," I thank you! Gwenda, my sister who "takes" the word and spreads it. Ehrai, my childhood friend who is always there for critical exchange. A.J. who never lets me forget the ecstasy of the Word, with whom I talk in the long hours of sleepless nights. Michele Wallace a colleague with whom I go to the wall. Saidiya whose encouragement sustains and makes the journey sweet. Cornel West a true friend of my mind. Paul Gilroy who helps me put the broken bits and pieces of my heart together again. And lastly those wild and funky theorists in the making, "the diva girls": I thank you. Especially, I thank Dionne whose courage and perserverance light the path, making a way for others. And lastly I am grateful to Tanya, Daughter of the Yam, my spiritual child, whom I have witnessed grow into liberatory consciousness. From student to teacher, she stands by my side—woman to woman, guiding me through the editing of this book, always challenging me to live out the truth of my words.

CONTENTS

Women yearn for change and will make great sacrifices for it.

—Lydia
A Dream Compels Us: Voices of Salvadoran Women

In this world-weary period of pervasive cynicisms, nihilisms, terrorisms, and possible extermination, there is a longing for norms and values that can make a difference, a yearning for principled resistance and struggle that can change our desperate plight.

—Cornel West
The American Evasion of Philosophy

I was moved by violent conflicts and yearnings, a need to be reassured in love that all but obscured any expression of loving.

—Robert Duncan

It was, gentleman, after a long absence—seven years to be exact, during which time I was studying in Europe—that I returned to my people. I learnt much and much passed me by—but that is another story. The important thing is that I return with a great yearning for my people in that small village at the bend of the Nile. For seven years I had longed for them, had dreamed of them, and it was an extraordinary moment when I at last found myself standing amongst them. They rejoiced at having me back and made a great fuss, and it was not long before I felt as though a piece of ice were melting inside of me, as though I were some frozen substance on which the sun had shone— that life warmth of the tribe which I had lost for a time...

—Tayeb Salih
Season of Migration to the North

1

LIBERATION SCENES

speak this yearning

Lorraine Hansberry's play *A Raisin in the Sun* was recently made into a film and shown to a mass audience on the PBS series *American Playhouse*. Opening on Broadway in 1959, it was a first. Lorraine Hansberry was the youngest American playwright, the fifth woman, the only black writer, and of course the first black woman writer to win the New York Drama Critics Circle Award for "Best Play of the Year." When it was first produced, *A Raisin in the Sun* was in many ways a counter-hegemonic cultural production. The play "interrogated" the fear within black people that being out of our place—not conforming to social norms, especially those set by white supremacy, would lead to destruction, even death. On a basic level, the play was about housing—the way racial segregation in a capitalist society meant that black folks were discriminated against when seeking places to live. It made it clear that the Younger family was not interested in being a part of white culture, in assimilation; they wanted better housing.

As counter-hegemonic cultural production, the play *A Raisin in the Sun* was full of contradictions. Though anti-assimilationist, it evoked the possibility of moving from one set of class values to another, working-class people aspiring to middle-class lifestyles. The play promises that the traditional black folk culture and value system epitomized and expressed by Mama will be maintained in the new location. These are the values that lead Mama to ask Walter Lee, who thinks only about a capitalist materialist sense of success, "Since when did money become life?" Warning against rooting one's sense of identity, culture, and value in materialism, Mama reminds her family that black people survived the holocaust of slavery because they had oppositional ways of thinking, ones that were different from the structures of domination determining so much of their lives. Critiques of materialism were crucial for black people seeking to preserve dignity in a rapidly developing consumer capitalist world. It is that world Walter Lee wants to join. His desire to take the insurance money and buy a liquor store links consumer capitalism with the production of a world of addiction. With visionary foresight, Hansberry suggests the possibility that substances (alcohol, drugs, etc.) and substance abuse threaten black solidarity, acting as a genocidal force in the black community.

In retrospect, *A Raisin in the Sun* prophetically hinted at the way consumer capitalism and racial integration would, in the near future, transform the lives of black people. Walter Lee as potential advanced capitalist monster, consumed as he is by desire for material things, symbolically represents the possible fate of poor black people in contemporary culture. He is saved by Mama and old world values. Walter Lee is consumed by "yearning." His longing for money, goods, power, and control over his destiny made him symbolic of the black American underclass in the fifties and early sixties. Ironically, when the play reached a contemporary public in the eighties, Walter Lee (played by Danny Glover) was portrayed as a crazed, angry, dangerous black man. Gone was Walter Lee as symbolic representation of collective black "yearning"; in his place stood the isolated black male terrorist, an image which lived up to a white audience's racist notions of contemporary black masculinity.

I was stunned by the way in which the contemporary re-visioning of Hansberry's play made it no longer a counter-hegemonic cultural production but a work that fit with popular racist stereotypes of black masculinity as dangerous, threatening, etc. Attempting to make this play accessible to a predominantly white mass audience, the work was altered so that the interpretation of specific roles would correspond with prefabricated notions of black identity, particularly black male identity. A powerful example of the way in which contemporary commodification of black culture strips work of the potential to be counter-hegemonic, this production received little critical attention. Even though it was "trashed" and critiqued in any number of personal conversations engaged in by black artists and intellectuals, no one made it the subject for extensive public cultural critique. Whenever a work by a black writer receives attention, acclaim, or recognition in mainstream cultural circles these days, black critics rarely respond with harsh critique. Or in the case of a drama, like *Driving Miss Daisy* created by a white writer with a major role for a black actor the tacit assumption seems to be that since the success of this play (which also became a film) catapulted black actors into greater stardom, it was above critical reproach. Again it was easier for black artists and intellectuals to challenge the sentimentalizing of race relations in this rather boring status quo cultural production in conversation among ourselves. Folks could admit to having been moved by the sentimental drama of *Driving Miss Daisy* in the same way some black viewers are touched by *Gone with the Wind,* even though politically they recognize the way the reproduction of cultural products which encourage and romanticize race relations that are rooted in domination dangerously undermines efforts to create critical consciousness of the need to eradicate racism.

Cultural criticism has historically functioned in black life as a force promoting critical resistance, one that enabled black folks to cultivate in everyday life a practice of critique and analysis that would disrupt and even deconstruct those cultural productions that were designed to promote and reinforce domination. In other words, a poor black family, like the one I was raised in, might sit around watching *Amos n' Andy*—enjoying it even as we simultaneously critiqued it—talking about the ways this cultural production served the interests of white supremacy. We knew we were not watching representations of ourselves created by black artists or progressive white folks. Within the context of an apartheid social structure where practically every aspect of black life was determined by the efforts of those in power to maintain white supremacy, black folks were incredibly vigilant. Not only was there in black life an obsessive concern with racial uplift (doing all that was necessary to improve the quality of black life), there was an ongoing recognition of the need to oppose and denounce representations of blackness created by racist white folks. When we sat in our living rooms in the fifties and early sixties watching those few black folks who appeared on television screens, we talked about their performance, but we always talked about the way the white folks were treating them. I have vivid memories of watching the Ed Sullivan show on Sunday nights, of seeing on that show the great Louis Armstrong. Daddy, who was usually silent, would talk about the music, the way Armstrong was being treated, and the political implications of his appearance. Watching television in the fifties and sixties, and listening to adult conversation, was one of the primary ways many young black folks learned about race politics.

Another vivid memory that comes to mind is watching *Imitation of Life* with my five sisters, one of the first screen dramas that linked issues of race, gender, and sexuality. Participating in household discussions about these works, many of us developed critical consciousness about the politics of race. Responding to televised cultural production, black people could express rage about racism as it informed representation, the construction of images. Then there was no passive consumption of images. How indeed could black viewers passively consume a film like *Birth of a Nation* when we lived daily with the threat of lynchings and the reality of racial murder. How could little black girls growing to womanhood in a segregated south so charged with sexualized violence—you knew every time you walked from your mama's place to your grandmama's to avoid any direct eye contact with white men in cars, and not to be caught in any secluded place alone with white men because you might be raped—not feel the sexual terrorism that is an underlying tension in *Imitation of Life*. Our gaze was not passive. The screen was not a place of escape. It was a place of confrontation and encounter.

No one has studied enough the extent to which racial integration changed black response to the culture industry and to cultural production. That collective critical black gaze, developed in the context of resistance to overt racist discrimination and racial violence, was altered in the late sixties and seventies as barriers were crossed and white folks behind the scenes of mass media (particularly television and film) suddenly realized that despite racism, perhaps even because of racial taboos, white viewers would in fact not only accept the presence of black images on the screen but actually be captivated by them. Media coverage of black civil rights struggles, the black power movement, race riots, and the like made for exciting news. Violence was on the screen in living color in a way that captured the attention of mass audiences. Black images were commodified as never before in history.

Unfortunately, all that counter-hegemonic cultural criticism that had been honed and developed in black living rooms, kitchens, barber shops, and beauty parlors did not surface in a different form. Black folks were not engaged in writing a body of critical cultural analysis that would keep pace with the proliferation of images. The primary form that black cultural criticism took was the question of good or bad images. This critical response corresponded with a political emphasis on reform. If the goal of reform-oriented black liberation struggle was equality within existing societal structures, then it followed that there would be passive acceptance of the commodification of black cultural life as long as the images produced were seen as "good" or "positive." And that would be determined by whether or not the images created were seen as helping to bring about racial inclusion in the mainstream.

Placing cultural critique by black critics solely in the reformist realm of debate about good and bad images effectively silenced more complex critical dialogue. No wonder then that there has not been, until very recently, concern about creating cultural spaces wherein larger numbers of black thinkers can be encouraged to do cultural critique. Current emphasis on the development of cultural studies in academic settings as well as the production of more and more publications that are willing to publish diverse perspectives on culture is helping create a climate where more black artists and intellectuals can do cultural criticism.

Changes in black responses to media created by consumer capitalism (we are a much more passive audience these days) must be talked about if we are to understand the ways black liberation struggles and, most particularly, the decolonizing of our minds is affected by media. In the introduction to *Cultural Politics In Contemporary America*, Ian Angus and Sut Jhally offer powerful reasons cultural critics must confront the power of representations as they affect the formation of social identity:

> In contemporary culture the media have become central to the constitution of social identity. It is not just that media messages have become important forms of influence on individuals. We also identify and construct ourselves as social beings through the mediation of images. This is not simply a case of people being dominated by images, but of people seeking and obtaining pleasure through the experience of the consumption of these images. An understanding of contemporary culture involves a focus on both the phenomenology of watching and the cultural form of images.

Within black communities, fundamental changes in conceptions of social identity occurred after the seventies. The collective critical black gaze that was central to an orally transmitted cultural politics of resistance was fundamentally altered. Replaced by an ethic in complete contradiction to those values stressed by Mama in *A Raisin in the Sun*, the emphasis was on finding work for black folks in the culture industry. And if indeed that work was well paid, then that would override any need to question the politics underlying certain representations.

Cultural critique is particularly relevant to black artists and/or intellectuals who see ourselves as committed to an ongoing black liberation struggle with a central emphasis on decolonization. Education for critical consciousness is the most important task before us. Working in the academy, as many of us do, it is through a liberatory pedagogy that we make useful critical intervention. Two important spaces for the transmission of our ideas are writing and speaking. In college and university settings, meeting the demands of one's profession often makes it difficult to do work that is fundamentally an expression of radical political commitment. Many academics involved with cultural studies do not see their work as emerging from an oppositional, progressive, cultural politic that seeks to link theory and practice, that has as its most central agenda sharing knowledge and information in ways that transform how we think about our social reality. Witnessing colleagues who are indifferent to the concrete needs of marginalized groups claim cultural studies as their privileged domain is disconcerting and potentially disillusioning. However, it does not cause me to despair, because I see the power of progressive cultural criticism in the classroom setting and recognize that location as a crucial site for critical intervention. Therefore it would be a grave mistake to abandon the field to those thinkers who are primarily concerned with professional advancement.

I have found that students are much more engaged when they are learning how to think critically and analytically by exploring concrete aspects of their reality, particularly their experience of popular culture. Teaching theory, I find that students may understand a particular paradigm in the abstract but are unable to see how to apply it to their lives. Focusing on popular culture has been one of the main ways to bridge this gap. When Spike Lee's film *Do The Right Thing* was initially shown, black students studying feminist theory with me, who had begun to apply a feminist analysis rooted in an understanding of race and class, felt conflicted. They enjoyed the film but were disturbed by aspects of the work. Black male students came to talk with me, bringing their buddies, because they were in conflict over their different interpretations of the film. They were deeply concerned with the issue of whether negative critique meant they were not supportive of a brother (i.e., Spike Lee) who is trying to make it and be in solidarity with blackness. Also they feared that disagreement among themselves might disrupt feelings of racial bonding and solidarity. Again, as we educate one another to acquire critical consciousness, we have the chance to see how important airing diverse perspectives can be for any progressive political struggle that is serious about transformation. Engaging in intellectual exchange where people hear a diversity of viewpoints enables them to witness first hand solidarity that grows stronger in a context of productive critical exchange and confrontation.

One issue that surfaces when teaching the skills of radical cultural critique to students is a sense of conflict between pleasure and analysis. Initially they often assume that if you are critiquing a subject it must mean that you do not like it. Since I have written critical essays on two Spike Lee films, students will often say "Hey, you're really down on Spike." Or even before they "get on my case," if I express a positive interest in Lee's work, they are surprised because they assume that the critical essays are an attack. In any liberatory pedagogy, students should learn how to distinguish between hostile critique that is about "trashing" and critique that's about illuminating and enriching our understanding. Critiques that offer critical insight without serving as a barrier to appreciation are necessary if black folks are to develop cultural products that will not be simply received, accepted, and applauded because of tokenism, a gesture which simply reinforces paternalistic notions of white supremacy.

The notion that cultural criticism by black folks must either be confined to the question of positive or negative representation or function in a self-serving manner (that is, if you are talking about a work by a black person then you must say something positive or risk being "silenced") must be continually challenged. Recently a filmmaker friend called me to say he had seen several anthologies of writing by black women on feminism and even those with black female editors did not include my work. He could not understand how my work could be excluded from works advertised as giving a critical overview. I responded by sharing that folks often do not like what I'm saying or the style of presentation and make that known by ignoring my work. Certainly one of the primary dangers arising from the reality that much critical and creative writing by black folks emerges from those of us housed in the academy is that the university is basically a politically conservative framework which often inhibits the production of diverse perspectives, new ideas, and different styles of thinking and writing. At times individual black folks who have gained power in the academy assume the role of the secret police, guarding ideas and work to make sure nothing is said that contradicts the status quo. Teaching and writing about the work of black women writers, I often meet tremendous resistance from students and colleagues when I suggest that we must do more than express positive appreciation for this work, that to engage it critically in a rigorous way is more a gesture of respect than is passive acceptance. When I ask students to think critically about the machinery of cultural production (how work is advertised, reviewed, disseminated, etc.) as it affects the current focus on black women writers, connecting these processes to the commodification of blackness, they are often disturbed. They want to see the current focus on black women writers solely in positive terms. They find it difficult to consider the possibility that work is not necessarily oppositional because it is created by a black person, that it may not necessarily offer a non-racist or non-sexist perspective. This desire to simplify one's critical response, to contain it within a dualistic model of good and bad, accepted and rejected, is an approach to ways of knowing that a liberatory pedagogy seeks to alter. Even though western metaphysical dualism as a paradigmatic philosophical approach provides the "logical" framework for structures of domination in this society (race, gender, class exploitation), individuals from oppressed and exploited groups internalize this way of thinking, inverting it. For example: some black people may reject the assumptions of white supremacy and replace them with notions of black superiority. Assuming such a standpoint, they may feel threatened by any critical approach that does not reinforce this perspective.

Cultural critics who are committed to a radical cultural politics (especially those of us who teach students from exploited and oppressed groups) must offer theoretical paradigms in a manner that connects them to contextualized political strategies. For me, critical pedagogy (expressed in writing, teaching, and habits of being) is fundamentally linked to a concern with creating strategies that will enable colonized folks to decolonize their minds and actions, thereby promoting the insurrection of subjugated knowledge. Trendy cultural critique that is in no way linked to a concern with critical pedagogy or liberation struggles hinders this process. When white critics write about black culture 'cause it's the "in" subject without interrogating their work to see whether or not it helps perpetuate and maintain racist domination, they participate in the commodification of "blackness" that is so peculiar to postmodern strategies of colonization. Jhally and Angus define postmodern culture as a "society where social identity is formed through mass-mediated images and where culture and economy have merged to form a single sphere." There is too little work which seeks to examine the impact of postmodernism on contemporary black culture. An oppositional cultural politic has always informed transformative black liberation struggle. More than ever before, cultural criticism that can illuminate and enrich our understanding of the social formation of black identity, the commodification of "blackness," is needed. It will not emerge solely from black critics but from all cultural critics who are concerned with the eradication of racism.

Within the field of cultural criticism there are very few African-American voices speaking out. There are more "black" voices, some from Europe and many from Third World countries. When these critics write about black American culture, they offer a valuable perspective, one that differs from that of African-Americans. Hence they do not "replace" absent or silenced African-American voices. Trendy notions of "difference" that lump all people of color together without distinguishing perspectives can serve to mask the absence of an African-American presence in the field of cultural studies. Cultural critics, especially those of us who are black, seeking to make a context for critical intervention that is linked with strategies for liberation, cannot ignore the issue of representation, as it determines who gets to speak to, with and for us about culture and be heard (with legitimacy) as cultural studies is more solidly institutionalized and commodified.

As I have already stated, cultural criticism is often the subject that most engages students in the classroom. There it is clear who the audience is and the impact on that audience. This is less the case with published cultural criticism. To avoid participating in the production of cultural criticism as a "hot" commodity to be exchanged in the academic marketplace, cultural critics can make an effort to publish work in places (magazines, newspapers, etc.) where it will potentially reach a different audience. Certainly, it's important for cultural critics to seize all opportunities to engage in oral dialogues and conversations with audiences outside the academy. If there is not a mutual exchange between the cultural subjects (African-Americans, for example) that are written about and the critics who write about them, a politic of domination is easily reproduced wherein intellectual elites assume an old colonizing role, that of privileged interpreter—cultural overseers. Entering the university as a writer concerned with acquiring credentials that would help me get a job, I am constantly aware of the way our very location in an academic setting, where one's work is periodically reviewed, judged, evaluated, etc., informs what we write about and how we write. On one hand, "cultural studies" has made writing about non-white culture more acceptable, particularly in the humanities; yet, on the other hand, this work does not emerge within a context that necessarily stresses the need to approach these subjects with a progressive politics or a liberatory pedagogy. Therein lies the danger. Cultural studies could easily become the space for the informers: those folks who appear to be allied with the disadvantaged, the oppressed, who are either spies or there to mediate between the forces of domination and its victims. Vigilant insistence that cultural studies be linked to a progressive radical cultural politics will ensure that it is a location that enables critical intervention. Ironically, though black writers and/or scholars have always been engaged in writing cultural criticism, the way it has been constituted as a new field of discourse in the academy tends to overlook these contributions or, when they are recognized, they tend to be devalued. The most productive response by black critics has to be the continued production of material and an ongoing expressed willingness to engage the discourse of cultural criticism on all fronts.

This collection of essays, *Yearning: Race, Gender, and Culture,* is the outcome of involvement with cultural criticism. Reading work by cultural critics both in and outside the academy, I was deeply troubled by the paucity of material by African-American women. Given current interest in fiction by black women writers, it is telling that there is not a corresponding desire to hear from us what we think about cultural production. Folks may be familiar with Michele Wallace's insightful cultural criticism, but they may not have read the essays of Hortense Spillers, Valerie Smith, Coco Fusco, or Lisa Jones, to name a few. Cultural studies and cultural criticism excite me because they are the obvious location for work that is inter-disciplinary, for feminist theory that seeks to combine multiple perspectives, for work that is written from a standpoint that includes analysis of race and class.

Some of the essays written for this collection were first published in *Z Magazine.* Yet the inspiration to write them usually came from concrete intellectual exchange in everyday life. Reluctant to see Spike Lee's film *Do The Right Thing* because the way in which it was advertised seemed like such a set-up (viewers were already being told what we would/should see when we watched the film), I had no desire to write about it. Finally, seeing it after all the fuss had subsided, I was determined not to write about it. When students and friends pleaded with me to respond to this film, to give them a critical framework that could serve as a catalyst, pushing them to think deeply about the work, I responded spontaneously in endless conversations, then by writing my thoughts. Writing cultural criticism as a response to engaged dialogue with friends, colleagues, and students is different from writing a piece so that it will enhance one's list of publications for a tenure process or any other process of academic evaluation. Since many of the white men with power in the institution where I teach "loved" *Do The Right Thing,* I was aware that being public in writing about my thoughts could possibly have negative consequences. Black thinkers and writers in the academy, like all other marginalized groups, are constantly subjected to scrutiny. Often colleagues read my work and arbitrarily conclude that "She hates white people." I share this so that folks can have some idea of why black scholars find it sometimes difficult to write, in whatever manner we choose, about everything we want to write about. And the same holds true for black cultural critics who are not in the academy. If you are trying to publish anything (book, article, review, etc.), usually there is a white hierarchy determining who will edit one's work. I did a piece recently on teaching women's studies courses to black students. When it was returned to me edited, I noticed that all the critical comments about white women feminists had been deleted.

We produce cultural criticism in the context of white supremacy. At times, even the most progressive and well-meaning white folks, who are friends and allies, may not understand why a black writer has to say something a certain way, or why we may not want to explain what has been said as though the first people we must always be addressing are privileged white readers. While writing these essays, I consciously thought about the process of decolonization, of what happens when black people begin to decolonize our minds, write from that perspective, and then turn work over to editors and publishers who may not have a clue as to what we are trying to say or who may try to rearrange the work so it says something else. Riding home from the movie theater after seeing Euzan Palcy's film *A Dry White Season* with my best buddy from childhood, I tried to describe the thoughts and feelings that welled up in me as I watched the film, yet found myself unable to articulate them clearly. After moments of violent weeping came a screaming rage about the way western contexts of covert censorship—white supremacy, the academy—make it hard to say what you really want to say. And every black writer knows that the people you may most want to hear your words may never read them, that many of them have never learned to read. Finally I found words to talk and write about this film, words lacking some of the fire I initially felt, though sparks remain. I share the background drama that lies behind some of these essays because I am always astounded by the fact that no amount of writing makes the difficulties of expression any less painful. Years ago I heard a Cuban writer Edmundo Desnoyez talk about the obsession citizens of the United States have with the issue of "censorship" in communist countries. There was little comment when it was pointed out that censorship takes place in this society in more subtle forms, a primary one being the process of editing and/or rejecting manuscripts. Often radical writers doing transgressive work are told not that it's too political or too "left," but simply that it will not sell or readers just will not be interested in that perspective.

When I wrote the essay on *Looking For Langston,* Issac Julien's latest film, I was not thinking about who would publish it. Annoyed that so much of what little was said about this work in the press did not give it serious regard, I wanted to express the way I experienced the film. When I sent this piece to *Z,* I enclosed a note saying that I realized it was not written in the style they think is most accessible to their readers, but I wanted to give readers this critical meditation on the film even if it seemed too poetic, too dreamy for *Z.* The note was really a plea for them to publish it "as is" without change. Being a worker in the academy, I can "steal" time to write long essays that may not be published anywhere. One reason more black writers are not doing cultural criticism is that it's hard to find time to write essays that might never make any money or be published. Certainly this is so for writers who are trying to make a living selling their work. And the extent to which writers are trying to "sell" work to pay the bills often determines their willingness to submit to undesired edits. It's a struggle sometimes.

Unlike other chi-chi collections on cultural criticism, *Yearning* includes feminist essays on race and gender. Writing about film and television, I now have readers who boldly tell me they just are not interested in that "feminist stuff" or that "race thing." Several essays in this collection discuss the way in which cultural criticism is at times seen as a way to get away from approaching subjects from a clearly politicized standpoint. Critics (Cornel West, Greg Tate, Lawrence Grossberg, Andrew Ross, Michele Wallace, Jane Gaines, to randomly name a few) who see no need to separate politics from the pleasure of reading a work intensely and critically celebrate the co-existence of these concerns. Certainly, I am most excited by writing and reading cultural criticism that is linked with a concern for transforming oppressive structures of domination. That's the kind of work I want to do, both as artist and critic.

Lastly, I gathered this group of essays under the heading *Yearning* because as I looked for common passions, sentiments shared by folks across race, class, gender, and sexual practice, I was struck by the depths of longing in many of us. Those without money long to find a way to get rid of the endless sense of deprivation. Those with money wonder why so much feels so meaningless and long to find the site of "meaning." Witnessing the genocidal ravages of drug addiction in black families and communities, I began to "hear" that longing for a substance as, in part, a displacement for the longed-for liberation—the freedom to control one's destiny. All too often our political desire for change is seen as separate from longings and passions that consume lots of time and energy in daily life. Particularly the realm of fantasy is often seen as completely separate from politics. Yet I think of all the time black folks (especially the underclass) spend just fantasizing about what our lives would be like if there were no racism, no white supremacy. Surely our desire for radical social change is intimately linked with the desire to experience pleasure, erotic fulfillment, and a host of other passions. Then, on the flip side, there are many individuals with race, gender, and class privilege who are longing to see the kind of revolutionary change that will end domination and oppression even though their lives would be completely and utterly transformed. The shared space and feeling of "yearning" opens up the possibility of common ground where all these differences might meet and engage one another. It seemed appropriate then to speak this yearning.

2

THE POLITICS OF
RADICAL BLACK SUBJECTIVITY

I often begin courses which focus on African-American literature, and sometimes specifically black women writers, with a declaration by Paulo Freire which had a profound liberatory effect on my thinking: "We cannot enter the struggle as objects in order to later become subjects." This statement compels reflection on how the dominated, the oppressed, the exploited make ourselves subject. How do we create an oppositional worldview, a consciousness, an identity, a standpoint that exists not only as that struggle which also opposes dehumanization but as that movement which enables creative, expansive self-actualization? Opposition is not enough. In that vacant space after one has resisted there is still the necessity to become—to make oneself anew. Resistance is that struggle we can most easily grasp. Even the most subjected person has moments of rage and resentment so intense that they respond, they act against. There is an inner uprising that leads to rebellion, however short-lived. It may be only momentary but it takes place. That space within oneself where resistance is possible remains. It is different then to talk about becoming subjects. That process emerges as one comes to understand how structures of domination work in one's own life, as one develops critical thinking and critical consciousness, as one invents new, alternative habits of being, and resists from that marginal space of difference inwardly defined.

Retrospective examination of black liberation struggle in the United States indicates the extent to which ideas about "freedom" were informed by efforts to imitate the behavior, lifestyles, and most importantly the values and consciousness of white colonizers. Much civil rights reform reinforced the idea that black liberation should be defined by the degree to which black people gained equal access to material opportunities and privileges available to whites—jobs, housing, schooling, etc. And even though the more radical 1960s black power movement repudiated imitation of whites, emphasizing pan-Africanist connections, their vision of liberation was not particularly distinctive or revolutionary. Certainly the core of Black Muslim liberatory efforts also centered around gaining access to material privileges (though from the standpoint of black self-determination and control), the kind of nation-building which would place black men in positions of authority and power.

Sexism has diminished the power of all black liberation struggles—reformist or revolutionary. Ironically, the more radical black nationalist liberation efforts were informed by a sexism much more severe than any present in earlier civil rights reform. The legacies of Fannie Lou Hamer, Septima Clark, Rosa Parks, Ella Baker, and many unknown black women testify to the force of their presence, the intensity and value of their contributions to civil rights struggle. The work of black women active in the 1960s black power movement was often appropriated by black males without acknowledgment or recognition. Witness the fate of Ruby Doris Smith Robinson (an excellent article on her involvement in the struggle was published in the 1988 student supplement of *SAGE: A Scholarly Journal on Black Women*). Commenting on Robinson's activism, Kathleen Cleaver suggests that she was subjected to a sexism that was fierce and unrelenting . Cleaver says, "She was destroyed by the movement."

Insistence on patriarchal values, on equating black liberation with black men gaining access to male privilege that would enable them to assert power over black women, was one of the most significant forces undermining radical struggle. Thorough critiques of gender would have compelled leaders of black liberation struggles to envision new strategies and to talk about black subjectivity in a visionary manner. Writer, activist, and feminist thinker Toni Cade Bambara participated in 1960s black liberation struggle, outspokenly emphasizing the undermining force of sexism as it informed the overall social status of black women, our participation in civil rights, as well as its debilitating impact on any attempt to radically re-vision black subjectivity. Her essay, "On the Issue of Roles" remains a forceful critique of sexism, documenting the demand for a different agenda. Bambara specifically cites as dangerous the sexist emphasis on black female submission and silence in the name of liberation. On the roles assigned black women, she asserts:

> She is being assigned an unreal role of mute servant that supposedly neutralizes the acidic tension that exists between Black men and Black women. She is being encouraged—in the name of revolution no less—to cultivate "virtues" that if listed would sound like personality traits of slaves. In other words, we are still abusing each other, aborting each other's nature—in the teeth of experiences both personal and historical that should alert us to the horror of a situation in which we profess to be about liberation but behave in a constricting manner; we rap about being correct but ignore the danger of having one half of our population regard the other with such condescension and perhaps fear that half finds it necessary to "reclaim his manhood" by denying her peoplehood. Perhaps we need to let go of all notions of manhood and femininity and concentrate on Blackhood. We have much, alas, to work against. The job of purging is staggering. It perhaps takes less heart to pick up the gun than to face the task of creating a new identity, a self, perhaps an androgynous self, via commitment to the struggle.

Unfortunately the 1960s conflict over the issue of gender roles was not fruitfully debated and resolved. Collectively, black women and men did not begin to move in a direction challenging sexist norms.

Contemporary feminist movement has not yet had revolutionary impact on black political thinking. Politically, black men continue to assume dominant leadership roles, rarely if ever paying lip service to the need for a change in thinking about gender. Even when Jesse Jackson emphasized gender issues in his recent campaign, his comments were most often perceived as being addressed to a white female constituency. Many Jesse Jackson supporters were black women, yet he never made any specific appeals to gender concerns that deeply affect our future, issues of poverty and childcare. Black male and female refusal to consider the importance of eradicating sexism has ongoing negative consequences for black solidarity.

On the cultural scene, a visible split has emerged between many black men and women, one that suggests our concerns are not similar, that we do not share a common ground where we can engage in critical dialogue about aesthetics, gender, feminist politics, etc. Viewers of the much talked-about play *The Colored Museum* cannot fail to note that much of the black cultural production that is ridiculed and mocked either represents black female concerns or refers to creative work by black women artists. Cultural examples that position black women and men in an ongoing adversarial relationship can be seen in

critical responses to Alice Walker's book *The Color Purple;* in Stanley
Crouch's scathing comments on Toni Morrison's *Beloved;* and in discussions of Spike Lee's films *She's Gotta Have It* and *School Daze.* The
latter contrasts two black males' engagement with male bonding via
involvement in global politics and sexist dehumanization of a black female as initiation rite which enables affirmation of black power and
brotherhood. Then there are the plays of August Wilson. *Fences*
poignantly portrays complex negative contradictions within black
masculinity in a white supremacist social context. However, patriarchy
is not critiqued, and even though tragic expressions of conventional
masculinity are evoked, sexist values are re-inscribed via the black
woman's redemption message as the play ends. Examples of brutal
conflict between black women and men abound in black women's fiction—*The Women of Brewster Place, The Bluest Eye, The Third Life of
Grange Copeland*—which highlights gender roles, especially the sexism of black male characters. Then there is the literary response to that
representation, works like Ishmael Reed's novel *Reckless Eyeballing*
and most recently Trey Ellis's *Platitudes.*

Many of the works I have cited in no way represent counter-hegemonic cultural practice. In some cases the veiled political agendas
affirmed in particular works are reactionary and conservative. Blackness does not mean that we are inherently oppositional. Our creative
work is shaped by a market that reflects white supremacist values and
concerns. It should be obvious to anyone writing in this social context
that novels highlighting black male oppression of black females while
downplaying white racist oppression of black people would be more
marketable than the reverse. Certainly the diverse inventive retelling of
gender conflict between black women and men, though often striking
and deeply moving, rarely suggests oppositional aesthetic directions
and possibilities. They are most often new takes on old themes, interesting in that they call attention to the need for visionary imaginative
works that expand our notions of self and identity as they themselves
often do not. They point to the way our struggle for subjectivity has
too long been mired in heterosexism, a narrative of selfhood contained within a paradigm of coupled relationships. Even so the realm
of cultural production continues to be the location for possible transformative thinking about the nature of black experience.

It is no mere accident of fate that the ground of current discourse
on black subjectivity is cultural terrain. Art remains that site of imaginative possibility where "anything goes," particularly if one is not seeking
to create a hot commodity for the marketplace. Black folks' inability to
envision liberatory paradigms of black subjectivity in a purely political

realm is in part a failure of critical imagination. Yet even on cultural ground discussions of black subjectivity are often limited to the topic of representation, good and bad images, or contained by projects concerned with reclaiming and/or inventing traditions (expressed in literary circles by the issue of canon formation). Interestingly, both these endeavors are not in any essential way oppositional. Focus on good and bad images may be more fundamentally connected to the western metaphysical dualism that is the philosophical underpinning of racist and sexist domination than with radical efforts to reconceptualize black cultural identities. Concurrently, focus on canon formation legitimates the creative work of black writers in academic circles while reinforcing white hegemonic authorial canonicity.

Perhaps the most fascinating constructions of black subjectivity (and critical thinking about the same) emerge from writers, cultural critics, and artists who are poised on the margins of various endeavors. I locate myself with this group, imagining I reside there with a wild crowd of known and unknown folks. We share commitment to left politics (yes, we critique capitalism and explore the revolutionary possibilities of socialism); we are concerned with ending domination in all its forms; we are into reading and deeply concerned with aesthetics (I mean, I have my own bumper sticker firmly stuck on my heart: "I die for style"); we are into all kinds of culture and do not fear losing our blackness; we see ourselves as one of the people, while simultaneously acknowledging our privileges, whatever they may be. Some of us are from working-class backgrounds, which makes our struggle for radical black subjectivity unique and intense because we have no intention of breaking ties with the world we come from. We all recognize the primacy of identity politics as an important stage in liberation process. We quote Audre Lorde, who said, "The master's tools will never dismantle the master's house" to claim the ground on which we are constructing "homeplace" (and we are not talking about ghettos or shantytowns). We are concerned about the fate of the planet, and some of us believe that living simply is part of revolutionary political practice. We have a sense of the sacred. The ground we stand on is shifting, fragile, and unstable. We are avant-garde only to the extent that we eschew essentialist notions of identity, and fashion selves that emerge from the meeting of diverse epistemologies, habits of being, concrete class locations, and radical political commitments. We believe in solidarity and are working to make spaces where black women and men can dialogue about everything, spaces where we can engage in critical dissent without violating one another. We are concerned with black culture and black identity.

Cultural identity has become an uncool issue in some circles. One of the very crowd I mentioned earlier suggests "the emphasis on culture is a sign of political defeat," whereas it seems to me a practical gesture to shift the scene of action if in fact the location of one's political practice does not enable change. We return to "identity" and "culture" for relocation, linked to political practice—identity that is not informed by a narrow cultural nationalism masking continued fascination with the power of the white hegemonic other. Instead identity is evoked as a stage in a process wherein one constructs radical black subjectivity. Recent critical reflections on static notions of black identity urge transformation of our sense of who we can be and still be black. Assimilation, imitation, or assuming the role of rebellious exotic other are not the only available options and never have been. This is why it is crucial to radically revise notions of identity politics, to explore marginal locations as spaces where we can best become whatever we want to be while remaining committed to liberatory black liberation struggle. A similar effort is taking place within feminist theory, where an identity politics based on essentialism is critiqued, while the connection between identity and politics is affirmed. Linda Alcoff problematizes it this way in her essay "Cultural Feminism versus Post-Structuralism: The Identity Crisis in Feminist Theory."

> Identity politics provides a decisive rejoinder to the generic
> human thesis and the mainstream methodology of Western
> political theory... If we combine the concept of identity politics
> with a conception of the subject as positionality, we can
> conceive of the subject as nonessentialized and emergent from a
> historical experience....

Such a standpoint would enable black folks to move away from narrow notions of black identity.

Assertions of identity that bring complexity and variety to constructions of black subjectivity are often negated by conservative policing forces—that is, black people who dismiss differences among us by labeling some folks black and others not. Growing up, whenever I thought about life in ways that differed from my familiar status quo, from our segregated black community norms, I was called "Miss White Girl." This process of social excommunication from "blackness" extends far beyond households. Folks who are concerned with preserving stereotypical identities can be most vicious in their condemnation of someone as not "black." Still, confronting these stereotypical forces which do not ever want to call attention to more fluid notions of black identity, or to marginal perspectives, is not nearly as frustrating as confrontation with the white avant-garde in politically charged cultural contexts in which they seek to appropriate and usurp radical efforts to subvert static notions of black identity. Such appropriation happens again and again. It takes the form of constructing African-American culture as though it exists solely to suggest new aesthetic and political directions white folks might move in. Michele Wallace calls it seeing African-American culture as "the starting point for white self-criticism."

An example which readily comes to mind from feminist movement centers on efforts made by women of color to call attention to white racism in the struggle as well as talking about racial identity from a standpoint which deconstructs the category "woman." Such discussions were part of the struggle by women of color to come to voice and also to assert new and different feminist narratives. Many white feminists responded by hearing only what was being said about race and most specifically about racism. Focusing solely on the issue of racism allowed for a re-centering of white authorial presence. White feminists could now centralize themselves by engaging in a discourse on race, "the Other," in a manner which further marginalized women of color, whose works were often relegated to the realm of the experiential. In actuality the theoretical groundwork for all reconsiderations of the category "woman" which consider race, as talked about in the work of theorists like Teresa de Lauretis and Elizabeth Spelman and many others, was laid by women of color. Among white feminist theoretical elites in the United States, the work of women of color is usually cited solely in relation to discussions of race. Our work is subordinated and used to reinforce their assertions about race and Otherness. Certainly my book *Feminist Theory: From Margin to Center* did not focus centrally on race, yet it is usually cited as though that was the most talked-about subject.

Radical black subjectivity can be recognized by others without ongoing political resistance only in a context where white people and Third World elites are not trying to maintain cultural hegemony, insisting that we be as they want us to be. Such contexts are rare. Recently, I heard Cornel West give a moving, insightful lecture, "De-centering Europe: The Crisis of Contemporary Culture." Though highly intellectual and theoretical in content, his manner of presentation was akin to a sermon mode popular in black communities, where such a style indicates depth and seriousness. In the context of white institutions, particularly universities, that mode of address is questionable precisely because it moves people. Style is equated in such a setting with a lack of substance. West not only transformed social space, legitimating an aspect of black experience in a context which rarely recognizes the value of black culture, he was also able to include non-scholarly members of the audience. His style of presentation required of the audience a shift in paradigms; a marginal aspect of black cultural identity was centralized. To understand what was happening, individuals had to assume a different literary standpoint. This is one example of counter-hegemonic cultural practice. It was an assertion of radical black subjectivity.

Often when black subjects give expression to multiple aspects of our identity, which emerge from a different location, we may be seen by white others as "spectacle." For example, when I give an academic talk without reading a paper, using a popular, performative, black story-telling mode, I risk being seen by the dominating white other as unprepared, as just entertainment. Yet their mode of seeing cannot be the factor which determines style of representation or the content of one's work. Fundamental to the process of decentering the oppressive other and claiming our right to subjectivity is the insistence that we must determine how we will be and not rely on colonizing responses to determine our legitimacy. We are not looking to that Other for recognition. We are recognizing ourselves and willingly making contact with all who would engage us in a constructive manner.

In an essay on counter-hegemonic cultural practice, I named marginality as a site of transformation where liberatory black subjectivity can fully emerge, emphasizing that there is a "definite distinction between that marginality which is imposed by oppressive structure and that marginality one chooses as site of resistance, as location of radical openness and possibility." Theorist Gayatri Spivak claims to be "moved by texts where so-called marginal groups, instead of claiming centrality, re-define the big word human in terms of the marginal." Such subversive play happens much more easily in the realm of "texts" than in the world of human interaction not focused on privatized reading, where such moves challenge, disrupt, threaten—where repression is real. I am moved by that confrontation with difference which takes place on new ground, in that counter-hegemonic marginal space where radical black subjectivity is *seen,* not overseen by any authoritative Other claiming to know us better than we know ourselves.

3

POSTMODERN BLACKNESS

Postmodernist discourses are often exclusionary even as they call attention to, appropriate even, the experience of "difference" and "Otherness" to provide oppositional political meaning, legitimacy, and immediacy when they are accused of lacking concrete relevance. Very few African-American intellectuals have talked or written about postmodernism. At a dinner party I talked about trying to grapple with the significance of postmodernism for contemporary black experience. It was one of those social gatherings where only one other black person was present. The setting quickly became a field of contestation. I was told by the other black person that I was wasting my time, that "this stuff does not relate in any way to what's happening with black people." Speaking in the presence of a group of white onlookers, staring at us as though this encounter were staged for their benefit, we engaged in a passionate discussion about black experience. Apparently, no one sympathized with my insistence that racism is perpetuated when blackness is associated solely with concrete gut level experience conceived as either opposing or having no connection to abstract thinking and the production of critical theory. The idea that there is no meaningful connection between black experience and critical thinking about aesthetics or culture must be continually interrogated.

My defense of postmodernism and its relevance to black folks sounded good, but I worried that I lacked conviction, largely because I approach the subject cautiously and with suspicion.

Disturbed not so much by the "sense" of postmodernism but by the conventional language used when it is written or talked about and by those who speak it, I find myself on the outside of the discourse looking in. As a discursive practice it is dominated primarily by the voices of white male intellectuals and/or academic elites who speak to and about one another with coded familiarity. Reading and studying their writing to understand postmodernism in its multiple manifestations, I appreciate it but feel little inclination to ally myself with the academic hierarchy and exclusivity pervasive in the movement today.

Critical of most writing on postmodernism, I perhaps am more conscious of the way in which the focus on "Otherness and difference" that is often alluded to in these works seems to have little concrete impact as an analysis or standpoint that might change the nature and direction of postmodernist theory. Since much of this theory has been constructed in reaction to and against high modernism, there is seldom any mention of black experience or writings by black people in this work, specifically black women (though in more recent work one may see a reference to Cornel West, the black male scholar who has most engaged postmodernist discourse). Even if an aspect of black culture is the subject of postmodern critical writing, the works cited will usually be those of black men. A work that comes immediately to mind is Andrew Ross's chapter "Hip, and the Long Front of Color" in *No Respect: Intellectuals and Popular Culture;* while it is an interesting reading, it constructs black culture as though black women have had no role in black cultural production. At the end of Meaghan Morris' discussion of postmodernism in her collection of essays *The Pirate's Fiance: Feminism and Postmodernism,* she provides a bibliography of works by women, identifying them as important contributions to a discourse on postmodernism that offer new insight as well as challenging male theoretical hegemony. Even though many of the works do not directly address postmodernism, they address similar concerns. There are no references to works by black women.

The failure to recognize a critical black presence in the culture and in most scholarship and writing on postmodernism compels a black reader, particularly a black female reader, to interrogate her interest in a subject where those who discuss and write about it seem not to know black women exist or even to consider the possibility that we might be somewhere writing or saying something that should be listened to, or producing art that should be seen, heard, approached with intellectual seriousness. This is especially the case with works that go on and on about the way in which postmodernist discourse has opened up a theoretical terrain where "difference and Otherness" can be considered legitimate issues in the academy. Confronting both the absence of recognition of black female presence that much postmodernist theory re-inscribes and the resistance on the part of most black folks to hearing about real connection between postmodernism and black experience, I enter a discourse, a practice, where there may be no ready audience for my words, no clear listener, uncertain then, that my voice can or will be heard.

During the sixties, black power movement was influenced by perspectives that could easily be labeled modernist. Certainly many of the ways black folks addressed issues of identity conformed to a modernist universalizing agenda. There was little critique of patriarchy as a master narrative among black militants. Despite the fact that black power ideology reflected a modernist sensibility, these elements were soon rendered irrelevant as militant protest was stifled by a powerful, repressive postmodern state. The period directly after the black power movement was a time when major news magazines carried articles with cocky headlines like "Whatever Happened to Black America?" This response was an ironic reply to the aggressive, unmet demand by decentered, marginalized black subjects who had at least momentarily successfully demanded a hearing, who had made it possible for black liberation to be on the national political agenda. In the wake of the black power movement, after so many rebels were slaughtered and lost, many of these voices were silenced by a repressive state; others became inarticulate. It has become necessary to find new avenues to transmit the messages of black liberation struggle, new ways to talk about racism and other politics of domination. Radical postmodernist practice, most powerfully conceptualized as a "politics of difference," should incorporate the voices of displaced, marginalized, exploited, and oppressed black people. It is sadly ironic that the contemporary discourse which talks the most about heterogeneity, the decentered subject, declaring breakthroughs that allow recognition of Otherness, still directs its critical voice primarily to a specialized audience that shares a common language rooted in the very master narratives it claims to challenge. If radical postmodernist thinking is to have a transformative impact, then a critical break with the notion of "authority" as "mastery over" must not simply be a rhetorical device. It must be reflected in habits of being, including styles of writing as well as chosen subject matter. Third world nationals, elites, and white critics who passively absorb white supremacist thinking, and therefore never notice or look at black people on the streets or at their jobs, who render us invisible with their gaze in all areas of daily life, are not likely to produce liberatory theory that will challenge racist domination, or promote a breakdown in traditional ways of seeing and thinking about reality, ways of constructing aesthetic theory and practice.

From a different standpoint, Robert Storr makes a similar critique in the global issue of *Art in America* when he asserts:

> To be sure, much postmodernist critical inquiry has centered precisely on the issues of "difference" and "Otherness." On the purely theoretical plane the exploration of these concepts has produced some important results, but in the absence of any sustained research into what artists of color and others outside the mainstream might be up to, such discussions become rootless instead of radical. Endless second guessing about the latent imperialism of intruding upon other cultures only compounded matters, preventing or excusing these theorists from investigating what black, Hispanic, Asian and Native American artists were actually doing.

Without adequate concrete knowledge of and contact with the non-white "Other," white theorists may move in discursive theoretical directions that are threatening and potentially disruptive of that critical practice which would support radical liberation struggle.

The postmodern critique of "identity," though relevant for renewed black liberation struggle, is often posed in ways that are problematic. Given a pervasive politic of white supremacy which seeks to prevent the formation of radical black subjectivity, we cannot cavalierly dismiss a concern with identity politics. Any critic exploring the radical potential of postmodernism as it relates to racial difference and racial domination would need to consider the implications of a critique of identity for oppressed groups. Many of us are struggling to find new strategies of resistance. We must engage decolonization as a critical practice if we are to have meaningful chances of survival even as we must simultaneously cope with the loss of political grounding which made radical activism more possible. I am thinking here about the postmodernist critique of essentialism as it pertains to the construction of "identity" as one example.

Postmodern theory that is not seeking to simply appropriate the experience of "Otherness" to enhance the discourse or to be radically chic should not separate the "politics of difference" from the politics of racism. To take racism seriously one must consider the plight of underclass people of color, a vast majority of whom are black. For African-Americans our collective condition prior to the advent of postmodernism and perhaps more tragically expressed under current postmodern conditions has been and is characterized by continued displacement, profound alienation, and despair. Writing about blacks and postmodernism, Cornel West describes our collective plight:

There is increasing class division and differentiation, creating on
the one hand a significant black middle-class, highly
anxiety-ridden, insecure, willing to be co-opted and
incorporated into the powers that be, concerned with racism
to the degree that it poses contraints on upward social
mobility; and, on the other, a vast and growing black
underclass, an underclass that embodies a kind of walking
nihilism of pervasive drug addiction, pervasive alcoholism,
pervasive homicide, and an exponential rise in suicide. Now
because of the deindustrialization, we also have a devastated
black industrial working class. We are talking here about
tremendous hopelessness.

This hopelessness creates longing for insight and strategies for
change that can renew spirits and reconstruct grounds for collective
black liberation struggle. The overall impact of postmodernism is that
many other groups now share with black folks a sense of deep alienation, despair, uncertainty, loss of a sense of grounding even if it is not
informed by shared circumstance. Radical postmodernism calls attention to those shared sensibilities which cross the boundaries of class,
gender, race, etc., that could be fertile ground for the construction of
empathy—ties that would promote recognition of common commitments, and serve as a base for solidarity and coalition.

Yearning is the word that best describes a common psychological state shared by many of us, cutting across boundaries of race, class,
gender, and sexual practice. Specifically, in relation to the post-mod-
ernist deconstruction of "master" narratives, the yearning that wells in
the hearts and minds of those whom such narratives have silenced is
the longing for critical voice. It is no accident that "rap" has usurped
the primary position of rhythm and blues music among young black
folks as the most desired sound or that it began as a form of "testimony" for the underclass. It has enabled underclass black youth to develop a critical voice, as a group of young black men told me, a
"common literacy." Rap projects a critical voice, explaining, demanding, urging. Working with this insight in his essay "Putting the Pop
Back into Postmodernism," Lawrence Grossberg comments:

The postmodern sensibility appropriates practices as boasts that
announce their own—and consequently our own—existence,
like a rap song boasting of the imaginary (or real—it makes no
difference) accomplishments of the rapper. They offer forms of
empowerment not only in the face of nihilism but precisely
through the forms of nihilism itself: an empowering nihilism, a

moment of positivity through the production and structuring of affective relations.

Considering that it is as subject one comes to voice, then the postmodernist focus on the critique of identity appears at first glance to threaten and close down the possibility that this discourse and practice will allow those who have suffered the crippling effects of colonization and domination to gain or regain a hearing. Even if this sense of threat and the fear it evokes are based on a misunderstanding of the postmodernist political project, they nevertheless shape responses. It never surprises me when black folks respond to the critique of essentialism, especially when it denies the validity of identity politics by saying, "Yeah, it's easy to give up identity, when you got one." Should we not be suspicious of postmodern critiques of the "subject" when they surface at a historical moment when many subjugated people feel themselves coming to voice for the first time. Though an apt and oftentimes appropriate comeback, it does not really intervene in the discourse in a way that alters and transforms.

Criticisms of directions in postmodern thinking should not obscure insights it may offer that open up our understanding of African-American experience. The critique of essentialism encouraged by postmodernist thought is useful for African-Americans concerned with reformulating outmoded notions of identity. We have too long had imposed upon us from both the outside and the inside a narrow, constricting notion of blackness. Postmodern critiques of essentialism which challenge notions of universality and static over-determined identity within mass culture and mass consciousness can open up new possibilities for the construction of self and the assertion of agency.

Employing a critique of essentialism allows African-Americans to acknowledge the way in which class mobility has altered collective black experience so that racism does not necessarily have the same impact on our lives. Such a critique allows us to affirm multiple black identities, varied black experience. It also challenges colonial imperialist paradigms of black identity which represent blackness one-dimensionally in ways that reinforce and sustain white supremacy. This discourse created the idea of the "primitive" and promoted the notion of an "authentic" experience, seeing as "natural" those expressions of black life which conformed to a pre-existing pattern or stereotype. Abandoning essentialist notions would be a serious challenge to racism. Contemporary African-American resistance struggle must be rooted in a process of decolonization that continually opposes re-inscribing notions of "authentic" black identity. This critique should not be made synonymous with a dismissal of the struggle of oppressed and exploited peoples to make ourselves subjects. Nor should it deny that in certain circumstances this experience affords us a privileged critical location from which to speak. This is not a re-inscription of modernist master narratives of authority which privilege some voices by denying voice to others. Part of our struggle for radical black sub-jectivity is the quest to find ways to construct self and identity that are oppositional and liberatory. The unwillingness to critique essentialism on the part of many African-Americans is rooted in the fear that it will cause folks to lose sight of the specific history and experience of Afri-can-Americans and the unique sensibilities and culture that arise from that experience. An adequate response to this concern is to critique es-sentialism while emphasizing the significance of "the authority of ex-perience." There is a radical difference between a repudiation of the idea that there is a black "essence" and recognition of the way black identity has been specifically constituted in the experience of exile and struggle.

When black folks critique essentialism, we are empowered to recognize multiple experiences of black identity that are the lived con-ditions which make diverse cultural productions possible. When this diversity is ignored, it is easy to see black folks as falling into two cate-gories: nationalist or assimilationist, black-identified or white-identi-fied. Coming to terms with the impact of postmodernism for black experience, particularly as it changes our sense of identity, means that we must and can rearticulate the basis for collective bonding. Given the various crises facing African-Americans (economic, spiritual, esca-lating racial violence, etc.), we are compelled by circumstance to reas-sess our relationship to popular culture and resistance struggle. Many of us are as reluctant to face this task as many non-black postmodern thinkers who focus theoretically on the issue of "difference" are to confront the issue of race and racism.

Music is the cultural product created by African-Americans that has most attracted postmodern theorists. It is rarely acknowledged that there is far greater censorship and restriction of other forms of cultural production by black folks—literary, critical writing, etc. Attempts on the part of editors and publishing houses to control and manipulate the representation of black culture, as well as the desire to promote the creation of products that will attract the widest audience, limit in a crippling and stifling way the kind of work many black folks feel we can do and still receive recognition. Using myself as an example, that creative writing I do which I consider to be most reflective of a postmodern oppositional sensibility, work that is abstract, fragmented, non-linear narrative, is constantly rejected by editors and publishers. It does not conform to the type of writing they think black women should be doing or the type of writing they believe will sell. Certainly I do not think I am the only black person engaged in forms of cultural production, especially experimental ones, who is constrained by the lack of an audience for certain kinds of work. It is important for postmodern thinkers and theorists to constitute themselves as an audience for such work. To do this they must assert power and privilege within the space of critical writing to open up the field so that it will be more inclusive. To change the exclusionary practice of postmodern critical discourse is to enact a postmodernism of resistance. Part of this intervention entails black intellectual participation in the discourse.

In his essay "Postmodernism and Black America," Cornel West suggests that black intellectuals "are marginal—usually languishing at the interface of Black and white cultures or thoroughly ensconced in Euro-American settings." He cannot see this group as potential producers of radical postmodernist thought. While I generally agree with this assessment, black intellectuals must proceed with the understanding that we are not condemned to the margins. The way we work and what we do can determine whether or not what we produce will be meaningful to a wider audience, one that includes all classes of black people. West suggests that black intellectuals lack "any organic link with most of Black life" and that this "diminishes their value to Black resistance." This statement bears traces of essentialism. Perhaps we need to focus more on those black intellectuals, however rare our presence, who do not feel this lack and whose work is primarily directed towards the enhancement of black critical consciousness and the strengthening of our collective capacity to engage in meaningful resistance struggle. Theoretical ideas and critical thinking need not be transmitted solely in written work or solely in the academy. While I work in a predominantly white institution, I remain intimately and passionately engaged with black community. It's not like I'm going to talk about writing and thinking about postmodernism with other academics and/or intellectuals and not discuss these ideas with underclass non-academic black folks who are family, friends, and comrades. Since I have not broken the ties that bind me to underclass poor black community, I have seen that knowledge, especially that which enhances daily life and strengthens our capacity to survive, can be shared. It means that critics, writers, and academics have to give the same critical attention to nurturing and cultivating our ties to black community that we give to writing articles, teaching, and lecturing. Here again I am really talking about cultivating habits of being that reinforce awareness that knowledge can be disseminated and shared on a number of fronts. The extent to which knowledge is made available, accessible, etc. depends on the nature of one's political commitments.

Postmodern culture with its decentered subject can be the space where ties are severed or it can provide the occasion for new and varied forms of bonding. To some extent, ruptures, surfaces, contextuality, and a host of other happenings create gaps that make space for oppositional practices which no longer require intellectuals to be confined by narrow separate spheres with no meaningful connection to the world of the everyday. Much postmodern engagement with culture emerges from the yearning to do intellectual work that connects with habits of being, forms of artistic expression, and aesthetics that inform the daily life of writers and scholars as well as a mass population. On the terrain of culture, one can participate in critical dialogue with the uneducated poor, the black underclass who are thinking about aesthetics. One can talk about what we are seeing, thinking, or listening to; a space is there for critical exchange. It's exciting to think, write, talk about, and create art that reflects passionate engagement with popular culture, because this may very well be "the" central future location of resistance struggle, a meeting place where new and radical happenings can occur.

4

THE CHITLIN CIRCUIT

on black community

O ne of the most intense, vivid memories of childhood re-
lives itself in my mind often, the memory of school deseg-
regation, which meant then the closing of black schools, our beloved
Booker T. Washington and Crispus Attucks, schools in segregated
black neighborhoods. We loved going to school then, from the moment we rushed out of the door in the morning to the lingering strolls
home. In that world, black children were allowed innocence. We did
not really understand the meaning of segregation, the brutal racism
that had created apartheid in this society, and no one explained it.
They wanted us to live childhood life not knowing. We only knew the
world we lived in, and as children we loved that world in a deep and
profound way.

It was the world of Southern, rural, black growing up, of folks
sitting on porches day and night, of folks calling your mama, 'cause
you walked by and didn't speak, and of the switch waiting when you
got home so you could be taught some manners. It was a world of single older black women schoolteachers, dedicated, tough; they had
taught your mama, her sisters, and her friends. They knew your people in ways that you never would and shared their insight, keeping us
in touch with generations. It was a world where we had a history.
There grandfathers and great-grandfathers, whose knees we sat on,
gave us everything wonderful they could think about giving. It was a
world where that something wonderful might be a ripe tomato, found
as we walked through the rows of Daddy Jerry's garden, or you
thought it was his garden then, 'cause you did not know that word you
would learn later—"sharecropper." You did not know then that it was

not his property. To your child mind it had to be his land, 'cause he worked it, 'cause he held that dirt in his hands and taught you to love it—land, that rich Kentucky soil that was good for growing things. It was a world where we had a history. At tent meetings and hot Sunday services we cooled ourselves with fans that waved familiar images back to us. Carried away by pure religious ecstasy we found ourselves and God. It was a sacred world, a world where we had a history.

That black world of my growing up began to fundamentally change when the schools were desegregated. What I remember most about that time is a deep sense of loss. It hurt to leave behind memories, schools that were "ours," places we loved and cherished, places that honored us. It was one of the first great tragedies of growing up. I mourned for that experience. I sat in classes in the integrated white high school where there was mostly contempt for us, a long tradition of hatred, and I wept. I wept throughout my high school years. I wept and longed for what we had lost and wondered why the grown black folks had acted as though they did not know we would be surrendering so much for so little, that we would be leaving behind a history.

Scenes in Paule Marshall's novel *Praisesong for the Widow* remind me of that loss; there the black couple is so intent on "making it" economically in the white world that they lose the sense of who they are, their history. Years later, older, and going through a process of self-recovery, the black woman has the insight that "they had behaved as if there had been nothing about themselves worth honoring." Contemplating the past, she thinks:

> Couldn't we have done differently? Hadn't there perhaps been another way! ...Would it have been possible to have done both? That is, to have wrested, as they had done all those years, the means to rescue them from Halsey Street and to see the children through, while preserving, safeguarding, treasuring those things that had come down to them over the generations, which had defined them in a particular way. The most vivid, the most valuable part of themselves.

That line "they had behaved as if there had been nothing about themselves worth honoring," echoes in my dreams. She could have been writing about us back then when we let our schools go, when no one talked about what we would be losing, when we did not make ways to hold on.

With no shame, I confess to bearing a deep nostalgia for that time, for that moment when I first stood before an audience of hundreds of my people in the gymnasium of Crispus Attucks and gave my first public presentation. I recited a long poem. We had these talent shows before pep rallies, where we performed, where we discovered our artistry. Nostalgia for that time often enters my dreams, wets my pillow (for a long time the man lying next to me, whose skin is almost soot black like my granddaddy's skin, woke me to say "stop crying, why you crying?") I cannot imagine daily life without the brown and black faces of my people.

Nostalgic for a sense of place and belonging and togetherness I want black folks to know again, I learn anew the meaning of struggle. Words hardly suffice to give memory to that time, the sweetness of our solidarity, the heaviness of our pain and sorrow, the thickness of our joy. We could celebrate then; we knew what a good time looked like.

For me, this experience, of growing up in a segregated small town, living in a marginal space where black people (though contained) exercised power, where we were truly caring and supportive of one another, was very different from the nationalism I would learn about in black studies classes or from the Black Muslims selling papers at Stanford University my first year there. That nationalism was linked to black capitalism. I had come from an agrarian world where folks were content to get by on a little, where Baba, mama's mother, made soap, dug fishing worms, set traps for rabbits, made butter and wine, sewed quilts, and wrung the necks of chickens; this was not black capitalism. The sweet communion we felt (that strong sense of solidarity shrouding and protecting my growing up years was something I thought all black people had known) was rooted in love, relational love, the care we had towards one another. This way of loving is best described by Linell Cady in her essay "A Feminist Christian Vision":

> Love is a mode of relating that seeks to establish bonds between the self and the other, creating a unity out of formerly detached individuals. It is a process of integration where the isolation of individuals is overcome through the forging of connections between persons. These connections constitute the emergence of a wider life including yet transcending the separate individuals. This wider life that emerges through the loving relationship between selves does not swallow up individuals, blurring their identities and concerns. It is not an undifferentiated whole that obliterates individuality. On the contrary, the wider life created by love constitutes a community of persons. In a community, persons retain their identity, and they also share a commitment to the continued well-being of the relational life uniting them.

It is this experience of relational love, of a beloved black community, I long to know again.

At this historical moment, black people are experiencing a deep
collective sense of "loss." Nostalgia for times past is intense, evoked by
awareness that feelings of bonding and connection that seemed to
hold black people together are swiftly eroding. We are divided. Assimilation rooted in internalized racism further separates us. Neonational-
ist responses do not provide an answer, as they return us to an
unproductive "us against them" dichotomy that no longer realistically
addresses how we live as black people in a postmodern world. Many
of us do not live in black neighborhoods. Practically all of us work for
white people. Most of us are not self-sufficient; we can't grow, build,
or fix nothing. Large numbers of us are educated in predominantly
white institutions. Inter-racial relations are more a norm. The "chitlin-
circuit"—that network of black folks who knew and aided one another—has been long broken. Clearly, as Marshall suggests in her
novel, things must be done differently. We cannot return to the past.
While it is true that we lost closeness, it was informed by the very
structure of racist domination black civil rights struggle sought to
change. It is equally true that this change has meant advancement, a
lessening of overt racist brutality towards all black people. Looking
back, it is easy to see that the nationalism of the sixties and seventies
was very different from the racial solidarity born of shared circumstance and not from theories of black power. Not that an articulation
of black power was not important; it was. Only it did not deliver the
goods; it was too informed by corrosive power relations, too mythic,
to take the place of that concrete relational love that bonded black
folks together in communities of hope and struggle.

Black women, writing from a feminist perspective, have worked
hard to show that narrow nationalism with its concomitant support of
patriarchy and male domination actually helped erode an organic
unity between black women and men that had been forged in struggles to resist racism begun in slavery time. Reinvoking black nationalism is not an adequate response to the situation of crisis we are facing
as a people. In many ways, ours is a crisis of identity, not that "I need
to find out who I am" lifestyle brand. The identity crisis we suffer has
to do with losing a sense of political perspective, not knowing how we
should struggle collectively to fight racism and to create a liberatory
space to construct radical black subjectivity. This identity has to do
with resistance, with reconstructing a collective front to re-vision and
renew black liberation struggle.

In his provocative book *The Death of Rhythm and Blues* Nelson George sees this crisis as informed by a split between assimilationists and those black folks who wish to be, as he calls it, self-sufficient. This simplistic account is problematic. There are many black people who are not positioned to be self-sufficient, who are also not assimilationist. It is not simply a matter of personal choice. Much of the "new racism" bombarding us undermines black solidarity by promoting notions of choice and individual rights in ways that suggest "freedom" for a black person can be measured by the degree to which we can base all decisions in life on individualistic concerns, what feels good or satisfies desire. This way of thinking militates against bonding that is rooted in relational love, nor is it countered by nationalism.

When black people collectively experienced racist oppression in similar ways, there was greater group solidarity. Racial integration has indeed altered in a fundamental way the common ground that once served as a foundation for black liberation struggle. Today black people of different classes are victimized by racism in distinctly different ways. Despite racism, privileged black people have available to them a variety of life choices and possibilities. We cannot respond to the emergence of multiple black experiences by advocating a return to narrow cultural nationalism. Contemporary critiques of essentialism (the assumption that there is a black essence shaping all African-American experience, expressed traditionally by the concept of "soul") challenge the idea that there is only "one" legitimate black experience. Facing the reality of multiple black experiences enables us to develop diverse agendas for unification, taking into account the specificity and diversity of who we are.

Teaching Black Studies, I find that students are quick to label a black person who has grown up in a predominantly white setting and attended similar schools as "not black enough." I am shocked and annoyed by the growing numbers of occasions where a white person explains to me that another black person is really "not black-identified." Our concept of black experience has been too narrow and constricting. Rather than assume that a black person coming from a background that is not predominantly black is assimilationist, I prefer to acknowledge that theirs is a different black experience, one that means that they may not have had access to life experiences more common to those of us raised in racially segregated worlds. It is not productive to see them as enemies or dismiss them by labeling them "not black enough." Most often they have not chosen the context of their upbringing, and they may be suffering from a sense of "loss" of not knowing who they are as black people or where they fit in. Teaching students from these backgrounds (particularly at Yale), I found myself referring often to traditional black folk experience and they would not know what I was talking about. It was not that they did not want to know—they did. In the interest of unity, of strengthening black community, it is important for us to recognize and value all black experiences and to share knowledge with one another. Those of us who have a particularly rich connection to black folk traditions can and should share.

Years ago I would begin my introduction to African-American literature classes by asking students to define blackness. Usually they simply listed stereotypes. Often folks evoke the experience of Southern rural black folks and make it synonymous with "authentic" blackness, or we take particular lifestyle traits of poor blacks and see them as "the real thing." Even though most black folks in the United States have Southern roots (let's not forget that for a long time ninety per cent of all black people lived in the agrarian South), today many know only an urban city experience. A very distinctive black culture was created in the agrarian South, by the experience of rural living, poverty, racial segregation, and resistance struggle, a culture we can cherish and learn from. It offers ways of knowing, habits of being, that can help sustain us as a people. We can value and cherish the "meaning" of this experience without essentializing it. And those who have kept the faith, who embody in our life practices aspects of that cultural legacy, can pass it on. Current trends in postmodernist cultural critiques devaluing the importance of this legacy by dismissing notions of authenticity or suggesting that the very concept of "soul" is illusory and not experientially based are disturbing. Already coping with a sense of extreme fragmentation and alienation, black folks cannot afford the luxury of such dismissal.

Philosopher Cornel West, an influential black scholar committed to liberation struggle, calls attention to the crisis we are facing in his discussions of postmodernism. Commenting on the nihilism that is so pervasive in black communities, he explains:

> Aside from the changes in society as a whole, developments like hedonistic consumerism and the constant need of stimulation of the body which make any qualitative human relationships hard to maintain, it is a question of a breakdown in resources, what Raymond Williams calls structures of meaning. Except for the church, there is no longer any potent tradition on which one can fall back in dealing with hopelessness and meaninglessness.

West is speaking about the black underclass, yet the patterns he cites are equally manifest among black people who have material privilege. Poverty alone does not create a situation of nihilism; black people have always been poor. We need to re-examine the factors that gave life meaning in the midst of deprivation, hardship, and despair. I have already cited relational love as one of these forces; that way of being can be consciously practiced.

We can begin to build anew black communal feelings and black community by returning to the practice of acknowledging one another in daily life. That way "downhome" black folks had of speaking to one another, looking one another directly in the eye (many of us had old folks tell us, don't look down, look at me when I'm talking to you) was not some quaint country gesture. It was a practice of resistance undoing years of racist teachings that had denied us the power of recognition, the power of the gaze. These looks were affirmations of our being, a balm to wounded spirits. They opposed the internalized racism or alienated individualism that would have us turn away from one another, aping the dehumanizing practices of the colonizer. There are many habits of being that were a part of traditional black folk experience that we can re-enact, rituals of belonging. To reclaim them would not be a gesture of passive nostalgia; it would reflect awareness that humanizing survival strategies employed then are needed now.

Another important practice we need to reconstruct is the sharing of stories that taught history, family genealogy, and facts about the African-American past. Briefly, during the contemporary black power movement, tremendous attention was given to the importance of learning history. Today young black people often have no knowledge of black history and are unable to identify important black leaders like Malcolm X. The arts remain one of the powerful, if not the most powerful, realms of cultural resistance, a space for awakening folks to critical consciousness and new vision. Crossover trends in black music, film, etc. that require assimilation have a devastating anti-black propagandistic impact. We need to call attention to those black artists who successfully attract diverse audiences without pandering to a white supremacist consumer market while simultaneously creating a value system where acquisition of wealth and fame are not the only measures of success.

The most important agenda for black people concerned with unity and renewed struggle is the construction of a visionary model of black liberation. To complete this task we would need to examine the impact of materialist thinking in black lives. Nowadays many black folks believe that it is fine to do anything that will make money. Many

of us have lost a needed sense of ethics, that morality Mama evokes in
A Raisin In The Sun when she asks Walter Lee, "Since when did
money become life?" Black people must critically examine our obsession with material gain and consumer goods. We need to talk about
the way living simply may be a necessary aspect of our collective self-
recovery. We need to look at the way addiction to drugs, food, alcohol
and a host of other substances undermine our our individual sense of
self and our capacity to relate to one another. Addiction must be seen
politically as both sickness and a manifestation of genocidal practices
that have a grip on black life and are destroying it.

     In *Freedom Charter*, a work which chronicles resistance strate-
gies in South Africa, the phrase "our struggle is also a struggle of memory against forgetting" is continually repeated. Memory need not be a
passive reflection, a nostalgic longing for things to be as they once
were; it can function as a way of knowing and learning from the past,
what Michael M.J. Fischer in his essay "Ethnicity and the Art of Memory" calls "retrospection to gain a vision for the future." It can serve as
a catalyst for self-recovery. We are talking about collective black self-
recovery. We need to keep alive the memory of our struggles against
racism so that we can concretely chart how far we have come and
where we want to go, recalling those places, those times, those people
that gave a sense of direction. If we fall prey to the contemporary
ahistorical mood, we will forget that we have not stayed in one place,
that we have journeyed away from home, away from our roots, that
we have lived drylongso and learned to make a new history. We have
not gone the distance, but we can never turn back. We need to sing
again the old songs, those spirituals that renewed spirits and made the
journey sweet, hear again the old testimony urging us to keep the
faith, to go forward in love.

5

HOMEPLACE

a site of resistance

When I was a young girl the journey across town to my grandmother's house was one of the most intriguing experiences. Mama did not like to stay there long. She did not care for all that loud talk, the talk that was usually about the old days, the way life happened then—who married whom, how and when somebody died, but also how we lived and survived as black people, how the white folks treated us. I remember this journey not just because of the stories I would hear. It was a movement away from the segregated blackness of our community into a poor white neighborhood. I remember the fear, being scared to walk to Baba's (our grandmother's house) because we would have to pass that terrifying whiteness—those white faces on the porches staring us down with hate. Even when empty or vacant, those porches seemed to say "danger," "you do not belong here," "you are not safe."

Oh! that feeling of safety, of arrival, of homecoming when we finally reached the edges of her yard, when we could see the soot black face of our grandfather, Daddy Gus, sitting in his chair on the porch, smell his cigar, and rest on his lap. Such a contrast, that feeling of arrival, of homecoming, this sweetness and the bitterness of that journey, that constant reminder of white power and control.

I speak of this journey as leading to my grandmother's house, even though our grandfather lived there too. In our young minds houses belonged to women, were their special domain, not as property, but as places where all that truly mattered in life took place—the warmth and comfort of shelter, the feeding of our bodies, the nurturing of our souls. There we learned dignity, integrity of being; there we

41

learned to have faith. The folks who made this life possible, who were our primary guides and teachers, were black women.

Their lives were not easy. Their lives were hard. They were black women who for the most part worked outside the home serving white folks, cleaning their houses, washing their clothes, tending their children—black women who worked in the fields or in the streets, whatever they could do to make ends meet, whatever was necessary. Then they returned to their homes to make life happen there. This tension between service outside one's home, family, and kin network, service provided to white folks which took time and energy, and the effort of black women to conserve enough of themselves to provide service (care and nurturance) within their own families and communities is one of the many factors that has historically distinguished the lot of black women in patriarchal white supremacist society from that of black men. Contemporary black struggle must honor this history of service just as it must critique the sexist definition of service as women's "natural" role.

Since sexism delegates to females the task of creating and sustaining a home environment, it has been primarily the responsibility of black women to construct domestic households as spaces of care and nurturance in the face of the brutal harsh reality of racist oppression, of sexist domination. Historically, African-American people believed that the construction of a homeplace, however fragile and tenuous (the slave hut, the wooden shack), had a radical political dimension. Despite the brutal reality of racial apartheid, of domination, one's homeplace was the one site where one could freely confront the issue of humanization, where one could resist. Black women resisted by making homes where all black people could strive to be subjects, not objects, where we could be affirmed in our minds and hearts despite poverty, hardship, and deprivation, where we could restore to ourselves the dignity denied us on the outside in the public world.

This task of making homeplace was not simply a matter of black women providing service; it was about the construction of a safe place where black people could affirm one another and by so doing heal many of the wounds inflicted by racist domination. We could not learn to love or respect ourselves in the culture of white supremacy, on the outside; it was there on the inside, in that "homeplace," most often created and kept by black women, that we had the opportunity to grow and develop, to nurture our spirits. This task of making a homeplace, of making home a community of resistance, has been shared by black women globally, especially black women in white supremacist societies.

I shall never forget the sense of shared history, of common anguish, I felt when first reading about the plight of black women domestic servants in South Africa, black women laboring in white homes. Their stories evoked vivid memories of our African-American past. I remember that one of the black women giving testimony complained that after traveling in the wee hours of the morning to the white folks' house, after working there all day, giving her time and energy, she had "none left for her own." I knew this story. I had read it in the slave narratives of African-American women who, like Sojourner Truth, could say, "When I cried out with a mother's grief none but Jesus heard." I knew this story. I had grown to womanhood hearing about black women who nurtured and cared for white families when they longed to have time and energy to give to their own.

I want to remember these black women today. The act of remembrance is a conscious gesture honoring their struggle, their effort to keep something for their own. I want us to respect and understand that this effort has been and continues to be a radically subversive political gesture. For those who dominate and oppress us benefit most when we have nothing to give our own, when they have so taken from us our dignity, our humanness that we have nothing left, no "homeplace" where we can recover ourselves. I want us to remember these black women today, both past and present. Even as I speak there are black women in the midst of racial apartheid in South Africa, struggling to provide something for their own. "We...know how our sisters suffer" (Quoted in the petition for the repeal of the pass laws, August 9, 1956). I want us to honor them, not because they suffer but because they continue to struggle in the midst of suffering, because they continue to resist. I want to speak about the importance of homeplace in the midst of oppression and domination, of homeplace as a site of resistance and liberation struggle. Writing about "resistance," particularly resistance to the Vietnam war, Vietnamese Buddhist monk Thich Nhat Hahn says:

> ....resistance, at root, must mean more than resistance against
> war. It is a resistance against all kinds of things that are like
> war...So perhaps, resistance means opposition to being invaded,
> occupied, assaulted and destroyed by the system. The purpose
> of resistance, here, is to seek the healing of yourself in order to
> be able to see clearly... I think that communities of resistance
> should be places where people can return to themselves more
> easily, where the conditions are such that they can heal
> themselves and recover their wholeness.

Historically, black women have resisted white supremacist domination by working to establish homeplace. It does not matter that sexism assigned them this role. It is more important that they took this conventional role and expanded it to include caring for one another, for children, for black men, in ways that elevated our spirits, that kept us from despair, that taught some of us to be revolutionaries able to struggle for freedom. In his famous 1845 slave narrative, Frederick Douglass tells the story of his birth, of his enslaved black mother who was hired out a considerable distance from his place of residence. Describing their relationship, he writes:

> I never saw my mother, to know her as such more than four or five times in my life; and each of these times was very short in duration, and at night. She was hired by Mr. Stewart, who lived about twelve miles from my house. She made her journeys to see me in the night, traveling the whole distance on foot, after the performance of her day's work. She was a field hand, and a whipping is the penalty of not being in the field at sunrise...I do not recollect of ever seeing my mother by the light of day. She was with me in the night. She would lie down with me and get me to sleep, but long before I waked she was gone.

After sharing this information, Douglass later says that he never enjoyed a mother's "soothing presence, her tender and watchful care" so that he received the "tidings of her death with much the same emotions I should have probably felt at the death of a stranger." Douglass surely intended to impress upon the consciousness of white readers the cruelty of that system of racial domination which separated black families, black mothers from their children. Yet he does so by devaluing black womanhood, by not even registering the quality of care that made his black mother travel those twelve miles to hold him in her arms. In the midst of a brutal racist system, which did not value black life, she valued the life of her child enough to resist that system, to come to him in the night, just to hold him.

Now I cannot agree with Douglass that he never knew a mother's care. I want to suggest that this mother, who dared to hold him in the night, gave him at birth a sense of value that provided a groundwork, however fragile, for the person he later became. If anyone doubts the power and significance of this maternal gesture, they would do well to read psychoanalyst Alice Miller's book, *The Untouched Key: Tracing Childhood Trauma in Creativity and Destructiveness*. Holding him in her arms, Douglass' mother provided, if only for a short time, a space where this black child was not the subject of dehumanizing scorn and devaluation but was the recipient of a quality of care that should have enabled the adult Douglass to look back and reflect on the political choices of this black mother who resisted slave codes, risking her life, to care for her son. I want to suggest that devaluation of the role his mother played in his life is a dangerous oversight. Though Douglass is only one example, we are currently in danger of forgetting the powerful role black women have played in constructing for us homeplaces that are the site for resistance. This forgetfulness undermines our solidarity and the future of black liberation struggle.

Douglass's work is important, for he is historically identified as sympathetic to the struggle for women's rights. All too often his critique of male domination, such as it was, did not include recognition of the particular circumstances of black women in relation to black men and families. To me one of the most important chapters in my first book, *Ain't I A Woman: Black Women and Feminism,* is one that calls attention to "Continued Devaluation of Black Womanhood." Overall devaluation of the role black women have played in constructing for us homeplaces that are the site for resistance undermines our efforts to resist racism and the colonizing mentality which promotes internalized self-hatred. Sexist thinking about the nature of domesticity has determined the way black women's experience in the home is perceived. In African-American culture there is a long tradition of "mother worship." Black autobiographies, fiction, and poetry praise the virtues of the self-sacrificing black mother. Unfortunately, though positively motivated, black mother worship extols the virtues of self-sacrifice while simultaneously implying that such a gesture is not reflective of choice and will, rather the perfect embodiment of a woman's "natural" role. The assumption then is that the black woman who works hard to be a responsible caretaker is only doing what she should be doing. Failure to recognize the realm of choice, and the remarkable re-visioning of both woman's role and the idea of "home" that black women consciously exercised in practice, obscures the political commitment to racial uplift, to eradicating racism, which was the philosophical core of dedication to community and home.

Though black women did not self-consciously articulate in written discourse the theoretical principles of decolonization, this does not detract from the importance of their actions. They understood intellectually and intuitively the meaning of homeplace in the midst of an oppressive and dominating social reality, of homeplace as site of resistance and liberation struggle. I know of what I speak. I would not be writing this essay if my mother, Rosa Bell, daughter to Sarah

Oldham, granddaughter to Bell Hooks, had not created homeplace in just this liberatory way, despite the contradictions of poverty and sexism.

In our family, I remember the immense anxiety we felt as children when mama would leave our house, our segregated community, to work as a maid in the homes of white folks. I believe that she sensed our fear, our concern that she might not return to us safe, that we could not find her (even though she always left phone numbers, they did not ease our worry). When she returned home after working long hours, she did not complain. She made an effort to rejoice with us that her work was done, that she was home, making it seem as though there was nothing about the experience of working as a maid in a white household, in that space of Otherness, which stripped her of dignity and personal power.

Looking back as an adult woman, I think of the effort it must have taken for her to transcend her own tiredness (and who knows what assaults or wounds to her spirit had to be put aside so that she could give something to her own). Given the contemporary notions of "good parenting" this may seem like a small gesture, yet in many post-slavery black families, it was a gesture parents were often too weary, too beaten down to make. Those of us who were fortunate enough to receive such care understood its value. Politically, our young mother, Rosa Bell, did not allow the white supremacist culture of domination to completely shape and control her psyche and her familial relationships. Working to create a homeplace that affirmed our beings, our blackness, our love for one another was necessary resistance. We learned degrees of critical consciousness from her. Our lives were not without contradictions, so it is not my intent to create a romanticized portrait. Yet any attempts to critically assess the role of black women in liberation struggle must examine the way political concern about the impact of racism shaped black women's thinking, their sense of home, and their modes of parenting.

An effective means of white subjugation of black people globally has been the perpetual construction of economic and social structures that deprive many folks of the means to make homeplace. Remembering this should enable us to understand the political value of black women's resistance in the home. It should provide a framework where we can discuss the development of black female political consciousness, acknowledging the political importance of resistance effort that took place in homes. It is no accident that the South African apartheid regime systematically attacks and destroys black efforts to construct homeplace, however tenuous, that small private reality where black

women and men can renew their spirits and recover themselves. It is
no accident that this homeplace, as fragile and as transitional as it may
be, a makeshift shed, a small bit of earth where one rests, is always
subject to violation and destruction. For when a people no longer
have the space to construct homeplace, we cannot build a meaningful
community of resistance.

Throughout our history, African-Americans have recognized the
subversive value of homeplace, of having access to private space
where we do not directly encounter white racist aggression. Whatever
the shape and direction of black liberation struggle (civil rights reform
or black power movement), domestic space has been a crucial site for
organizing, for forming political solidarity. Homeplace has been a site
of resistance. Its structure was defined less by whether or not black
women and men were conforming to sexist behavior norms and more
by our struggle to uplift ourselves as a people, our struggle to resist
racist domination and oppression.

That liberatory struggle has been seriously undermined by contemporary efforts to change that subversive homeplace into a site of
patriarchal domination of black women by black men, where we
abuse one another for not conforming to sexist norms. This shift in
perspective, where homeplace is not viewed as a political site, has had
negative impact on the construction of black female identity and political consciousness. Masses of black women, many of whom were not
formally educated, had in the past been able to play a vital role in
black liberation struggle. In the contemporary situation, as the paradigms for domesticity in black life mirrored white bourgeois norms
(where home is conceptualized as politically neutral space), black
people began to overlook and devalue the importance of black female
labor in teaching critical consciousness in domestic space. Many black
women, irrespective of class status, have responded to this crisis of
meaning by imitating leisure-class sexist notions of women's role, focusing their lives on meaningless compulsive consumerism.

Identifying this syndrome as "the crisis of black womanhood" in
her essay, "Considering Feminism as a Model for Social Change,"
Sheila Radford-Hill points to the mid-sixties as that historical moment
when the primacy of black woman's role in liberation struggle began
to be questioned as a threat to black manhood and was deemed unimportant. Radford-Hill asserts:

> Without the power to influence the purpose and the direction of
> our collective experience, without the power to influence our
> culture from within, we are increasingly immobilized, unable to
> integrate self and role identities, unable to resist the cultural

imperialism of the dominant culture which assures our continued oppression by destroying us from within. Thus, the crisis manifests itself as social dysfunction in the black community—as genocide, fratricide, homicide, and suicide. It is also manifested by the abdication of personal responsibility by black women for themselves and for each other...The crisis of black womanhood is a form of cultural aggression: a form of exploitation so vicious, so insidious that it is currently destroying an entire generation of black women and their families.

This contemporary crisis of black womanhood might have been avoided had black women collectively sustained attempts to develop the latent feminism expressed by their willingness to work equally alongside black men in black liberation struggle. Contemporary equation of black liberation struggle with the subordination of black women has damaged collective black solidarity. It has served the interests of white supremacy to promote the assumption that the wounds of racist domination would be less severe were black women conforming to sexist role patterns.

We are daily witnessing the disintegration of African-American family life that is grounded in a recognition of the political value of constructing homeplace as a site of resistance; black people daily perpetuate sexist norms that threaten our survival as a people. We can no longer act as though sexism in black communities does not threaten our solidarity; any force which estranges and alienates us from one another serves the interests of racist domination.

Black women and men must create a revolutionary vision of black liberation that has a feminist dimension, one which is formed in consideration of our specific needs and concerns. Drawing on past legacies, contemporary black women can begin to reconceptualize ideas of homeplace, once again considering the primacy of domesticity as a site for subversion and resistance. When we renew our concern with homeplace, we can address political issues that most affect our daily lives. Calling attention to the skills and resources of black women who may have begun to feel that they have no meaningful contribution to make, women who may or may not be formally educated but who have essential wisdom to share, who have practical experience that is the breeding ground for all useful theory, we may begin to bond with one another in ways that renew our solidarity.

When black women renew our political commitment to homeplace, we can address the needs and concerns of young black women who are groping for structures of meaning that will further their growth, young women who are struggling for self-definition. Together, black women can renew our commitment to black liberation struggle, sharing insights and awareness, sharing feminist thinking and feminist vision, building solidarity.

With this foundation, we can regain lost perspective, give life new meaning. We can make homeplace that space where we return for renewal and self-recovery, where we can heal our wounds and become whole.

6

CRITICAL INTERROGATION

talking race, resisting racism

Within black street culture, *fresh* is a word used to express aesthetic evaluation of the unnamed forces behind a style, a concept, that add something new to our way of seeing—enhancing the visual experience of the look, the gaze. In *Radiance from the Waters,* art historian Sylvia Boone writes about the place of *neku*—freshness as one of the core concepts within the aesthetic culture of the Mende peoples of Sierra Leone and Liberia. A critical cultural tension emerges between this African sense of "freshness" and the African-American aesthetic. Different cultural locations evoke links, sensibilities, and longings contained within diverse structures of representation and meaning. These connections raise issues regarding race and culture similar to those James Clifford writes about in *The Predicament of Culture.* Appearing at a time when race is the "hot" topic, the "in" subject, these two works offer new insight and direction. They subvert and disrupt, challenging us to think critically about race and culture, about aesthetics.

Anyone witnessing the current cultural and academic focus on race has to note the new way race is being talked about, as though it were in no way linked to cultural practices that reinforce and perpetuate racism, creating a gap between attitudes and actions. There is even a new terminology to signal the shift in direction: the buzz words are *difference, the Other, hegemony, ethnography.* It's not that these words were not always around, but that they now are in style. Words like *Other* and *difference* are taking the place of commonly known words deemed uncool or too simplistic, words like *oppression, exploitation,*

and *domination*. *Black* and *white* in some circles are becoming definite no-nos, perpetuating what some folks see as stale and meaningless binary oppositions. Separated from a political and historical
context, *ethnicity* is being reconstituted as the new frontier, accessible
to all, no passes or permits necessary, where attention can now be focused on the production of a privileged, commodifiable discourse in
which race becomes synonymous with culture. There would be no
need, however, for any unruly radical black folks to raise critical ob-
jections to the phenomenon if all this passionate focus on race were
not so neatly divorced from a recognition of racism, of the continuing
domination of blacks by whites, and (to use some of those out-of-date,
uncool terms) of the continued suffering and pain in black life.

Powerful expressions of these contradictions are found in popular culture, ranging from the seemingly innocuous to the aggressively
racist. Just recently, for instance, in *Vogue* magazine, there was an article wherein the writer referred to Tracy Chapman's "Buckwheat"
hairdo. In terms of today's ethnic cool, I imagine the writer thought he
sounded cute, like he was in the know. *Excuse me!* Buckwheat has
never been recovered by black people as a positive representation of
their reality.

But let's not stop there. Opening the February issue of *Interview*,
I read, "Yoko: Life After Lennon." Ono is talking about Japan's economy when suddenly interviewer Kevin Sessums asks: "What is it about
Japanese women, Oriental women, that Caucasian men find so fascinating?" Nothing in the text suggests that Ono responds critically to
this line of questioning. Ono's answer begins, "Maybe the Western
man is intriguing to the Oriental woman..." Sessum's response:
"Maybe Oriental women are just better in bed. They know more positions." Is the insertion that tells the readers that Ono "laughs" intended
to mediate this racist remark, to make the remark appear nouveau ethnic cool? The point is that neither of these comments reflects a critical
consciousness about race. And come on, Yoko Ono, you know better!
For on the very next page, Ono cuts to the heart of the matter:

> I did about five interviews yesterday because the documentary
> *Imagine* is opening in Europe... Anyway, I woke up this
> morning with this kind of *pain* that I had never realized before. I
> said to myself, How *dare* they! Every time I have an interview I
> am asked this question: "The world hated you. You've been
> called the Dragon Lady for the past twenty years. How do you
> feel about it? Why do you think that happened?" You know what
> that is like? It's like somebody battering a woman and then
> saying, "All of us battered you, but why do you think we did it?"

I'm the one responsible for telling them why I was battered?
Well, let *them* tell *me*. They're the ones who did it. The other
side of it was Asian-bashing—it was as simple as that.

Precisely.

Later that same day, I walked to the local bookstore (and I live in
a small town) and picked up a new book on film and television—
Boxed In—in which the white male author, Mark Crispin Miller, talks
about images of blacks (in a way) presented as enlightened critique, as
though he had some special understanding of the way "black Others"
see themselves. I didn't stop there. I went on to the drama section and
actually sat down and read Alfred Uhry's Pulitzer Prize-winning *Driving Miss Daisy*—an integrated play by a white playwright. I had been
told that the play was about a sexual relationship between the two
main characters. Well, it is not. No! The play just hints at the possibility
that white Miss Daisy and her black chauffeur are sweet on each other.
Reading the play, it was easy to see the way it relies on those old stereotypes about Southern black men lusting after white ladies to titillate, without interrogating these images.

Whether blatantly racist or condescending to represent the
Other, these examples (and there are many more) give an idea of the
attitudes underlying popular culture. And, in many ways, a certain un-
consciousness about these attitudes has also characterized—even informed—intellectual inquiry into race and racism. To begin, what does
it mean when primarily white men and women are producing the discourse around Otherness?

Years ago, when I first left my segregated neighborhood for college, it seemed that the vast majority of college liberal whites were
confused: on the one hand, eager to make connections with black
people, and on the other, uncertain about the nature of the contact.
They were, however, confident that they were not racists. Wasn't their
desire for contact proof that they had transcended racism? As the black
liberation struggle waned, feminism emerged as a new terrain of radical politics. By the early eighties, women of color, particularly black
women, were challenging the assumption of shared oppression based
on gender. After a period of resistance, individual white women began
to discuss the issues of racism—developing "unlearning racism" work-
shops—and feminist scholars called attention to the work of black
novelists and poets.

Black male literary critics joined the discussion, at times appropriating the subject in ways that made it appear as though they—and
not black women—had been at the forefront demanding consideration
of these topics. And as male scholars from various backgrounds and

disciplines focused more on culture, particularly popular culture, post-colonial discourse and the work of Third World scholars and critics began to receive widespread attention.

The upshot of all this has been the unprecedented support among scholars and intellectuals for the inclusion of the Other—in theory. Yes! Everyone seems to be clamoring for "difference," only too few seem to want any difference that is about changing policy or that supports active engagement and struggle (another no-no word; recently a member of the new radical chic announced to me her sense that "struggle" is a tired term, and she's just not into it). Too often, it seems, the point is to promote the *appearance* of difference within intellectual discourse, a "celebration" that fails to ask who is sponsoring the party and who is extending the invitations. For who is controlling this new discourse? Who is getting hired to teach it, and where? Who is getting paid to write about it?

One change in direction that would be real cool would be the production of a discourse on race that interrogates whiteness. It would just be so interesting for all those white folks who are giving blacks their take on blackness to let them know what's going on with whiteness. In far too much contemporary writing—though there are some outstanding exceptions—race is always an issue of Otherness that is not white; it is black, brown, yellow, red, purple even. Yet only a persistent, rigorous, and informed critique of whiteness could really determine what forces of denial, fear, and competition are responsible for creating fundamental gaps between professed political commitment to eradicating racism and the participation in the construction of a discourse on race that perpetuates racial domination. Many scholars, critics, and writers preface their work by stating that they are white, as though mere acknowledgement of this fact were sufficient, as though it conveyed all we need to know of standpoint, motivation, direction. I think back to my graduate years when many of the feminist professors fiercely resisted the insistence that it was important to examine race and racism. Now many of these very same women are producing scholarship focusing on race and gender. What process enabled their perspectives to shift? Understanding that process is important for the development of solidarity; it can enhance awareness of the epistemological shifts that enable all of us to move in new and oppositional directions. Yet none of these women write articles reflecting on their critical process, showing how their attitudes have changed.

Let's take a look at a recent front-page spread in the *New York Times Book Review* from January 8, 1989, featuring historian Elizabeth Fox-Genovese's new work, *Within the Plantation Household: Black and White Women of the Old South.* Talking about her work, Fox-Genovese "conceded that it felt a bit odd at times to be a white woman writing about black women. 'On the other hand,' she said, 'I am deeply committed to the idea that we all have to be able to study any subject provided we are honest.' " While valorizing the notion of intellectual freedom, the comment obscures the more crucial issues involved when a member of a privileged group "interprets" the reality of members of a less powerful, exploited, and oppressed group.

Given a framework of domination, let's look at some concrete negative manifestations that occur when these issues are not addressed. First of all, let's acknowledge that few nonwhite scholars are being awarded grants to investigate and study all aspects of white culture from a standpoint of "difference"; doesn't this indicate just how tightly the colonizer/colonized paradigm continues to frame the discourse on race and the "Other"? At the same time, just as it has been necessary for black critical thinkers to challenge the idea that black people are inherently oppositional, are born with critical consciousness about domination and the will to resist, white thinkers must question their assumption that the decision to write about race and difference necessarily certifies antiracist behavior. And third, isn't it time to look closely at how and why work by white scholars about nonwhite people receives more attention and acclaim than similar work produced by nonwhite scholars (while at the same time, the latter's work is devalued—for being too "angry"—even as it's appropriated)? Many people who are into Clifford's work have never read Boone, for instance. Finally, the tendency to overvalue work by white scholars, coupled with the suggestion that such work constitutes the only relevant discourse, evades the issue of potential inaccessible locations—spaces white theorists cannot occupy. Without reinscribing an essentialist standpoint, it is crucial that we neither ignore nor deny that such locations exist.

If much of the recent work on race grows out of a sincere commitment to cultural transformation, there is serious need for immediate and persistent self-critique. Committed cultural critics—whether white or black, scholars or artists—can produce work that opposes structures of domination, that presents possibilities for a transformed future by willingly interrogating their own work on aesthetic and political grounds. This interrogation itself becomes an act of critical intervention, fostering a fundamental attitude of vigilance rather than denial.

7

REFLECTIONS ON RACE AND SEX

Race and sex have always been overlapping discourses in the United States. That discourse began in slavery. The talk then was not about black men wanting to be free so that they would have access to the bodies of white women—that would come later. Then, black women's bodies were the discursive terrain, the playing fields where racism and sexuality converged. Rape as both right and rite of the white male dominating group was a cultural norm. Rape was also an apt metaphor for European imperialist colonization of Africa and North America.

Sexuality has always provided gendered metaphors for colonization. Free countries equated with free men, domination with castration, the loss of manhood, and rape—the terrorist act re-enacting the drama of conquest, as men of the dominating group sexually violate the bodies of women who are among the dominated. The intent of this act was to continually remind dominated men of their loss of power; rape was a gesture of symbolic castration. Dominated men are made powerless (i.e., impotent) over and over again as the women they would have had the right to possess, to control, to assert power over, to dominate, to fuck, are fucked and fucked over by the dominating victorious male group.

There is no psychosexual history of slavery that explores the meaning of white male sexual exploitation of black women or the politics of sexuality, no work that lays out all the available information. There is no discussion of sexual sado-masochism, of the master who forced his wife to sleep on the floor as he nightly raped a black woman in bed. There is no discussion of sexual voyeurism. And what were the sexual lives of white men like who were legally declared "insane" because they wanted to marry black slave women with whom they were sexually and romantically involved? Under what conditions did sexuality serve as a force subverting and disrupting power relations, unsettling the oppressor/oppressed paradigm? No one seems to know how to tell this story, where to begin. As historical narrative it was long ago supplanted by the creation of another story (pornographic sexual project, fantasy, fear, the origin has yet to be traced). That story, invented by white men, is about the overwhelming desperate longing black men have to sexually violate the bodies of white women. The central character in this story is the black male rapist. Black men are constructed, as Michael Dyson puts it, as "peripatetic phalluses with unrequited desire for their denied object—white women." As the story goes, this desire is not based on longing for sexual pleasure. It is a story of revenge, rape as the weapon by which black men, the dominated, reverse their circumstance, regain power over white men.

Oppressed black men and women have rarely challenged the use of gendered metaphors to describe the impact of racist domination and/or black liberation struggle. The discourse of black resistance has almost always equated freedom with manhood, the economic and material domination of black men with castration, emasculation. Accepting these sexual metaphors forged a bond between oppressed black men and their white male oppressors. They shared the patriarchal belief that revolutionary struggle was really about the erect phallus, the ability of men to establish political dominance that could correspond to sexual dominance. Careful critical examination of black power literature in the sixties and early seventies exposes the extent to which black women and men were using sexualized metaphors to talk about the effort to resist racist domination. Many of us have never forgotten that moment in *Soul on Ice* when Eldridge Cleaver, writing about the need to "redeem my conquered manhood," described raping black women as practice for the eventual rape of white women. Remember that readers were not shocked or horrified by this glamorization of rape as a weapon of terrorism men might use to express rage about other forms of domination, about their struggle for power with other men. Given the sexist context of the culture, it made sense. Cleaver was able to deflect attention away from the misogynist sexism of his assertions by poignantly justifying these acts as a "natural" response to racial domination. He wanted to force readers to confront the agony and suffering black men experience in a white supremacist society. Again, freedom from racial domination was expressed in terms of redeeming black masculinity. And gaining the right to assert one's manhood was always about sexuality.

During slavery, there was perhaps a white male who created his own version of *Soul on Ice*, one who confessed how good it felt to assert racial dominance over black people, and particularly black men, by raping black women with impunity, or how sexually stimulating it was to use the sexual exploitation of black women to humiliate and degrade white women, to assert phallocentric domination in one's household. Sexism has always been a political stance mediating racial domination, enabling white men and black men to share a common sensibility about sex roles and the importance of male domination. Clearly both groups have equated freedom with manhood, and manhood with the right of men to have indiscriminate access to the bodies of women. Both groups have been socialized to condone patriarchal affirmation of rape as an acceptable way to maintain male domination. It is this merging of sexuality with male domination within patriarchy that informs the construction of masculinity for men of all races and classes. Robin Morgan's book, *The Demon Lover: On The Sexuality of Terrorism,* begins with rape. She analyses the way men are bonded across class, race, and nationalities through shared notions of manhood which make masculinity synonymous with the ability to assert power-over through acts of violence and terrorism. Since terrorist acts are most often committed by men, Morgan sees the terrorist as "the logical incarnation of patriarchal politics in a technological world." She is not concerned with the overlapping discourses of race and sex, with the interconnectedness of racism and sexism. Like many radical feminists, she believes that male commitment to maintaining patriarchy and male domination diminishes or erases difference.

Much of my work within feminist theory has stressed the importance of understanding difference, of the ways race and class status determine the degree to which one can assert male domination and privilege and most importantly the ways racism and sexism are interlocking systems of domination which uphold and sustain one another. Many feminists continue to see them as completely separate issues, believing that sexism can be abolished while racism remains intact, or that women who work to resist racism are not supporting feminist movement. Since black liberation struggle is so often framed in terms that affirm and support sexism, it is not surprising that white women are uncertain about whether women's rights struggle will be diminished if there is too much focus on resisting racism, or that many black women continue to fear that they will be betraying black men if they support feminist movement. Both these fears are responses to the equation of black liberation with manhood. This continues to be a central way black people frame our efforts to resist racist domination; it must be critiqued. We must reject the sexualization of black liberation in ways that support and perpetuate sexism, phallocentrism, and male domination. Even though Michele Wallace tried to expose the fallacy of equating black liberation with the assertion of oppressive manhood in *Black Macho and the Myth of the Superwoman*, few black people got the message. Continuing this critique in *Ain't I A Woman:Black Women and Feminism*, I found that more and more black women were rejecting this paradigm. It has yet to be rejected by most black men, and especially black male political figures. As long as black people hold on to the idea that the trauma of racist domination is really the loss of black manhood, then we invest in the racist narratives that perpetuate the idea that all black men are rapists, eager to use sexual terrorism to express their rage about racial domination.

Currently we are witnessing a resurgence of such narratives. They are resurfacing at a historical moment when black people are bearing the brunt of more overt and blatant racist assaults, when black men and especially young black men are increasingly disenfranchised by society. Mainstream white supremacist media make it appear that a black menace to societal safety is at large, that control, repression, and violent domination are the only effective ways to address the problem. Witness the use of the Willie Horton case to discredit Dukakis in the 1988 Presidential election. Susan Estrich in her post-campaign articles has done a useful job of showing how racist stereotypes were evoked to turn voters against Dukakis, and how Bush in no way denounced this strategy. In all her articles she recounts the experience of being raped by a black man fifteen years ago, describing the way racism determined how the police responded to the crime, and her response. Though her intent is to urge societal commitment to anti-racist struggle, every article I have read has carried captions in bold print emphasizing the rape. The subversive content of her work is undermined and the stereotype that all black men are rapists is re-inscribed and reinforced. Most people in this society do not realize that the vast majority of rapes are not inter-racial, that all groups of men are more likely to rape women who are the same race as themselves.

Within popular culture, Madonna's video "Like a Prayer" also makes use of imagery which links black men with rape, reinforcing this representation in the minds of millions of viewers—even though she has said that her intention is to be anti-racist, and certainly the video suggests that not all black men who are accused of raping white women are guilty. Once again, however, this subversive message is undermined by the overall focus on sexually charged imagery of white female sexuality and black male lust. The most subversive message in the video has nothing to do with anti-racism; it has to do with the construction of white females as desiring subjects who can freely assert sexual agency. Of course the taboo expression of that agency is choosing to be sexual with black men. Unfortunately this is a continuation of the notion that ending racist domination is really about issues of interracial sexual access, a myth that must be critiqued so that this society can confront the actual material, economic, and moral consequences of perpetuating white supremacy and its traumatic genocidal impact on black people.

Images of black men as rapists, as dangerous menaces to society, have been sensational cultural currency for some time. The obsessive media focus on these representations is political. The role it plays in the maintenance of racist domination is to convince the public that black men are a dangerous threat who must be controlled by any means necessary, including annihilation. This is the cultural backdrop shaping media response to the Central Park rape case, and the media has played a major role in shaping public response. Many people are using this case to perpetuate racial stereotypes and racism. Ironically, the very people who claim to be shocked by the brutality of this case have no qualms about suggesting that the suspects should be castrated or killed. They see no link between this support of violence as a means of social control and the suspects' use of violence to exercise control. Public response to this case highlights the lack of understanding about the interconnectedness of racism and sexism.

Many black people, especially black men, using the sexist paradigm that suggests rape of white women by black men is a reaction to racist domination, view the Central Park case as an indictment of the racist system. They do not see sexism as informing the nature of the crime, the choice of victim. Many white women have responded to the case by focusing solely on the brutal assault as an act of gender domination, of male violence against women. A piece in the *Village Voice* written by white female Andrea Kannapell carried captions in bold print which began with the statement in all capitals for greater emphasis, "THE CRIME WAS MORE SEXIST THAN RACIST..." Black women responding to the same issue all focused on the sexist nature of the crime, often giving examples of black male sexism. Given the work black women have done within feminist writing to call attention to the reality of black male sexism, work that often receives little or no attention or is accused of attacking black men, it is ironic that the brutal rape of a white woman by a group of young black males serves as the catalyst for admission that sexism is a serious problem in black communities. Lisa Kennedy's piece, "Body Double: The Anatomy of a Crime," also published in the *Village Voice,* acknowledges the convergence of racism and sexism as politics of domination that inform this assault. Kennedy writes:

> If I accept the premise of the coverage, that this rape is more
> heartbreaking than all the rapes that happen to women of color,
> then what happens to the value of my body? What happens to
> the quality of my blackness?

These questions remain unanswered, though she closes with "a call for a sophisticated feminist offensive." Such an offensive should begin with cultivating critical awareness of the way racism and sexism are interlocking systems of domination.

Public response to the Central Park case reveals the extent to which the culture invests in the kind of dualistic thinking that helps reinforce and maintain all forms of domination. Why must people decide whether this crime is more sexist than racist, as if these are competing oppressions? Why do white people, and especially feminist white women, feel better when black people, especially black women, disassociate themselves from the plight of black men in white supremacist capitalist patriarchy to emphasize opposition to black male sexism? Cannot black women remain seriously concerned about the brutal effect of racist domination on black men and also denounce black male sexism? And why is black male sexism evoked as though it is a special brand of this social disorder, more dangerous, more abhorrent and life-threatening than the sexism that pervades the culture as a whole, or the sexism that informs white male domination of women? These questions call attention to the either/or ways of thinking that are the philosophical underpinning of systems of domination. Progressive folks must then insist, wherever we engage in discussions of this crime or of issues of race and gender, on the complexity of our experience in a racist sexist society.

The Central Park crime involves aspects of sexism, male domination, misogyny, and the use of rape as an instrument of terror. It also involves race and racism; it is unlikely that young black males growing up in this society, attacking a white woman, would see her as "just a woman"—her race would be foremost in their consciousness as well as her sex, in the same way that masses of people hearing about this crime were concerned with identifying first her race. In a white supremacist sexist society all women's bodies are devalued, but white women's bodies are more valued than those of women of color. Given the context of white supremacy, the historical narratives about black male rapists, the racial identities of both victim and victimizers enable this tragedy to be sensationalized.

To fully understand the multiple meanings of this incident, it must be approached from an analytical standpoint that considers the impact of sexism and racism. Beginning there enables many of us to empathize with both the victim and the victimizers. If one reads *The Demon Lover* and thinks again about this crime, one can see it as part of a continuum of male violence against women, of rape and terror as weapons of male domination—yet another horrific and brutal expression of patriarchal socialization. And if one considers this case by combining a feminist analysis of race and masculinity, one sees that since male power within patriarchy is relative, men from poorer groups and men of color are not able to reap the material and social rewards for their participation in patriarchy. In fact they often suffer from blindly and passively acting out a myth of masculinity that is life-threatening. Sexist thinking blinds them to this reality. They become victims of the patriarchy. No one can truly believe that the young black males involved in the Central Park incident were not engaged in a suicidal ritual enactment of a dangerous masculinity that will ultimately threaten their lives, their well-being.

If one reads again Michael Dyson's piece "The Plight of Black Men," focusing especially on the part where he describes the reason many young black men form gangs—"the sense of absolute belonging and unsurpassed love"—it is easy to understand why young black males are despairing and nihilistic. And it is rather naive to think that if they do not value their own lives, they will value the lives of others. Is it really so difficult for folks to see the connection between the constant pornographic glorification of male violence against women that is represented, enacted, and condoned daily in the culture and the Central Park crime? Does racism create and maintain this blindspot or does it allow black people and particularly black men to become the scapegoats, embodying society's evils?

If we are to live in a less violent and more just society, then we must engage in anti-sexist and anti-racist work. We desperately need to explore and understand the connections between racism and sexism. And we need to teach everyone about those connections so that they can be critically aware and socially active. Much education for critical consciousness can take place in everyday conversations. Black women and men must participate in the construction of feminist thinking, creating models for feminist struggle that address the particular circumstances of black people. Still, the most visionary task of all re-

mains that of re-conceptualizing masculinity so that alternative, transformative models are there in the culture, in our daily lives, to help
boys and men who are working to construct a self, to build new identities. Black liberation struggle must be re-visioned so that it is no
longer equated with maleness. We need a revolutionary vision of
black liberation, one that emerges from a feminist standpoint and addresses the collective plight of black people.

Any individual committed to resisting politics of domination, to
eradicating sexism and racism, understands the importance of not promoting an either/or competition between the oppressive systems. We
can empathize with the victim and the victimizers in the Central Park
case, allowing that feeling to serve as a catalyst for renewed commitment to anti-sexist and anti-racist work. Yesterday I heard this story. A
black woman friend called to say that she had been attacked on the
street by a black man. He took her purse, her house keys, her car keys.
She lives in one of the poorest cities in the United States. We talked
about poverty, sexism, and racial domination to place what had happened in a perspective that will enable both individual healing and
political understanding of this crime. Today I heard this story. A white
woman friend called to say that she had been attacked in her doorway
by a black man. She screamed and he ran away. Neighbors coming to
her aid invoked racism. She refused to engage in this discussion even
though she was shocked by the intensity and degree of racism expressed. Even in the midst of her own fear and pain, she remained politically aware, so as not to be complicit in perpetuating the white
supremacy that is the root of so much suffering. Both of these women
feel rage at their victimizers; they do not absolve them even as they
seek to understand and to respond in ways that will enrich the struggle
to end domination—so that sexism, sexist violence, racism, and racist
violence will cease to be an everyday happening.

8

REPRESENTATIONS

feminism and black masculinity

R ecently in conversation with a feminist white woman friend I mentioned that I had just completed Ishmael Reed's book of essays *Writin' is Fightin'* and found it interesting, especially his comments on race and culture. Her response was to emphasize (as though I were too naive to have a clue) that he is considered by most feminists to be "horribly misogynist," that she had given up on his work long ago. As she put it, "I just don't read the man." Confessing that I not only read his work but teach it, I fondly recalled several long intense conversations with him when I lived in the Bay area, where we talked about feminism. This conversation with the white woman feminist served as the catalyst for a reflection on the problem of censorship within feminist movement. Teaching women's studies classes, I often encounter students who do not want to read a particular writer's work because they consider it sexist or misogynist. Whenever that happens I use the occasion to talk about the danger of passing judgment in ways that suggest we should not read a writer because of his or her political stance on a particular issue, the danger of using hearsay to negate a work. Encouraging students to go to the source and critique from there, I reiterate that knowledge is more powerful than hearsay.

Over the years I have noticed that students in women's studies are often quick to pass judgments about writing by black men even though they have not read a wide range of literature by black male authors. Often students take a course I teach on black women writers and are resentful when I suggest that before they enter this field of study they need to fully understand the African-American literary tradition; this means they need to have read works by black women and men. Their desire to focus solely on works by black women is a response that feeds the erroneous notion that racism and sexism are two radically different forms of oppression, that one can be eradicated while the other remains intact. Listening to mature feminists make similar comments abut Reed and other black male writers, I call attention to their willingness to pass judgment on black male writers when it is rare to hear such condemnation of white male writers. Within literary studies racism often shapes this response. White women who cannot imagine excluding Chaucer, Shakespeare, or Joyce from their reading list (even though their works reflect sexism and racism) easily use this criterion to defend their ignorance of writing by black men. Currently in the academic world, the trend among women interested in critical theory, or post-colonial discourse, is to overlook as much as possible the sexism and racism of white male thinkers whose work is deemed "important" (Derrida, Foucault, Jameson, Said, for example). This response is as problematic as that reaction which would encourage women to ignore the work of these writers. If we are ever to construct a feminist movement that is not based on the premise that men and women are always at war with one another, then we must be willing to acknowledge the appropriateness of complex critical responses to writing by men even if it is sexist. Clearly women can learn from writers whose work is sexist, even be inspired by it, because sexism may be simply one dimension of that work. Concurrently fiercely critiquing the sexism does not mean that one does not value the work.

In this essay I want to focus on feminist responses to black men and black male sexism. Since many black men believe that feminist movement threatens to erase their voices, to usurp focus on racial oppression, it is in the interest of feminist movement to examine the negative implications of attempts to censor their work, or to overly condemn a particular group of men.

Censorship or condemnation of a particular writer's work within feminist circles has never focused solely on male writing. When my first book was published, an established black feminist writer wrote a review urging readers not to buy it, and most importantly not to read it. Another black feminist poet and essayist wrote the publishers a letter telling them that their publication of this work was, to use her words, "a criminal act." Shocked by these attempts to censor and/or repress the introduction into feminist discourse of a perspective and style of writing deemed unacceptable (at that time it was not fashionable to criticize the nature and direction of feminist movement), I began to realize that even in the realm of feminist thinking there existed a hegemonic discourse censoring dissident voices. Ironically, years later, the very issues I had raised in ways that unsettled and offended have become acceptable, in vogue even. Positive feminist critical appreciation of my work has not obliterated the memory of what it meant to have one's writing casually and brutally dismissed. This experience informs my concern that there be a space within feminist movement for the production, dissemination, and discussion of diverse ideas and perspectives. This includes focusing on black male thinkers and writers. I can understand the dissident black male voices who indict feminist thinkers for condemning their work without giving it serious critical appraisal, without seeking to understand where they are coming from. To be truly productive such understanding must be reciprocal. Black men must also seek to fully explore feminist thinking.

While I found Ishmael Reed's essays on race and culture compelling, I noted that he consciously placed the work in a masculinist exclusionary framework. The book is subtitled "Thirty-Seven Years of Boxing on Paper." His choice of metaphor, his use of fighting, and more particularly "boxing" to frame his work, coupled with all the direct references solely to black men (there are a few black women boxers, yet they are not a part of his "in" group) structurally set up the book in a manner declaring a particular solidarity with black male writers that presumably he does not feel toward black women. Dedicating the book to three men "who fought the good fight," he then reiterates and stresses his focus on black men by prefacing the work with four short quotes, all by men: Chester Himes saying, "A fighter fights, and a writer writes." Paul Lofty saying, "A black man is born with his guard up." Muhammad Ali's quote provides the title, "Writin' is Fightin'." And finally Larry Holmes saying, "Don't bite your tongue about it." It could not be more obvious to the aware reader that Reed is indeed responding to the attention black women have received by lavishly placing black men at the center of his work, and self-consciously calling attention to that placement.

Rather than construct his text in a way which might bridge tensions between black male writers and their female counterparts, he exploits these concerns, enhancing public representation of himself as writing in opposition to black women and to feminist thinking.

Reed's colorful essay "Steven Spielberg Plays Howard Beach" seeks on the one hand to counter feminist charges that he is sexist and misogynist even as it includes comments that could be easily interpreted as anti-feminist. For example:

> Gloria Steinem, media-appointed high priest person of American
> feminism, set the tone for the current group libel campaign
> against black men when she said, in the June 2, l982 issue of
> "Ms.", that the characterizations of black men in Walker's book
> represented "Truth-telling." Since then this "truth-telling" line has
> been picked up by other feminists, womanists, and their male
> allies: bimps and wimps.

Since sarcasm and ridicule are ways of talking about women that reinforce male sexism and domination, it is easy to see why many feminists view Reed as an enemy. However, this essay raises a crucial issue, one that it does not fully explore—whether or not feminist focus on black male chauvinism is harsher and more brutal than critiques of patriarchy in general.

Fundamentally, Reed is critically on the mark when he calls attention to a differentiation in reactions to black and white male sexism within feminist movement. Contemporary feminists do tend to act as though black male sexism is more heinous than white male sexism. Given white female racism, which has shaped the direction of much feminist movement, it is not surprising that the early radical focus on rape tended to project the racist stereotype that the male most to be feared was black. I will never forget listening to a feminist radio show where this was stated on the air. White women discussing rape cautioned female listeners who were hitch-hikers to avoid accepting rides from black men, the implication being that they were more likely to rape than their white counterparts. This bit of information was not supported with any statistical evidence showing that higher numbers of black men raped white female hitch-hikers. Studies show that white women are more likely to be raped by men of the same racial group than by men of color. This is one example of the way in which racism has informed feminist perceptions of black males; there are many more. To some extent, insightful critiques of racism within feminist movement have helped create a progressive political climate where white feminist thinkers (and black women as well) are more likely to reflect on how they talk about race and black male sexism. Still, the tendency to harshly critique black male sexism in ways that suggest it is the most harmful expression of patriarchal power (which it is not) surfaces in feminist discussions, even in the writings of black women.

Much of the public debate about Alice Walker's novel *The Color Purple* focused on whether the portrayal of black men as brutal misogynists was accurate. Even though the novel shows the transformation of Mister—he moves from being a brutal male chauvinist to a compassionate caring person—Walker's shift in representation was rarely acknowledged. Completely overshadowed by Steven Spielberg's cinematic interpretation of the novel, audiences seemed to forget Walker's position. In the film version of the novel, Speilberg did not choose to graphically portray Mister's transformation. Instead he highlighted images that readily resembled existing racist stereotypes depicting black masculinity as threatening and dangerous. This has been the case in filmmaking from *Birth of a Nation* to contemporary films like *Witness*. These images "work" in movies. Within a white supremacist culture, it is logical that white audiences feel more engaged with a scary film when the villain is a black male.

Witness is a prime example of a film which exploits racial stereotypes to enhance its "thriller" dimension. Audiences are literally sitting on the edge of their seats when the black male character (played by Danny Glover) commits a brutal murder in the presence of a little white boy who watches, unseen. After the murder, the black male searches the stalls to make sure he was not observed. Racial difference is exploited to create dramatic tension. As he reaches his hand into the stall where the innocent "beautiful" little white boy is hiding, the camera zooms in for a close up of the black hand, moving from that image to the scared white face of the little boy, playing on the contrasts between terrifying blackness and pure, innocent whiteness. Cinematically, the movie version of *The Color Purple* operates in a similar manner. When the film begins, the innocence of the young black girls appears more poignant and authentic when contrasted with the brutal images of dominating black masculinity.

Spielberg's representation of black men cannot be dismissed as though it has no political implications, as though it is rooted solely in neutral artistic choices. Whatever the factors which personally motivated him to downplay and in some ways almost completely ignore the transformation of Mister, it had the political impact of transforming Walker's text (which was not anti-black male, which did not portray black men as if they are not complex individuals) into a one-dimensional frame where black males were depicted in a conventional, stereotypically racist Hollywood manner. In this film, black masculinity was portrayed as brutish and animalistic.

Much of the debate about race and representation sparked by *The Color Purple,* both the book and the film, focused primarily on the representation of black masculinity. Those works, as well as writing by contemporary black women writers in general, were seen as being anti-black male, as consciously promoting negative representations. Unfortunately, most of these discussions were superficial, taking the form of an emphasis on purity, whether or not images were "good" or "bad." Producing images of blacks in a racist context is politically charged. Black women have been accused of acting in complicity with "the man" (i.e., white male systems of domination) when creating images of black men. Whether or not images of black femaleness in contemporary work by black women are "positive" is never a concern voiced by black men. The concern is with the black male image, who will control it, who will represent it. A central aspect of black male aesthetics has always been the construction of an image, particularly the dissembling image. Given this concern, it follows that most black men would respond with intense defensiveness when they perceive other groups gaining "control" over representations of black masculinity. Those black men who approach the issue from a patriarchal mindset fundamentally disapprove of autonomous black women creating images without first seeking their approval. From a sexist perspective, that in and of itself is seen as an indication that black men have no power, since it suggests that they can't control "their women."

Black women writers have responded to the charges that they consciously portray black men "negatively" by defensively pointing to the accuracy of their representations or by invoking the notion of a transcendent artist who is somehow divinely inspired and therefore not fully accountable for the images emerging in her work. After masses of black people watched the film version of *The Color Purple,* all around the United States there were public discussions in black communities, debates about the film and the book. Black women testified that they had known black men like Mister, that we are victims of incest, rape, and brutal physical abuse. Black males responded with the challenge that the issue of representation was not accuracy but rather whether certain aspects of black life should be talked about (i.e., revealed) in a non-black context. Nationalist responses questioned the value of showing one's dirty laundry in public, though rarely did they offer a context where such discussions would be more acceptable. Certainly Walker's book was not the catalyst for the discussion, but a white male's interpretation, a fact which suggests that black men are more concerned with how they are seen by white men than by black women. Overall the discussions of race, representation, and gender that these debates sparked did little to enhance collective understanding of the issues. There was little meaningful communication between the two groups. A major barrier was the unwillingness of black men to take sexism seriously, to acknowledge that it is and can be as detrimental as racism.

This discussion continues. As recently as July 14, 1989, the Phil Donahue show featured five black women writers and thinkers (Maya Angelou, Angela Davis, Ntozake Shange, Alice Walker, and Michele Wallace) who were there to discuss the issue of whether or not black women writers create "negative" images of black men. Much of the debate focused once again on *The Color Purple*. As public spectacle the show gave the impression that there is tremendous hostility between black women and men; that black women writers are responsible for disrupting solidarity between the two groups; and finally that there is little or no communication taking place. Again this discussion conveyed the message that any exploration of race and representation should focus solely on the issue of good and bad imagery, made synonymous with the construction of black male characters. Certainly a racist white media would be inclined to highlight the apparent confusions and tensions around gender among black people rather than establish a climate where there might be a more rigorous engaged dialogue, one that would focus less on issues of purity, good and bad images, and more on the question of representation, what function it serves, whose interests. The black women writers present on the Donahue show, particularly Alice Walker, were called upon to "defend" their portrayals of black men, not to discuss their motivations, ways they think about gender. Feminism was never mentioned. When Walker commented about the transformation of Mister in her book from a misogynist brute into a caring compassionate man, there was no response. It may very well be that sexist black men do not consider Mister's cultivating habits of being usually associated with females, (tenderness, compassion, absence of physical force) as positive. To them it may seem as though he is castrated. None of the black men speaking to Alice Walker and the other writers talked about the ways they would like to see black masculi-nity portrayed.

While I do not share the assumption that contemporary black women writers maliciously create negative images of black masculinity, it is true that whenever these images appear in their work they risk appropriation by the popular racist white imagination. Representations of black men in mass media usually depict them as more violent than other men, super-masculine (television characters like Hawk and Mr. T.). These images appeal to white audiences, who simultaneously fear them and are fascinated by them. It does not diminish the literary value of black women's fiction that many white consumers of this work, particularly white females, are perhaps unconsciously drawn to characterizations of black men emphasizing similar stereotypical qualities. Many works of contemporary black female fiction portray a black male rapist. Popular works like Nancy Friday's study of white female sexual fantasies reveal that one of the most consistent images is that of the black male seducer/rapist. It is consistent with racism that this imagery has so much power to captivate, titillate, and simultaneously horrify. Given the popularity of an anti-male reactionary aspect of radical feminism, there is an audience for works highlighting and exposing male violence. When black women writers suggest that the most exploitative and oppressive force in the lives of black females is black men, white society is free from the burden of responsibility; they can easily ignore the painful and brutal impact of racism.

Black readers of African-American fiction are not trespassing on the sacred ground of artistic freedom when we raise political concerns about the content of contemporary writing produced by black writers in a white supremacist, capitalist economy, where we are all acutely aware that some images "sell" better than others. We must be wary of those critics who belittle attempts by black people to critically interrogate the terrain of representation. Interviewed for a special issue of *Wedge* on "The Imperialism of Representation, the Representation of Imperialism," Edward Said reminds readers that "representations are put to use in the domestic economy of an imperial society." Speaking of his schooling in classrooms where he was taught English history and culture but "nothing about my own history, Arab history," he states: "I couldn't help but come to understand representation as a discursive system involving political choices and political forces, authority in one form or another." Attention to the politics of representation has been crucial for colonized groups globally in the struggle for self-determination. The political power of representations cannot be ignored. African-Americans have understood this without fully allowing this knowledge to shape the nature and direction of our analysis of representation. Discussions of representation among African-Americans usually occur within the context of emerging identity politics, again with the central focus on whether images are considered "good" or "bad." The idea of a good image is often informed simply by whether or not it differs from a racist stereotype. A television character like Dr. Huxtable on the Cosby Show is usually uncritically seen as "positive." There is little recognition that his benevolent patriarchal role is problematic. Since the primary stereotypical image of black men in the white supremacist imagination is that of rapist, then any characterization of black men in such a role risks being seen as a "bad" image. Issues of context, form, audience, experience (all of which inform the construction of images) are usually completely submerged when judgments are made solely on the basis of good or bad imagery.

This seems to be especially so in the ongoing debate around black female portrayal, both fictive and otherwise, of black masculinity.

Black woman talk show host Oprah Winfrey received criticism from viewers suggesting her show is a forum where black men are consistently "dogged" and "trashed," subjected to unrelenting critique. According to black male viewers, they are always portrayed negatively. Winfrey hosted an entire show featuring black men who critiqued this pattern, giving their responses. This was serious public spectacle. In most cases, individual black men who were guests, as well as those who spoke from the audience, verbally sought to challenge representations that suggest that black men are dominating, sexist, etc., even though they responded in a manner which implied such accusations are well founded. At times the entire show seemed to be mere farce, poking fun at African-American attempts to confront gender issues, ridiculing both black men and women.

In his contribution to the collection of essays *Watching Television,* "We Keep America on Top of the World," Daniel Hallin cautions viewers to remember that television influences the public's political consciousness. Certainly since many people live in racially segregated environments, they learn about race and racism from the tube. Hallin's comments on television news are equally true of the talk show: "One of the things that is most distinctive about TV news is the extent to which it is an ideological medium, providing not just information or entertainment, but 'pockets of consciousness'—frameworks for interpreting and clues for reacting to social and political reality." Since television is one of the primary propaganda machines used within this white supremacist state, African-Americans need to consider whose interests are served when the predominant representation of black culture both on television news and in talk shows suggests that the black family is disintegrating and that a hostile gender war is taking place between black women and men. In fact much of the hostility between the two groups has been generated in arenas of political spectacle that are not designed to be forums where gender issues can be approached in a progressive and serious manner. Why does a television program like the Donahue show decide to bring to the public five diverse black women writers and want them to discuss only the subject of whether black men are portrayed negatively or unfairly in their work? And suddenly the Donahue audience, which is usually all white, is peopled predominantly by black men wearing suits and ties. Who is manipulating these images and to what end? Debates about whether or not black women, and particularly those who advocate feminist politics, are representing black men negatively serve to undermine any fruitful discus-

sion of the way sexism functions in black communities, of the ways a
patriarchal system supporting male domination empowers black men
even as racism disempowers them, or the place of feminist movement
in black liberation struggle. Most importantly, debates which are mere
spectacle prevent us from collectively discussing what contexts and in
what manner black people can best discuss issues of black male sexism as it is manifest in the politics of everyday life, in extreme cases of
abuse and domination.

A few years ago I began work on a book of essays about masculinity, interviewing a number of black men. One of them made the
comment: "Sexism is the last thing black men want to deal with." We
talked about the fact that many black men feel daily hounded by racism and the impact of capitalism on their status as workers; they feel
they must continually face horrendous barriers which make life hard.
In keeping with these sentiments Ishmael Reed ends his piece "Steven
Spielberg Plays Howard Beach" with the declaration:

> I hope that the Howard Beach tragedy will persuade black
> feminists and womanists to understand that the criticisms of such
> films as *The Color Purple* (which made over $100 million, more
> than the annual revenues of many smokestack industries!) are
> not always based upon "envy" or spite, but just may be a
> justifiable paranoia. Film and television, besides being sources of
> entertainment, are the most powerful instruments of propaganda
> ever created by man, and the Nazi period has proved that, in
> sinister hands, they can be used to harm unpopular groups and
> scapegoats. On television, black men are typically shown naked
> from the waist up, handcuffed, and leaning over a police car.

Feeling as though they are constantly on edge, their lives always in
jeopardy, many black men truly cannot understand that this condition
of "powerlessness" does not negate their capacity to assert power over
black females in a way that is dominating and oppressive; nor does it
justify and condone sexist behavior. Coming home from a hard day of
work at a low-paying job, or after a day of searching for work or feeling the burden of unemployment, an individual black man demanding, in a coercive or aggressive way, that his wife serve him may not
see his actions as sexist or involving the use of power. This "not seeing" can be, and often is, a process of denial that helps maintain patriarchal structures.

Black men are not alone in being unwilling to confront sexism.
Many black women feel that black males have borne the brunt of racist oppression and that nothing that women endure could possibly

equal male pain. Many of us were raised in homes where black mothers excused and explained male anger, irritability, and violence by calling attention to the pressures black men face in a racist society where they are collectively denied full access to economic power. They clearly believed, as do many black men, that racism is harder on males than females, even though many of these black women worked for low wages in circumstances where they were daily humiliated and mistreated. Assumptions that racism is more oppressive to black men than black women, then and now, are fundamentally based on acceptance of patriarchal notions of masculinity.

Many people continue to believe that black men are particularly wounded by racist practices that deny many of them employment in high-paying jobs, thereby depriving them of the capacity to be providers and heads of households. Yet societal attitudes towards work have altered. It is no longer a norm to have a male primary provider, but these assumptions still hold sway in the larger culture and in black communities. It has been difficult for black men and women to dialogue about gender issues, especially in the context of discussions focusing on racial uplift and black liberation struggle. One barrier to such discussions is the continued acceptance of conventional gender norms as the prevailing standard by which we must judge racial progress. Uncritical acceptance of patriarchy makes it easy to ignore the reality of changing circumstances, both in the labor force and in private households, that no longer equate a positive masculinity with traditional norms of male behavior shaped by sexist thinking. There are many individual black male "heads of households" who continue to bear the pain of living in a racist society; that suffering is not altered by successful fulfillment of sexist-defined roles. Yet we have not begun to create new norms of masculine behavior, blueprints for the construction of self that would be liberating to black men.

Until black men can face the reality that sexism empowers them despite the impact of racism in their lives, it will be difficult to engage in meaningful dialogue about gender. Listening to black men talk about their social reality, one often hears narratives of victimization. Even very successful black men will talk about their lives as though racism is denying them access to forms of power they cannot even describe, that seem almost mythic. Seeing themselves solely as victims, or potential victims, they may be blind to all that they have accomplished. This is not unlike the self-perception of many privileged white women within feminist movement who were so determined to create awareness of the ways they were victimized within patriarchy that they could not accept any analysis of their experience that was more com-

plex, that showed the forms of power they maintain even in the face
of sexist exploitation—class and race privilege. Discussions of gender
roles in black communities, particularly those that spontaneously erupt
in response to a specific cultural product or event, do not begin with a
focus on defining sexism, how it functions within patriarchy and
within black communities and households. Yet this is the critical
framework that is the necessary backdrop that can bring intellectual
rigor and seriousness to discussions of gender that have heretofore
culminated in a politics of blame, black men accusing black women of
standing in the way of their progress and vice versa.

Historically the language used to describe the way black men are
victimized within racist society has been sexualized. When words like
castration, emasculation, impotency are the commonly used terms to
describe the nature of black male suffering, a discursive practice is established that links black male liberation with gaining the right to participate fully within patriarchy. Embedded in this assumption is the
idea that black women who are not willing to assist black men in their
efforts to become patriarchs are "the enemy." Such assistance would
take the form of black women consciously choosing to act subordi-
nate, to be the woman behind the man. In the early seventies individual black women decided that they could repair the damages done to
black men within this racist society by repressing their advancement
and assuming a secondary, supportive role; they found themselves in
relationships where black males exercised power in ways that were
dominating and coercive. Black female willingness to assume a subor-
dinate position did not transform male aggression or violence. Ultimately most of these black women ended up feeling as though they
were in a "no win" situation.

Solidarity between black women and men has diminished as
more black men have uncritically accepted assumptions that black
women are advancing at their expense. Despite the prevalence of female-headed households in the society as a whole, when those households are black the assumption is that black males have failed.
Conservative white supremacist politicians, and even some black
folks, attempt to link high black male unemployment with the rise in
female-headed households, placing responsibility onto black women
for a situation we have certainly not created. Such thinking also carries
with it the assumption that the only reason black heterosexual people
should couple and share a life is economic. Clearly there are multiple
reasons to explain the existence of female-headed households. Black
people have created a variety of meaningful and productive lifestyles
that do not conform to white societal norms. Failure to document

healthy productive households that do not conform to prevailing notions of the nuclear family helps further the erroneous assumption that any household that deviates from the accepted pattern is destructive. No effort is made to study ways black men perceive family and their participation, so there is no way to know why males making high incomes still choose not to spend that money providing for families. No one has really done extensive surveys among black men to discover whether or not they wish to head households. Do black men long to be providers? Is there any affirmative space for black men who want to be househusbands, to stay home maintaining households and/or raising children? These are some of the gender issues that must be addressed by black people who want to interrogate ways our experiences are represented by the dominating white elite, who hope to create new futures for black families and revise notions of masculinity in ways that break with sexism.

Until black women and men begin to seriously confront sexism in black communities, as well as within black individuals who live in predominantly white settings, we will continue to witness mounting tensions and ongoing divisiveness between the two groups. Masculinity as it is conceived within patriarchy is life-threatening to black men. Careful interrogation of the way in which sexist notions of masculinity legitimize the use of violence to maintain control, male domination of women, children, and even other men, will reveal the connection between such thinking and black-on-black homicide, domestic violence, and rape.

We need to hear from black men who are interrogating sexism, who are striving to create different and oppositional visions of masculinity. Their experience is the concrete practice that may influence others. Progressive black liberation struggle must take seriously feminist movement to end sexism and sexist oppression if we are to restore to ourselves, to future generations of black people, the sweet solidarity in struggle that has historically been a redemptive subversive challenge to white supremacist capitalist patriarchy.

9

SITTING AT THE FEET OF THE MESSENGER

remembering Malcolm X

When I was a young college student in the early seventies, the book I read which revolutionized my thinking about race and politics was the *The Autobiography of Malcolm X*. His awakening to critical consciousness, lived through by many readers, stimulated our awakening. As readers we witnessed his struggles to throw off the yoke of internalized racism, following him through various stages of self-recovery. Towards the end of the book he appears to be a transformed man, liberated and engaged in revolutionary struggle, working to free those who remained in bondage. Like nineteenth-century slave narratives, his story stands as living testimony of the movement from slavery to freedom. Only Malcolm X charts the decolonization of a black mind in a manner that far surpasses any experience described in slave narratives. Most readers of *The Autobiography* are moved by his quest for self-realization, by the frank and direct way he communicates his rage and his profound commitment to black liberation struggle. Even after his trip to Mecca, which transformed his sense of religious experience, Malcolm X remained true to his political concerns, declaring:

> No religion will ever make me forget the conditions of our people in this country. No religion will ever make me forget the continued fighting with dogs against our people in this country. No religion will ever make me forget the police clubs that come up 'side our heads. No God, no religion, no nothing will make me forget it until it stops, until it's finished, until it's eliminated.

This statement was not meant to diminish the importance of religious experience in Malcolm's life; it was meant to demonstrate that devout spirituality was not altering his militant commitment to liberation struggle. Any reader of *The Autobiography* can see that the two major concerns in his life were the commitment to black liberation and his personal struggle for religious fulfillment.

The Autobiography of Malcolm X narrates his political journey from slavery to freedom and it also narrates his religious quest, the journey of self-realization as felt and experienced in spiritual terms. It was years after I first read this autobiography that I began to think of it as telling these two stories. Since so many people had written and talked about Malcolm's political conversion, I wanted to critically explore the spiritual awakening this work describes. When he begins the narrative, Malcolm portrays himself as a man growing from childhood to maturity concerned only with satisfying material needs, the longing for food, clothing, shelter; the needs of the spirit have no place. Nearly half of *The Autobiography* is a graphic depiction of the way in which processes of dehumanization warp, distort, and when successful, break the spirit. In keeping with the tradition of narratives that depict spiritual awakening, Malcolm wanders in the wilderness, lost in an abyss. His wandering ceases not because he wills it, but through his arrest and subsequent imprisonment. At this point he tells readers:

> I want to say before I go on that I have never previously told anyone my sordid past in detail. I haven't done it now to sound as though I might be proud of how bad, how evil, I was.
>
> But people are always speculating—why am I as I am? To understand that of any person, his whole life, from birth, must be reviewed. Everything that ever happened to us is an ingredient.
>
> Today, when everything that I do has an urgency, I would not spend one hour in the preparation of a book which had the ambition to perhaps titillate some readers. But I am spending hours because the full story is the best way that I know to have it seen, and understood, that I had sunk to the very bottom of the American white society when—soon, now, in prison—I found Allah and the religion of Islam and it completely transformed my life.

Confinement in prison provides the space where Malcolm can engage in uninterrupted critical reflection on his life, where he can contemplate the meaning and significance of human existence. During this period of confinement, he comes face to face with the emptiness of his life, the nihilism. This time for him is akin to "a dark night of the soul." It is a time when he experiences deep grief for the past and an anguish of spirit. Like Saint John of the Cross, Buddha, and other seekers on the path, he is overwhelmed with longing, without knowing for what he longs. It is in that space of need that he is offered Islam. His brothers share with him their involvement with the Nation of Islam, urging him to pray, to speak with Allah about his personal salvation. This was the beginning of his conversion, but it was a difficult process. He states:

> For evil to bend its knees, admitting its guilt, to implore the forgiveness of God, is the hardest thing in the world. It's easy for me to see and say that now. But then, when I was the personification of evil, I was going through it. Again, again, I would force myself back down into the praying-to-Allah posture. When finally I was able to make myself stay down—I didn't know what to say to Allah.

Malcolm's uncertainty is also echoed in the writings of other seekers after God who feel uncertain. St. Augustine pondered, "In me what space or room is there into which my God should come." In part Malcolm doubts his worthiness and is uncertain about whether his prayers can be heard.

Perhaps it was the fear that not only was he not worthy to appear before Allah but that he did not know what to say, that motivated him to write a daily letter to Elijah Muhammad, to contemplate his picture just as many contemporary devotees contemplate the photo of a guru, a spiritual teacher, the way many Christians sit in churches where they stare directly at portraits of Christ. Long before Malcolm encountered Elijah Muhammad in the flesh, he had fully accepted him as his spiritual teacher and mentor. When his brother, Reginald, who had helped lead Malcolm into the fold of Islam, first criticized Elijah Muhammad, Malcolm was shocked. His faith was in no way shaken. Shortly after this conflict with his brother, Malcolm had a vision. It was not his teacher, Elijah Muhammad, who appeared before him; instead he saw a vision of Muhammad's spiritual mentor, W.D. Fard. Malcolm felt this visitation confirmed that he was journeying on the right path.

He left prison filled with the longing to meet the messenger, his spiritual liberator, Elijah Muhammad. Remembering the first sight of him, he writes:

> I was totally unprepared for the Messenger Elijah Muhammad's physical impact upon my emotions. From the rear of Temple Number Two, he came toward the platform. The small, sensitive, gentle brown face that I had studied in photographs, until I had

dreamed about it, was fixed straight ahead as the Messenger
strode, encircled by the marching strapping Fruit of Islam guards.
The Messenger, compared to them, seemed fragile, almost tiny...

I stared at the great man who had taken the time to write to me
when I was a convict whom he knew nothing about. He was the
man whom I had been told had spent years of his life in suffering
and sacrifice to lead us, the black people, because he loved us so
much. And then, hearing his voice, I sat leaning forward, riveted
upon his words...

Mesmerized by seeing and hearing his teacher, Malcolm became all
the more devout. He wanted to live his life in a manner that would reflect the depth of his commitment and devotion to Islam, but especially to Elijah Muhammad.

In many ways the Nation of Islam was a revolutionary theology.
It became for many underclass black people the perfect mix of religi-
osity and political training. It was a Theology of Liberation. Defining
this term, Pablo Richard, a Chilean sociologist of religion, asserts in a
March, 1985 interview in *Dialogo Social:*

The most fundamental form of Theology of Liberation, in the
religious consciousness of the poor and believing people on our
continent, is spirituality. Spirituality is the experience of God in
popular struggle and movements. The experience of the poor is
a privileged position of encounter with God, and God is lived
and celebrated as the God of the poor.

Even though liberation theology, for Richard and most people, is primarily associated with Christianity, whether one speaks about the
Islam of Elijah Muhammad or the Islam of Ayatollah Khomeini it expressed itself in the form of a politicized religious faith that promised
liberation. In the United States, public focus on the conversion of African-Americans to Islam via the Nation of Islam rarely called attention
to the religious nature of this experience and always focused on the
issue of race. Black Muslim rhetoric naming white folks as evil, as dev-
ils, was far more fascinating to the white public as it still meant they
were the central focus. They were not interested in the significance of
Islamic religious teachings and ceremony and their impact on black
life.

Malcolm always strove to call attention to religious experience
within the Nation of Islam. In an effort to bring this aspect of the faith
into the foreground, he rejected the use of the term Black Muslim:

The public mind fixed on "Black Muslims." From Mr. Muhammad
on down, the name "Black Muslims" distressed everyone in the
Nation of Islam. I tried for at least two years to kill off that "Black
Muslims." Every newspaper and magazine writer and
microphone I got close to: "No! We are black people here in
America. Our religion is Islam. We are properly called 'Muslims'!"
But that "Black Muslims" name never got dislodged.

Overt anti-Muslim racist sentiment in the United States determined the
way black people converting to Islam were seen. The white power
structure's contemptuous ridicule of the Nation of Islam was part of an
overall cultural effort to discredit Islam, to make it appear to be a
mock religion. This particular western imperialist racist reading of
Islam was most evident when the press was covering the situation of
Americans held hostage in Iran. It was no accident that the aspect of
the Nation of Islam that least interested the American public was the
focus on daily prayer and spiritual practice.

The extent to which Malcolm valued Islamic religious worship is
revealed in the second part of his autobiography. Clearly he desired
there to be a perfect harmony between that worship and the political
efforts of the Nation to decolonize black minds. The devotion Malcolm
gave to Elijah Muhammad was not that of a citizen towards a political
leader. In fact Malcolm did not see Elijah Muhammad as a political figure. First and foremost, in Malcolm's mind and heart, Elijah Muhammad was the spiritual messenger, the embodiment of the Divine. He
represents, for Malcolm, the Beloved, the One, who within Sufism, Islamic mystical tradition, the lover (i.e., the seeker on the spiritual path)
cares for so passionately that he willingly gives his life, or as commonly expressed in Sufi tradition, offers his head to be chopped off as
a sign of devotion and complete submission to the will of the spiritual
master. Malcolm had such devotion for Elijah Muhammad. He comments, "I believed so strong in Mr. Muhammad that I would have
hurled myself between him and an assassin."

Throughout *The Autobiography*, Malcolm expresses his intense
love and devotion for Elijah Muhammad, assuring readers, "I had more
faith in Elijah Muhammad than I could ever have in any other man
upon this earth." Mr. Muhammad's influence on Malcolm was so great
that he seemed at times to have truly given over his own will to that of
his spiritual teacher. Taking a vow of celibacy was one of the ways
Malcolm expressed this devotion. He sought no personal love relationships because he felt they would interfere with his spiritual quest, with
his commitment to serve his master:

In my twelve years as a Muslim minister, I had always taught so
strongly on the moral issues that many Muslims accused me of
being "anti-woman." The very keel of my teaching, and my most
bone-deep personal belief, was that Elijah Muhammad in every
aspect of his existence was a symbol of moral, mental, and
spiritual reform among the American black people. For twelve
years, I had taught that within the entire Nation of Islam; my own
transformation was the best example I knew of Mr. Muhammad's
influence upon me, I had never touched a woman.

Undoubtedly there are many individuals who would question that a
public male figure as charismatic and dynamic as Malcolm X could
have remained celibate for so many years. But unlike other significant
black political figures, no one has uncovered a past that would cast
doubt on the truth of this assertion. These twelve years of celibacy ex-
emplify the depth of Malcolm's emotional and spiritual engagement
with Elijah Muhammad. And it must be remembered that prior to his
conversion Malcolm was a man of "the streets." He had probably engaged in all manner of illicit taboo sexual activity, some of which he
describes in his autobiography. It is possible to see in Malcolm's celibacy a desire to suppress and deny those earlier years of hedonistic
sexual practice, the memory of which clearly evoked shame and guilt.
Celibacy alongside rigid standards for sexual behavior may have been
Malcolm's way of erasing all trace of that sexual past.

Ironically, it was precisely the question of sexual morality that
was to shake Malcolm's faith in his spiritual teacher. When many followers of the Nation were leaving the faith because they had witnessed or knew of Elijah Muhammad's illicit sexual affairs, Malcolm
could not even consider the possibility that his spiritual master could
betray his faith:

I don't think I could say anything which better testifies to my
depth of faith in Mr. Muhammad than that I totally and absolutely
rejected my own intelligence. I simply refused to believe...

No one in the world could have convinced me that Mr.
Muhammad would betray the reverence bestowed upon him by
all of the mosques full of poor, trusting Muslims nickeling and
diming up to faithfully support the Nation of Islam. When many
of these faithful were scarcely able to pay their own rents.

Even when Malcolm finally faced the truth of the accusations against
Elijah Muhammad, he remained steadfast and devoted. Rather than re-

proach his spiritual messenger when he learned that he had strayed from the path of Islam, Malcolm struggled to find a way to re-interpret and understand Elijah Muhammad's actions. He wanted to convince other followers that they should keep the faith:

> I thought of one bridge that could be used if and when the
> shattering disclosure became public. Loyal Muslims could be
> taught that a man's accomplishments in his life outweigh his
> personal, human weaknesses. Wallace Muhammad helped me to
> review the Quran and the Bible for documentation. David's
> adultery with Bathsheba weighed less on history's scales, for
> instance, than the positive fact of David's killing of Goliath.
> Thinking of Lot, we think not of incest, but of his saving the
> people from the destruction of Sodom and Gomorrah. Or, our
> image of Noah isn't of his getting drunk—but of his building the
> ark and teaching people to save themselves from the flood, nor
> of Moses' adultery with Ethiopian women. In all of the cases I
> reviewed, the positive outweighed the negative.

Malcolm's love was so great that he took upon himself the challenge of speaking to Elijah Muhammad about the charges against him. In fact he saw this as the only honorable action a devotee could make:

> He was the Messenger of Allah. When I was a vile vicious
> convict, so evil that other convicts called me Satan, this man had
> rescued me. He was the man who had trained me, who had
> treated me as if I were his own flesh and blood. He was the man
> who had given me wings—to go places, to do things I otherwise
> never would have dreamed of…

Malcolm's ongoing commitment to Elijah Muhammad, even after the period of disillusionment, in part sets up the deep sense of betrayal he has later when the messenger does not remain loyal to his spiritual child.

When Elijah Muhammad turns away from Malcolm, ostensibly because the "child" is beginning to assert too much autonomy and not following orders, this rejection nearly drives Malcolm insane. Again he plunges into a dark night of the soul, an anguish of spirit, generated by a momentary loss of faith. It is painful to read autobiographical passages where Malcolm conveys the deep sense of bewilderment and loss that overcomes him, when he must come to terms with the reality that the messenger of Allah, to whom he had devoted years of service, has not only strayed from the path but is extremely jealous and threatened by the power of his pupil, so threatened he turns against him.

Ironically, Elijah Muhammad seems to have been most threatened by the depth of Malcolm's religious beliefs and his spiritual practice. Perhaps the teacher feared that the more spiritually devout pupil might someday have a greater following.

Malcolm's spiritual anguish is vividly evoked in autobiographical passages where he talks about the nature of his devotion, the way he believed in the messenger more than he believed in himself. Importantly, Malcolm continues to obey the will of his spiritual master, even after he learns about the sexual affairs, even as he suspects that the teacher wishes to strip him of power. Had Malcolm no longer felt intense loyalty and commitment to Muhammad and the Nation of Islam, he could have responded with rebellion to the spiritual messenger's silencing of him over his statement about "the chickens coming home to roost." Instead he submits. His obedience in this circumstance conveyed to the public that he still saw himself as a good and faithful servant, the true spiritual devotee, willing only as his master wills.

Reading Malcolm's autobiography as a narrative of spiritual quest, his spiritual anguish, occasioned by the loss of faith, can be viewed as part of the initiation a seeker undergoes before he achieves spiritual enlightenment. The betrayal by Elijah Muhammad can be seen as a trial by fire, testing Malcolm's spiritual commitment. Although it is not explicitly stated in the book, the shattering of his faith in the spiritual messenger must have led him to question the meaning of religious experience and spiritual practice in a corrupt world. During this time, Malcolm so anguished in spirit, felt he was losing his mind. Shattered and broken in spirit, he is more tormented than he was during the time of his confinement. He is spiritually tried. The spiritual lesson Malcolm learns from this trial is that divine power can never be seen as exclusively embodied in one individual. After his break with the Nation of Islam, he goes to Mecca, making the journey to express and renew his faith. That journey also provides a space where he can contemplate all that has happened:

> In Mecca, too, I had played back for myself the twelve years I
> had spent with Elijah Muhammad as if it were a motion picture. I
> guess it would be impossible for anyone even to realize fully
> how complete was my belief in Elijah Muhammad. I believed in
> him not only as a leader in the ordinary human sense, but also I
> believed in him as a divine leader. I believed he had no human
> weaknesses or faults, and that, therefore, he could make no
> mistakes and that he could do no wrong. There on a Holy World
> hilltop, I realized how very dangerous it is for people to hold any

human being in such esteem, especially to consider anyone
some sort of "divinely guided" and "protected" person.

In this passage Malcolm repudiates the belief that humans can embody
the divine. Had he lived long enough to encounter other spiritual mes-
sengers, different from Elijah Muhammad, he might have altered this
perception.

Significantly, it is the break with Elijah Muhammad that prepares
the way for Malcolm to proceed on his "true" spiritual path and make
the pilgrimage to Mecca. From a Christian standpoint the betrayal by
Muhammad and Malcolm's anguish can be likened to the experience
of Christ, the anguish he feels in the garden of Gethsemane, expressed
in his tortured cry, "My God, my God, why hast thou forsaken me?"
Undergoing a period of spiritual anguish, a dark night of the soul, in-
tensifies Malcolm's spiritual humility. Much of the public arrogance
that was part of his political persona changed after the journey to
Mecca. The trial by fire had managed to cut through what Tibetan
Buddhist monk Chögyam Trungpa calls "spiritual materialism." It is
this break with the ego and its attachments that enables Malcolm to
reach the final stage of his spiritual journey. The quest ends. The journey restores his faith and renews his spirit. It is this renewal of spiritual
commitment combined with an ever abiding commitment to radical
political change, the liberation of black people, that readers witness at
the end of *The Autobiography*.

Just as Martin Luther King spoke of going to the mountaintop before his death as a metaphor for reaching a certain understanding with
God and a sweet spiritual bliss which prepares him to accept death, in
retrospect Malcolm's journey seems to have been a preparation for a
similar acceptance. Had he chosen to abandon his spiritual journey, to
retreat into a reclusive life, Malcolm might be alive today. Yet he chose
the path that he knew would ultimately test him, require of him a spiritual submission that would necessitate offering his life. He gave that
life to us freely, to the people, that we would know in our hearts the
meaning of spiritual and political commitment, the union of love that
he felt between religious aspiration and progressive political struggle,
the passionate longing for black liberation.

10

THIRD WORLD DIVA GIRLS

politics of feminist solidarity

C oming from a Southern black working-class background, one that remains a place I consider "home," I brought with me to feminist movement a certain style of being that grows out of black cultural traditions, like signifying. In the P.C. (politically correct) world of feminism, signifying tends to provoke negative feedback, as there has been so much emphasis on a notion of friendship and sisterly bonding that is based on principles of "seamless harmony." No one really speaks about the way in which class privilege informs feminist notions of social behavior, setting standards that would govern all feminist interaction. Often the "nice, nice" behavior privileged white women had rebelled against in their relationships with white men was transposed onto relations between white women and women of color. It was a common occurrence at feminist events for women of color to be accused of having said or done the wrong thing (especially in confrontational encounters where white women cried). Feelings of social awkwardness intensified when black women found that our social and cultural codes were neither respected nor known in most arenas of feminist movement. Moving in academic circles, spaces often inhabited by not too interesting smart people, a few intellectuals here and there, and in artistic circles peopled mainly by folks from privileged class backgrounds or the up and coming greedy folk who are wanting as much as they can get for as little cost, I often feel my class background. I struggle with the politics of location—pondering what it means for individuals from underclass and poor backgrounds to enter social terrains dominated by the ethos and values of privileged class experience.

Assimilation makes it very easy for those of us from working-class backgrounds to acquire all the trappings that make us seem like we come from privilege, especially if we are college educated and talk the right kinda talk (every time I try to get clever and throw some vernacular black speech into my essays, they are perceived as errors and "corrected"). Until recently I felt that was alright, I'd been happy to keep that speech for private spaces of my life. Now, I recognize how disempowering it is for people from underprivileged backgrounds to consciously censor our speech so as to "fit better" in settings where we are perceived as not belonging. It's easy enough for folks from working-class backgrounds to step into the world of privilege and realize we've made a mistake and to go right back where we came from. There's a certain inverse status to be had by retreating back into one's problematic roots bearing the message that it's really better there, a more righteous place (where you might not be fully understood but where you at least have ties). Better to be there than to be with those privileged "others" who don't have a clue where you're coming from.

Faced with the choice of assimilating or returning to my roots, I would catch the first train home. There is another more difficult and less acceptable choice, that is to decide to maintain values and traditions that emerge from a working-class Southern black folk experience while incorporating meaningful knowledge gained in other locations, even in those hierarchical spaces of privilege. This choice makes a lot of people uncomfortable. It makes it hard for them to put you in a neat little category and keep you there. In a troubled voice, my grandmother asked me the last time I saw her before she died, "How can you live so far away from your people?" In her mind, "my people" were not synonymous with a mass of black people, but with particular black folks that one is connected to by ties of blood and fellowship, the folks with whom we share a history, the folks who talk our talk (the patois of our region), who know our background and our ways. Her comment silenced me. I felt a pain in my heart as though I had been pierced by a sharp blade. My grandmother's words were like that; they felt to me like little knives. My silent response was tacit agreement that only misguided confused folks would live away from their people, their own.

I often think about my people, especially the womenfolk, the way we were raised, when I participate in feminist meetings and conferences. I am startled by the dichotomy between the rhetoric of sisterhood and the vicious way nice, nice, politically correct girls can deal with one another, do one another in, in ways far more brutal than I ever witnessed in shoot and cut black communities. With no body of feminist theory shaping her actions, my mama was determined to raise her daughters to value our connections to one another. Often she would "preach" on the subject of sisterhood. She would tell us about households of women, sisters usually, where they were always quarreling with one another, fighting, back-stabbing, working out some "serious" female rivalry. Mama made it clear there was gonna be none of that in our house. We were gonna learn how to respect and care for one another as women. It was not an easy task; her six girls were very different. Despite her efforts, now and then envy and little hatreds would surface, but for the most part we learned how to bond as sisters across our differences. We all had to become grown women to look back and see the importance of this early home training 'cause it takes being a woman to know just what we can do to wound one another. Now that we are grown black women, we can sit on the porch at family reunions and groove on the strength of our ties, that we are close despite differences of class, experience, values, attitudes, sexual practice, education, and so on. At those times I remember mama's hard work, teaching us tolerance, compassion, generosity, sisterly ways to love one another.

Growing up in a household full of black females, it was impossible to cultivate any sense of being "exotic." 'Cause folk will laugh at you in a minute and tell you your shit is just common. This does not mean that within our collective family setting one's uniqueness was not acknowledged or valued—it was—but it did not give anybody the right to assert dominating power over other folks. Moving in and out of segregated black communities into predominantly white circles, I have observed how easy it is for individual black females deemed "special" to become exoticized, objectified in ways that support types of behavior that on home turf would just be considered out of control. Basically in white culture black women get to play two roles. We are either the bad girls, the "bitches," the madwomen (how many times have you heard folks say that a particularly assertive black woman is "crazy") seen as threatening and treated badly, or we are the supermamas, telling it like it is and taking care of everybody, spreading our special magic wherever we go. Certainly the most outstanding contemporary example of the way this particular image is codified in popular culture and commodified is in the construction of Oprah Winfrey as beloved black "mammy" icon. Everyone tries to destroy the bad girls, who are constantly checked and kept in line, and the supermamas, who are sometimes "vamps" (witness the change in Oprah's image after she lost weight—take the 1989 Revlon ad, for example) on their off time, and get to do whatever they want; after all they are "special."

Unless we remain ever vigilant about the ways representations of black womanhood (especially those of successful individuals) are appropriated and exploited in white supremacist capitalist patriarchy, we may find ourselves falling into traps set by the dominant culture.

In the past few years I have received greater attention for my feminist writing, more public recognition, and it makes me understand how easy it is to become self-enthralled, to believe that somehow one deserves to be set apart from others and in some cases to "lord it over them" especially those who seem to be less enlightened, less knowing. Now and then I have to "check" myself, look at my behavior and engage in some downhome critical feedback, or I have to check things with comrades to make sure I'm not getting out of line. It seems to me that one of the real danger zones is that space where one encounters black women/women of color outside home communities in predominantly white space. Often we meet in these arenas and treat each other as adversaries. Often in white settings we are like siblings fighting for the approval of "white parents" whose attention we now have. It's serious. Recently I attended a major conference on "Third World feminism" where I was one of several "women of color" invited to speak (I put that label in quotes because I rarely use it. I mostly identify myself as a black woman). When I arrived at the conference, I was mingling and heard a number of participants talk about how they had come to see the fireworks, the negative confrontations that they were confident would take place between women of color there. Their comments and expectations reminded me of the many scenes fictively portrayed in African-American literature where black people, most often males, fight one another publicly, to entertain white folks, making of themselves a dehumanized spectacle.

Fearful that just such a happening might take place at this conference, I was particularly sensitive to whether or not I and other women of color were relating to one another with recognition, care, and respect, appreciating those women who were engaged in a similar process. We were acting out an ethical commitment to feminist solidarity that begins first with our regarding one another with respect. Throughout most of the conference, as though by collective mutual consent, Third World feminist speakers maintained an impressive positive interaction with one another even in situations where dialogue was rigorously critical. Folks disagreed but not in ways that were trashing of one another, silencing, or disenabling. On the final day of the conference, this sense of care was completely disrupted by the actions of one Third World woman scholar—behaving towards women of color, particularly black women, in ways that were disrespectful (for example she was always quick to point out perceived intellectual inadequacies in their comments) setting the stage for the competitive spectacle many of us had worked hard to avoid.

In the aftermath of this encounter, as folks were digging up the bodies and trying to lay blame, I was chastised by many people for having behaved in a positive respectful manner towards this critic throughout the conference. She is a scholar whose work I respect and from my cultural tradition an "elder" whom I should respect on principle. I was surprised by all this criticism directed at me for being "too nice." Suddenly the usual bourgeois insistence on decorum that is a tedious norm in most public academic settings was deemed non-applicable to this situation and participants seemed really glad to have had an occasion to witness the spectacle of one woman of color "putting down," mind you in very fancy ways, black women and black people. Indeed the girl was out of control. Of course, in the aftermath, she placed the blame on "us," more specifically me, saying it was something I said that just upset her. Naturally she could have decided to work out with me, in a another setting, whatever was bothering her, but dare I say "that would have been too much, right." The point however is that this business of blaming the black women for why "you have to abuse us" sounds so familiar. Similarly, when black women challenge racism within feminist movement the dominant response is one of hostility and anger. We are most often accused of inviting this hostility whenever we confront to resist. Black women resisting racism in feminist movement were trashed and then told "You made me do it." Frequently white women use this tactic to mask their complicity with racist structures of domination. A parallel paradigm is often enacted in interactions between powerful Third World elites and black Americans in predominantly white settings. This was certainly taking place at the conference, nor was it surprising that it was initiated by the Third World woman scholar whose work has received the most extensive legitimation in privileged white academic circles.

The current popularity of post-colonial discourse that implicates solely the West often obscures the colonizing relationship of the East in relation to Africa and other parts of the Third World. We often forget that many Third World nationals bring to this country the same kind of contempt and disrespect for blackness that is most frequently associated with white western imperialism. While it is true that many Third World nationals who live in Britain and the United States develop through theoretical and concrete experience knowledge of how they are diminished by white western racism, that does not always lead them to interrogate the way in which they enter a racialized hierarchy where in the eyes of whites they automatically have greater status and privilege than individuals of African descent. Within feminist movement Third World nationals often assume the role of mediator or interpreter, explaining the "bad" black people to their white colleagues or helping the "naive" black people to understand whiteness. For example: in a women's studies program where the black woman is seen by white colleagues as hostile and angry, they go to the Third World national and express concern saying, "Why can't she be like you." She responds by saying: "In my country we have a long tradition of diplomacy; therefore I am in a better position to cope with the politics of difference." Confident that she cares about the fate of her black colleague, she then shares this conversation with her and offers advice. Unwittingly assuming the role of go-between, of mediator, she re-inscribes a colonial paradigm. Such an action disrupts all possibility that feminist political solidarity will be sustained between women of color cross-culturally. Certainly many of us left the conference on Third World feminism feeling as though a rift had been created between black women and Third World nationals that remained unexamined and unresolved.

Weeks after the conference ended, I was still defending my position that it was important for women of color to treat one another with respect, even if that meant extending oneself beyond what might normally be seen as appropriate behavior. Audre Lorde makes this point again and again in her insightful essay "Eye to Eye," reminding readers that in patriarchal white supremacist context, this gesture, whether it be black women dealing with one another with respect, or women of color in general, is an act of political resistance. It is an indication that we reject and oppose the internalized racism that would have us work against one another.

Feminist solidarity between black women/women of color must be constructed in ways that enable us to engage in meaningful critique and rigorous intellectual exchange, without brutally trashing or negating one another. To maintain this commitment to solidarity we must be ever vigilant, living as we do in a society where internalized racism and sexism make it a norm for us to treat one another harshly and with disrespect. So often we are in settings with well-known Third World feminists, writers, thinkers who are able to be gracious to white women (even if they consider them racist) but who completely downgrade or dismiss the women of color in their midst, especially if they are perceived as not showing proper deference. I was told a very disheartening story recently that demonstrates the behavior I am describing. A little-known black woman scholar participated in a summer institute for college professors in an ivy league university setting. She went to the program already in conflict about her "place" place within the academy. She was hoping to have a learning experience that would reassure her that her presence, her voice mattered. Bonding with another black woman participant helped. Together they attended a lunch for a celebrated black woman writer with white women feminists.

At one point her black woman friend was speaking, sharing ideas, when she was suddenly aggressively told by the famous black woman writer to "shut up." This dismissal shocked and wounded the black women. The white women present acted as though they did not hear this comment and were apparently completely enthralled with the writer. Feeling erased and humiliated on two accounts, first that their presence was not seen as important and second that it was not important that their voices be heard, they left feeling all the more alienated. Ironically, the well-known black woman writer may have responded as she did because she is probably accustomed to being the only black woman in such settings, the "voice of authority," and she may have been threatened by the presence of other voices with potentially equal authority based on shared knowledge and experience. And these black women may not have been giving her the same quality of "adoration" that white women give. It's difficult to know what her experience was. Often well-known black women find we are present in settings where white audiences hang on our every word, and it may be difficult to move into settings with people of color where this is not taking place. Of course we need to interrogate "reverence," for idolization can be another way one is objectified and not really taken seriously. For example: some famous black women receive standing ovations even if they give talks that are generally perceived to be lacking in power or uninteresting. In such cases, audience feedback does not enable the speaker to accurately interrogate her impact. While this incident describes conflict between the well-known black woman and the unknown audience and/or peers, where power was used to hurt, often the opposite occurs.

Sometimes it is easier for well-known women, feminists, to be most caring and protective towards individuals who do not share the same status and are not in a position to claim the limelight. In such circumstances a benevolent hierarchy surfaces, where power-over becomes the occasion for the assertion of a generosity, even as the hierarchy is maintained. Usually the famous or well-known person accepts the assertion of dominating power as part of her due, as the rewards of status. Within the United States this is part of what lets you know you've made it, you're a star. One of the perks is that you are often allowed to treat others badly, to be offensively narcissistic, and though folks may hate you, they rarely call you on your shit. In this culture we are socialized to believe that really important people have a right to be self-absorbed, to think their needs and concerns are more important than others'. This may be especially problematic for black women who become stars because there are so few of us in any arena. It is difficult because stardom on a broad scale means simultaneous isolation and fame. This then breeds fierce territorialism since we operate within a social matrix that is always telling us that only one of us can be at the top. Since many black women/women of color have usually overcome grave obstacles to arrive at a point where we receive recognition, we can easily have a false sense of entitlement.

Working as we do in a capitalist environment, writers, especially well-known women of color, are acutely aware that white people represent the largest possible group of consumers for the "products" we make. This can translate into: "they" are the people who should receive attention and feedback. How many times have we heard the woman of color feminist talk privately about how much easier it is to relate to white women? Often it is easier to make connections with white women because they may be acting out of a kind of racial fear and guilt that leads them to respond positively to negative behavior and/or accept any kind of treatment to keep a friendship with a woman of color. Often white women agree uncritically about all issues pertaining to race when speaking with an individual black woman/woman of color. This limited deference allows them to feel anti-racist and yet be intellectually domineering and condescending around their perceived area of expertise. Usually a black woman involved in this kind of relationship is invested to some degree in assimilationist white-identification leading her to believe that this kind of tokenism will enhance her status. On another level it may at times be easier for progressive white women scholars to accept differences in perspectives among themselves even as they and women of color police women of color. Often harsh, mean-spirited critiques are made by women of color about women of color. While no woman of color wrote a harsh unrelenting critique of Elizabeth Fox-Genovese's work *Within the Plantation Household,* similar work by black women scholars has been brutally trashed. How often does one hear that the work of Rosalyn Terborg-Penn or Paula Giddings is somehow less than adequate, not sufficiently academically rigorous.

Writing about the way black women relate to one another, about policing that leads us to vent an anger deeper than any we let loose on other groups, Audre Lorde raises these questions: "Why does that anger unleash itself more tellingly against another Black woman at the least excuse? Why do I judge her in a more critical light that any other, become enraged when she does not measure up?" Black women may "police" one another because many of us were raised in communities where we were taught that it was a gesture of care to "oversee" each other's actions. When many of us were growing up it was common for elders to monitor the behavior of those younger. Sometimes this monitoring was helpful, but it was often repressive. In different locations such gestures may be less an expression of care and more an attempt to maintain the status quo. Black women often police one another to maintain positions of power and authority, especially in professional settings. Unfortunately, the legacy of being the "exception" damages our ability to relate to one another. Usually, gifted brilliant black women work in settings where it is easy to begin thinking of oneself as different from and superior to other black women. Many of us are repeatedly told by white "superiors" that we are different, special. Internalizing this message can make it difficult to share space with another black woman. Hooked on being the "exception" this individual may need to expose or undermine other black female peers, to show that she is better. This can lead to horribly negative interactions in work settings. Since black women (like almost everyone raised in this society) are usually taught to believe competition is necessary for success, it's easy for folks to feel particularly gratified by having one-upped a colleague; that may be even more the case if that person is another black woman/woman of color. Also we appear more qualified and trustworthy in the eyes of white people when we function as overseer, willing to crack the whip harder on each other.

When asked to submit a list of ten names from which three would be chosen to evaluate me in a tenure process, I felt most wary of naming black women. I named only one, whom I felt could be trusted not to judge my work unfairly, which is not to say that I thought she would only make positive comments. My wariness is a response to negative encounters with black women peers, who often see differing opinions and lifestyles as reason to viciously trash, excommunicate, and ostracize other black women. This seems ironic since most black women, especially those of us who are reluctant to advocate feminism, often chauvinistically insist that we have had this tradition of mutual support and closeness and did not need feminist thinking to create such ties. There is some truth in this assertion, although it is usually forgotten that these ties often emerge in a homogeneous setting. Many of us learned how to bond with females who were like us, who shared similar values and experiences. Often these close-knit groups used the power of their intimacy to trash women outside the chosen circle.

Like all women within patriarchal society, black women have to develop oppositional feminist strategies that will indeed enable us to accept, respect, and even honor peers who are not like us. We must understand that through active work, such solidarity should lead to the formation of different strategies that make productive communication possible. Many women who are high achievers have learned the rugged individualist model of success. This is true of many black women. They may feel that any gestures of bonding with other women threaten that success. Sometimes black women in positions of authority and power impose internalized racist assumptions on those folks whom they have power to influence. They may share downgrading messages that they once received and used as a challenge, a goad for further productivity. Unfortunately, that is not the way most of us respond to negative feedback. In Nikki Giovanni's "Woman Poem" she has a line that reads, "I ain't shit, you must be lower than that to care." Confronting internalized racism and sexism must be a central agenda for both feminist and black liberation struggle. An important stage in this process is developing skills that enable us to look at ourselves critically and observe how we behave towards others.

Recently, at a dinner where a well-known black woman writer was present, I said in conversation with the person I was sitting next to that I had sent a novel to several publishers and it had been rejected. The famous black woman writer (whose work has inspired and excited me both as a writer and a teacher) interrupted the conversation she was having to say loudly to me, in a hostile tone of voice, "Probably it's just a bad novel." Since she had been behaving all evening as though no one had anything to say worth listening to but herself, I was not surprised by this not-so-subtle attack. I was grateful, however, that I had not met her at a time in life when I was longing for a black woman mentor, for affirmation that I should continue writing. No interaction between us indicated that she was familiar with my writing. I pondered how damaging this negative feedback could have been for a fledgling writer. Her hostility saddened me. Though we were in a group that was predominantly white and were hearing many of the usual comments made in such settings (some of them naively racist), she did not direct critical comments to these speakers. In fact she was most gracious to the white men present. Audre Lorde's question: "Why does that anger unleash itself most tellingly against another black woman at the least excuse" came to mind. To answer that question we would need to critically examine the dynamics of black female interaction from a feminist perspective.

When I later spoke with other guests, who had again relished this spectacle, I was told that I must have done something to invite such hostility. Their need to absolve the well-known writer of responsibility for her actions seemed linked to the longing to maintain their idealized notions of powerful black womanhood. When you are well-known, surrounded by fans and adoring followers, few people offer critical feedback. Most folks tend to graciously overlook abusive and dominating behavior by famous "feminist" thinkers, even if our work is based on a critique of domination. Feminist analysis of the way patriarchy manifests itself in everyday life highlights the subtle and seemingly trivial incidents where men exercise coercive control and domination over women as important arenas of political struggle. Individual men changing their dominating behavior serve as necessary examples for their peers. Often women engaged with feminism critique behavior in men that is acceptable to them when done by women. Much of the dominating and abusive behavior that happens in feminist circles where there are gradations of power would be immediately challenged and critiqued if the perpetrators were men.

As feminist movement has progressed and individuals have even begun to talk about post-feminism, many women are forgetting one of the most important dimensions of feminist struggle, the focus on feminist ethics. That focus was rooted in the recognition of the way in which patriarchal sexist thinking distorts women's relation to one another. Commitment to feminist politics was a corrective process. Consciousness-raising groups were once settings where women engaged in dialectical exchange about these issues. Nowadays there is a tendency to act as though it is no longer important how women deal with one another. In the place of the community-based consciousness-raising group, we have feminist stars who are leaders in that they shape feminist thinking and action. Yet these women are often the least willing to participate in sessions where their feminist practice might be interrogated. The emergence of a feminist star system, one that has concrete material rewards (royalties from book publication, paid lectures, high-paying jobs, etc.), means that women jockey for power within feminist circles, and women of color are most often competing with one another.

When feminism becomes a means for opportunistic self-advancement, it means that prominent spokespeople can easily lose sight of the need to share critical feminist thought with masses of people. Much of the small amount of feminist writing done by women of

color is directed towards a white audience. Thus it comes as no surprise that we are not working as hard as we should be to spread the
feminist message to large groups of people of color. It also means that
we are rarely engaged in the types of mentor relationships that would
produce a new group of feminist thinkers and theorists who would be
women and men of color. Those who are deeply committed to feminist struggle must be ever mindful of the reality that this commitment
is actively manifest when we share knowledge, resources, and strategies for change with those who have the least access.

Working with a brilliant group of young women of color who
are struggling to deepen their critical consciousness, to learn ways to
be politically active, who are striving to develop intellectually, I lov-
ingly called them "Third World diva girls," a title which gives expression to their uniqueness and importance. We use the word "girl" in
that way it is used in traditional African-American culture as a sign of
intense womanist affection, not as a put down. It is an evocation to
and of intimacy, based on proud recognition of gender. And we use
the term "diva" because of the special role women have had in opera.
(See Catherine Clement's *Opera: The Undoing of Women.*) It both
names specialness but carries with it the connotation of being just a bit
out of control, stuck on oneself. We wanted it as a reminder of how
easy it is to imagine we are superior to others and therefore deserve
special treatment or have the right to dominate.

I began to think about writing this essay when one of the diva
girls called me weeping wildly after she had been at a talk given by a
prominent black feminist thinker. The audience was predominantly
white. During the question period she spoke even though she was terrified to do so in a public setting. The speaker ridiculed and dismissed
her words. She felt crushed. On another day yet another diva girl
called to share a painful interaction between herself and a black Third
World national whose scholarship is grounded in analysis of the experiences of African-American women. All her attempts to critically engage this scholar, especially in encounters where she seeks
recognition of their different cultural standpoints, are heard as attempts to usurp power and are rebuffed. She too left this encounter
feeling crushed, wondering why prominent black women scholars of
all ethnicities so rarely mentor black women students. How can prominent women of color engaged in feminist movement be surprised that
there is so little participation in the movement by folks like us if we
behave as though feminism is only for those of us who are "special?"
Or if we behave as though feminism is a turf we have conquered, a
field of power where we can maintain authority and presence, and

reap rewards only if there are a few of us present, if we are always a rare commodity.

A clear distinction must be made between receiving the respect and recognition exceptional women of color active in feminist movement rightfully deserve and the misuse of power and presence. Speaking about this in relation to black women, Lorde reminds us:

> Often we give lip service to the idea of mutual support between black women because we have not yet crossed the barriers to these possibilities, nor fully expressed the angers and fears that keep us from realizing the power of a real Black sisterhood. And to acknowledge our dreams is to sometimes acknowledge the distance between those dreams and our present situation.

If "Third World diva girls," whoever they may be—emerging writers and thinkers or the already famous and well-known—want to know whether we are cultivating the kind of sisterhood based on feminist solidarity and informed by feminist ethics, we must look and listen, observe and hear the response around us. We must engage in ongoing self-critique. When I give a talk and no one raises challenging questions, then I consider how I've represented myself. When I'm doing talks and folks tell me that I'm not the way they thought I would be, I ask them to explain. Sometimes they want to let me know that I'm not power tripping like the way they thought I might, since so many of us do. I am especially gratified when I receive a letter that clarifies how I am perceived. One came recently. After hearing me speak at the university where she works, a black woman listener wrote these words:

> Your lecture raised my consciousness of the world in which we live to a much higher level. I was so deeply touched by your words and your obvious "black pride." I have had no female or male black role models... So hearing you speak was monumental... I don't see you as the "celebrity figure" you are but as a true sister who knows her roots and herself and is proud of it. I believe you have appeared in my life for a reason.

This letter inspires me, strengthens the conviction that feminist solidarity has reality and substance.

Sometimes I act like a diva girl in the worst way—that is narcissistic, self-focused, or wanting others to serve me. Home with my family recently I was wanting attention and my sisters let me know it was getting out of hand. Tired from intense months of teaching, writing, and being on the lecture circuit, I did indeed want to be pampered and waited on, to get that special care the divas of our imagination merit because they are so unique. My sisters were willing to give that care, to affirm my specialness, even as they let me know there were limits, boundaries beyond which I would be placing them in the role of subordinates. The difficulties women of color face in a white supremacist capitalist patriarchy are intense. We can only respect and admire all among us who manage to resist, who become self-actualized. We need to cherish and honor those among us who emerge as "stars," not because they are above us but because they share with us light that guides, providing insight and necessary wisdom. To be a star, a diva, carries with it responsibility; one must learn to know and respect boundaries, using power in ways that enrich and uplift. In these times that are fundamentally more anti-feminist than post-feminist, feminist movement needs activists who can carry on the work of liberation, diva girls who are on the front line.

11

AN AESTHETIC OF BLACKNESS

strange and oppositional

T his is the story of a house. It has been lived in by many people. Our grandmother, Baba, made this house living space. She was certain that the way we lived was shaped by objects, the way we looked at them, the way they were placed around us. She was certain that we were shaped by space. From her I learn about aesthetics, the yearning for beauty that she tells me is the predicament of heart that makes our passion real. A quiltmaker, she teaches me about color. Her house is a place where I am learning to look at things, where I am learning how to belong in space. In rooms full of objects, crowded with things, I am learning to recognize myself. She hands me a mirror, showing me how to look. The color of wine she has made in my cup, the beauty of the everyday. Surrounded by fields of tobacco, the leaves braided like hair, dried and hung, circles and circles of smoke fill the air. We string red peppers fiery hot, with thread that will not be seen. They will hang in front of a lace curtain to catch the sun. Look, she tells me, what the light does to color! Do you believe that space can give life, or take it away, that space has power? These are the questions she asks which frighten me. Baba dies an old woman, out of place. Her funeral is also a place to see things, to recognize myself. How can I be sad in the face of death, surrounded by so much beauty? Death, hidden in a field of tulips, wearing my face and calling my name. Baba can make them grow. Red, yellow, they surround her body like lovers in a swoon, tulips everywhere. Here a soul on fire with beauty burns and passes, a soul touched by flame. We see her leave. She has taught me how to look at the world and see beauty. She has taught me "we must learn to see."

Years ago, at an art gallery in San Francisco near the Tassajara restaurant, I saw rooms arranged by Buddhist monk Chögyam Trungpa. At a moment in my life when I had forgotten how to see, he reminds me to look. He arranges spaces. Moved by an aesthetic shaped by old beliefs. Objects are not without spirit. As living things they touch us in unimagined ways. On this path one learns that an entire room is a space to be created, a space that can reflect beauty, peace, and a harmony of being, a spiritual aesthetic. Each space is a sanctuary. I remember. Baba has taught me "we must learn to see."

Aesthetics then is more than a philosophy or theory of art and beauty; it is a way of inhabiting space, a particular location, a way of looking and becoming. It is not organic. I grew up in an ugly house. No one there considered the function of beauty or pondered the use of space. Surrounded by dead things, whose spirits had long ago vanished since they were no longer needed, that house contained a great engulfing emptiness. In that house things were not to be looked at, they were to be possessed—space was not to be created but owned—a violent anti-aesthetic. I grew up thinking about art and beauty as it existed in our lives, the lives of poor black people. Without knowing the appropriate language, I understood that advanced capitalism was affecting our capacity to see, that consumerism began to take the place of that predicament of heart that called us to yearn for beauty. Now many of us are only yearning for things.

In one house I learned the place of aesthetics in the lives of agrarian poor black folks. There the lesson was that one had to understand beauty as a force to be made and imagined. Old folks shared their sense that we had come out of slavery into this free space and we had to create a world that would renew the spirit, that would make it life-giving. In that house there was a sense of history. In the other house, the one I lived in, aesthetics had no place. There the lessons were never about art or beauty, but always only to possess things. My thinking about aesthetics has been informed by the recognition of these houses: one which cultivated and celebrated an aesthetic of existence, rooted in the idea that no degree of material lack could keep one from learning how to look at the world with a critical eye, how to recognize beauty, or how to use it as a force to enhance inner well-being; the other which denied the power of abstract aestheticism. Living in that other house where we were so acutely aware of lack, so conscious of materiality, I could see in our daily life the way consumer capitalism ravaged the black poor, nurtured in us a longing for things that often subsumed our ability to recognize aesthetic worth or value.

Despite these conditions, there was in the traditional southern racially segregated black community a concern with racial uplift that continually promoted recognition of the need for artistic expressiveness and cultural production. Art was seen as intrinsically serving a political function. Whatever African-Americans created in music, dance, poetry, painting, etc., it was regarded as testimony, bearing witness, challenging racist thinking which suggested that black folks were not fully human, were uncivilized, and that the measure of this was our collective failure to create "great" art. White supremacist ideology insisted that black people, being more animal than human, lacked the capacity to feel and therefore could not engage the finer sensibilities that were the breeding ground for art. Responding to this propaganda, nineteenth-century black folks emphasized the importance of art and cultural production, seeing it as the most effective challenge to such assertions. Since many displaced African slaves brought to this country an aesthetic based on the belief that beauty, especially that created in a collective context, should be an integrated aspect of everyday life, enhancing the survival and development of community, these ideas formed the basis of African-American aesthetics. Cultural production and artistic expressiveness were also ways for displaced African people to maintain connections with the past. Artistic African cultural retentions survived long after other expressions had been lost or forgotten. Though not remembered or cherished for political reasons, they would ultimately be evoked to counter assertions by white supremacists and colonized black minds that there remained no vital living bond between the culture of African-Americans and the cultures of Africa. This historical aesthetic legacy has proved so powerful that consumer capitalism has not been able to completely destroy artistic production in underclass black communities.

Even though the house where I lived was ugly, it was a place where I could and did create art. I painted, I wrote poetry. Though it was an environment more concerned with practical reality than art, these aspirations were encouraged. In an interview in *Callaloo* painter Lois Mailou Jones describes the tremendous support she received from black folks: "Well I began with art at a very early stage in my life. As a child, I was always drawing. I loved color. My mother and father, realizing that I had talent, gave me an excellent supply of crayons and pencils and paper—and encouraged me." Poor black parents saw artistic cultural production as crucial to the struggle against racism, but they were also cognizant of the link between creating art and pleasure. Art was necessary to bring delight, pleasure, and beauty into lives that were hard, that were materially deprived. It mediated the harsh conditions of poverty and servitude. Art was also a way to escape one's plight. Protestant black churches emphasized the parable of the talents, and commitment to spirituality also meant appreciating one's talents and using them. In our church if someone could sing or play the piano and they did not offer these talents to the community, they were admonished.

Performance arts—dance, music, and theater—were the most accessible ways to express creativity. Making and listening to black music, both secular and sacred, was one of the ways black folks developed an aesthetic. It was not an aesthetic documented in writing, but it did inform cultural production. Analyzing the role of the "talent show" in segregated black communities, which was truly the community-based way to support and promote cultural production, would reveal much about the place of aesthetics in traditional black life. It was both a place for collective display of artistry and a place for the development of aesthetic criteria. I cite this information to place African-American concern with aesthetics in a historical framework that shows a continuity of concern. It is often assumed that black folks first began to articulate an interest in aesthetics during the sixties. Privileged black folks in the nineteenth and early twentieth centuries were often, like their white counterparts, obsessed with notions of "high art." Significantly, one of the important dimensions of the artistic movement among black people, most often talked about as the Harlem Renaissance, was the call for an appreciation of popular forms. Like other periods of intense focus on the arts in African-American culture, it called attention to forms of artistic expression that were simply passing away because they were not valued in the context of a conventional aesthetic focusing on "high art." Often African-American intellectual elites appropriated these forms, reshaping them in ways suited to different locations. Certainly the spiritual as it was sung by Paul Robeson at concerts in Europe was an aspect of African-American folk culture evoked in a context far removed from small, hot, Southern church services, where poor black folks gathered in religious ecstasy. Celebration of popular forms ensured their survival, kept them as a legacy to be passed on, even as they were altered and transformed by the interplay of varied cultural forces.

Conscious articulation of a "black aesthetic" as it was constructed by African-American artists and critics in the sixties and early seventies was an effort to forge an unbreakable link between artistic production and revolutionary politics. Writing about the interconnectedness of art and politics in the essay "Frida Kahlo and Tina Modottit," Laura Mulvey describes the way an artistic avant-garde

> ...was able to use popular form not as a means of communication but as a means of constructing a mythic past whose effectiveness could be felt in the present. Thereby it brought itself into line with revolutionary impetus towards constructing the mythic past of the nation.

A similar trend emerged in African-American art as painters, writers, musicians worked to imaginatively evoke black nationhood, a homeland, re-creating bonds with an African past while simultaneously evoking a mythic nation to be born in exile. During this time Larry Neal declared the Black Arts Movement to be "the cultural arm of the black revolution." Art was to serve black people in the struggle for liberation. It was to call for and inspire resistance. One of the major voices of the black aesthetic movement, Maulana Karenga, in his *Thesis on Black Cultural Nationalism,* taught that art should be functional, collective, and committed.

The black aesthetic movement was fundamentally essentialist. Characterized by an inversion of the "us" and "them" dichotomy, it inverted conventional ways of thinking about otherness in ways that suggested that everything black was good and everything white bad. In his introduction to the anthology *Black Fire,* Larry Neal set the terms of the movement, dismissing work by black artists which did not emerge from black power movement:

> A revolutionary art is being expressed today. The anguish and aimlessness that attended our great artists of the forties and fifties and which drove most of them to early graves, to dissipation and dissolution, is over. Misguided by white cultural references (the models the culture sets for its individuals), and the incongruity of these models with black reality, men like Bird were driven to willful self-destruction. There was no program. And the reality-model was incongruous. It was a white reality-model. If Bird had had a black reality-model, it might have been different...In Bird's case, there was a dichotomy between his genius and the society. But that he couldn't find the adequate model of being was the tragic part of the whole thing.

Links between black cultural nationalism and revolutionary politics led ultimately to the subordination of art to politics. Rather than serving as a catalyst promoting diverse artistic expression, the Black Arts Movement began to dismiss all forms of cultural production by African-Americans that did not conform to movement criteria. Often this led to aesthetic judgments that did not allow for recognition of multiple black experience or the complexity of black life, as in the case of Neal's critical interpretation of jazz musician Charlie Parker's fate. Clearly, the problems facing Parker were not simply aesthetic concerns, and they could not have been resolved by art or critical theories about the nature of black artistic production. Ironically, in many of its aesthetic practices the Black Arts Movement was based on the notion that a people's art, cultural production for the masses, could not be either complex, abstract, or diverse in style, form, content, etc.

Despite its limitations, the Black Arts Movement provided useful critique based on radical questioning of the place and meaning of aesthetics for black artistic production. The movement's insistence that all art is political, that an ethical dimension should inform cultural production, as well as the encouragement of an aesthetic which did not separate habits of being from artistic production, were important to black thinkers concerned with strategies of decolonization. Unfortunately, these positive aspects of the black aesthetic movement should have led to the formation of critical space where there could have been more open discussion of the relevance of cultural production to black liberation struggle. Ironically, even though the Black Arts Movement insisted that it represented a break from white western traditions, much of its philosophical underpinning re-inscribed prevailing notions about the relationship between art and mass culture. The assumption that naturalism or realism was more accessible to a mass audience than abstraction was certainly not a revolutionary position. Indeed the paradigms for artistic creation offered by the Black Arts Movement were most often restrictive and disempowering. They stripped many artists of creative agency by dismissing and devaluing their work because it was either too abstract or did not overtly address a radical politic. Writing about socialist attitudes towards art and politics in *Art and Revolution*, John Berger suggests that the relationship between art and political propaganda is often confused in the radical or revolutionary context. This was often the case in the Black Arts Movement. While Berger willingly accepts the truism "that all works of art exercise an ideological influence—even works by artists who profess to have no interest outside art," he critiques the idea that simplicity of form or content necessarily promotes critical political consciousness or leads to the development of a meaningful revolutionary art. His words of caution should be heeded by those who would revive a prescriptive black aesthetic that limits freedom and restricts artistic development. Speaking against a prescriptive aesthetic, Berger writes:

> When the experience is "offered up," it is not expected to be in any way transformed. Its apotheosis should be instant, and as it

were invisible. The artistic process is taken for granted: it always remains exterior to the spectator's experience. It is no more than the supplied vehicle in which experience is placed so that it may arrive safely at a kind of cultural terminus. Just as academicism reduces the process of art to an apparatus for artists, it reduces it to a vehicle for the spectator. There is absolutely no dialectic between experience and expression, between experience and its formulations.

The black aesthetic movement was a self-conscious articulation by many of a deep fear that the power of art resides in its potential to transgress boundaries.

Many African-American artists retreated from black cultural nationalism into a retrogressive posture where they suggested there were no links between art and politics, evoking outmoded notions of art as transcendent and pure to defend their position. This was another step backwards. There was no meaningful attempt to counter the black aesthetic with conceptual criteria for creating and evaluating art which would simultaneously acknowledge its ideological content even as it allowed for expansive notions of artistic freedom. Overall the impact of these two movements, black aesthetics and its opponents, was a stifling of artistic production by African-Americans in practically every medium with the exception of music. Significantly, avant-garde jazz musicians, grappling with artistic expressivity that demanded experimentation, resisted restrictive mandates about their work, whether they were imposed by a white public saying their work was not really music or a black public which wanted to see more overt links between that work and political struggle.

To re-open the creative space that much of the black aesthetic movement closed down, it seems vital for those involved in contemporary black arts to engage in a revitalized discussion of aesthetics. Critical theories about cultural production, about aesthetics, continue to confine and restrict black artists, and passive withdrawal from a discussion of aesthetics is a useless response. To suggest, as Clyde Taylor does in his essay "We Don't Need Another Hero: Anti-Theses On Aesthetics," that the failure of black aesthetics or the development of white western theorizing on the subject should negate all African-American concern with the issue is to once again repeat an essentialist project that does not enable or promote artistic growth. An African-American discourse on aesthetics need not begin with white western traditions and it need not be prescriptive. Cultural decolonization does not happen solely by repudiating all that appears to maintain connection with the colonizing culture. It is really important to dispel the notion that white western culture is "the" location where a discussion of aesthetics emerged, as Taylor suggests; it is only one location.

Progressive African-Americans concerned with the future of our cultural production seek to critically conceptualize a radical aesthetic that does not negate the powerful place of theory as both that force which sets up criteria for aesthetic judgment and as vital grounding that helps make certain work possible, particularly expressive work that is transgressive and oppositional. Hal Foster's comments on the importance of an anti-aesthetic in the essay "Postmodernism: A Preface" present a useful paradigm African-Americans can employ to interrogate modernist notions of aesthetics without negating the discourse on Aesthetics. Foster proposes this paradigm to critically question "the idea that aesthetic experience exists apart, without 'purpose,' all but beyond history, or that art can now affect a world at once (inter) subjective, concrete, and universal—a symbolic totality." Taking the position that an anti-aesthetic "signals a practice, cross-disciplinary in nature, that is sensitive to cultural forms engaged in a politic (e.g., feminist art) or rooted in a vernacular—that is, to forms that deny the idea of a privileged aesthetic realm," Foster opens up the possibility that work by marginalized groups can have a greater audience and impact. Working from a base where difference and otherness are acknowledged as forces that intervene in western theorizing about aesthetics to reformulate and transform the discussion, African-Americans are empowered to break with old ways of seeing reality that suggest there is only one audience for our work and only one aesthetic measure of its value. Moving away from narrow cultural nationalism, one leaves behind as well racist assumptions that cultural productions by black people can only have "authentic" significance and meaning for a black audience.

Black artists concerned with producing work that embodies and reflects a liberatory politic know that an important part of any decolonization process is critical intervention and interrogation of existing repressive and dominating structures. African-American critics and/or artists who speak about our need to engage in ongoing dialogue with dominant discourses always risk being dismissed as assimilationist. There is a grave difference between that engagement with white culture which seeks to deconstruct, demystify, challenge, and transform and gestures of collaboration and complicity. We cannot participate in dialogue that is the mark of freedom and critical agency if we dismiss all work emerging from white western traditions. The assumption that the crisis of African-Americans should or can only be addressed by us must also be interrogated. Much of what threatens our collective well-being is the product of dominating structures. Racism is a white issue as much as it is a black one.

Contemporary intellectual engagement with issues of "otherness and difference" manifest in literary critique, cultural studies, feminist theory, and black studies indicates that there is a growing body of work that can provide and promote critical dialogue and debate across boundaries of class, race, and gender. These circumstances, coupled with a focus on pluralism at the level of social and public policy, are creating a cultural climate where it is possible to interrogate the idea that difference is synonymous with lack and deprivation, and simultaneously call for critical re-thinking of aesthetics. Retrospective examination of the repressive impact a prescriptive black aesthetic had on black cultural production should serve as a cautionary model for African-Americans. There can never be one critical paradigm for the evaluation of artistic work. In part, a radical aesthetic acknowledges that we are constantly changing positions, locations, that our needs and concerns vary, that these diverse directions must correspond with shifts in critical thinking. Narrow limiting aesthetics within black communities tend to place innovative black artistry on the margins. Often this work receives little or no attention. Whenever black artists work in ways that are transgressive, we are seen as suspect, by our group and by the dominant culture. Rethinking aesthetic principles could lead to the development of a critical standpoint that promotes and encourages various modes of artistic and cultural production.

As artist and critic, I find compelling a radical aesthetic that seeks to uncover and restore links between art and revolutionary politics, particularly black liberation struggle, while offering an expansive critical foundation for aesthetic evaluation. Concern for the contemporary plight of black people necessitates that I interrogate my work to see if it functions as a force that promotes the development of critical consciousness and resistance movement. I remain passionately committed to an aesthetic that focuses on the purpose and function of beauty, of artistry in everyday life, especially the lives of poor people, one that seeks to explore and celebrate the connection between our capacity to engage in critical resistance and our ability to experience pleasure and beauty. I want to create work that shares with an audience, particularly oppressed and marginalized groups, the sense of agency artistry offers, the empowerment. I want to share the aesthetic inheritance handed down to me by my grandmother and generations of black ancestors, whose ways of thinking about the issue have been globally shaped in the African diaspora and informed by the experience of exile and domination. I want to reiterate the message that "we must learn to see." Seeing here is meant metaphysically as heightened awareness and understanding, the intensification of one's capacity to experience reality through the realm of the senses.

Remembering the houses of my childhood, I see how deeply my concern with aesthetics was shaped by black women who were fashioning an aesthetic of being, struggling to create an oppositional world view for their children, working with space to make it livable. Baba, my grandmother, could not read or write. She did not inherit her contemplative preoccupation with aesthetics from a white western literary tradition. She was poor all her life. Her memory stands as a challenge to intellectuals, especially those on the left, who assume that the capacity to think critically, in abstract concepts, to be theoretical, is a function of class and educational privilege. Contemporary intellectuals committed to progressive politics must be reminded again and again that the capacity to name something (particularly in writing terms like aesthetics, postmodernism, deconstruction, etc.) is not synonymous with the creation or ownership of the condition or circumstance to which such terms may refer.

Many underclass black people who do not know conventional academic theoretical language are thinking critically about aesthetics. The richness of their thoughts is rarely documented in books. Innovative African-American artists have rarely documented their process, their critical thinking on the subject of aesthetics. Accounts of the theories that inform their work are necessary and essential; hence my concern with opposing any standpoint that devalues this critical project. Certainly many of the revolutionary, visionary critical perspectives on music that were inherent to John Coltrane's oppositional aesthetics and his cultural production will never be shared because they were not fully documented. Such tragic loss retards the development of reflective work by African-Americans on aesthetics that is linked to enabling politics. We must not deny the way aesthetics serves as the foundation for emerging visions. It is, for some of us, critical space that inspires and encourages artistic endeavor. The ways we interpret that space and inhabit it differ.

As a grown black woman, a guest in my mother's house, I explain that my interior landscape is informed by minimalism, that I cannot live in a space filled with too many things. My grandmother's house is only inhabited by ghosts and can no longer shelter or rescue me. Boldly I declare that I am a minimalist. My sisters repeat this word with the kind of glee that makes us laugh, as we celebrate together that particular way language, and the "meaning" of words is transformed when they fall from the hierarchical space they inhabit in certain locations (the predominantly white university setting) into the mouths of vernacular culture and speech, into underclass blackness, segregated communities where there is much illiteracy. Who can say what will happen to this word "minimalist." Who knows how it will be changed, re-fashioned by the thick patois that is our Southern black tongue. This experience cannot be written. Even if I attempt description it will never convey process.

One of my five sisters wants to know how it is I come to think about these things, about houses, and space. She does not remember long conversations with Baba. She remembers her house as an ugly place, crowded with objects. My memories fascinate her. She listens with astonishment as I describe the shadows in Baba's house and what they meant to me, the way the moon entered an upstairs window and created new ways for me to see dark and light. After reading Tanizaki's essay on aesthetics "In Praise of Shadows," I tell this sister in a late night conversation that I am learning to think about blackness in a new way. Tanizaki speaks of seeing beauty in darkness and shares this moment of insight: "The quality that we call beauty, however, must always grow from the realities of life, and our ancestors, forced to live in dark rooms, presently came to discover beauty in shadows, ultimately to guide shadows towards beauty's end." My sister has skin darker than mine. We think about our skin as a dark room, a place of shadows. We talk often about color politics and the ways racism has created an aesthetic that wounds us, a way of thinking about beauty that hurts. In the shadows of late night, we talk about the need to see darkness differently, to talk about it in a new way. In that space of shadows we long for an aesthetic of blackness—strange and oppositional.

12

AESTHETIC INHERITANCES

history worked by hand

To write this piece I have relied on fragments, bits and pieces of information found here and there. Sweet late night calls to mama to see if she "remembers when." Memories of old conversations coming back again and again, memories like reused fabric in a crazy quilt, contained and kept for the right moment. I have gathered and remembered. I wanted one day to record and document so that I would not participate in further erasure of the aesthetic legacy and artistic contributions of black women. This writing was inspired by the work of artist Faith Ringgold, who has always cherished and celebrated the artistic work of unknown and unheralded black women. Evoking this legacy in her work, she calls us to remember, to celebrate, to give praise.

Even though I have always longed to write about my grandmother's quiltmaking, I never found the words, the necessary language. At one time I dreamed of filming her quilting. She died. Nothing had been done to document the power and beauty of her work. Seeing Faith Ringgold's elaborate story quilts, which insist on naming, on documentation, on black women telling our story, I found words. When art museums highlight the artistic achievement of American quiltmakers, I mourn that my grandmother is not among those named and honored. Often representation at such shows suggests that white women were the only group truly dedicated to the art of quiltmaking. This is not so. Yet quilts by black women are portrayed as exceptions; usually there is only one. The card identifying the maker reads "anonymous black woman." Art historians focusing on

quiltmaking have just begun to document traditions of black female
quiltmakers, to name names, to state particulars.

My grandmother was a dedicated quiltmaker. That is the very
first statement I want to make about Baba, mama's mother, pro-
nounced with the long "a" sound. Then I want to tell her name, Sarah
Hooks Oldham, daughter of Bell Blair Hooks. They were both
quiltmakers. I call their names in resistance, to oppose the erasure of
black women—that historical mark of racist and sexist oppression.
We have too often had no names, our history recorded without specificity, as though it's not important to know who—which one of us—
the particulars. Baba was interested in particulars. Whenever we were
"over home," as we called her house, she let us know "straight up" that
upon entering we were to look at her, call her name, acknowledge her
presence. Then once that was done we were to state our "particulars"—who we were and/or what we were about. We were to name
ourselves—our history. This ritualistic naming was frightening. It felt
as though this prolonged moment of greeting was an interrogation. To
her it was a way we could learn ourselves, establish kinship and connection, the way we would know and acknowledge our ancestors. It
was a process of gathering and remembering.

Baba did not read or write. She worked with her hands. She
never called herself an artist. It was not one of her words. Even if she
had known it, there might have been nothing in the sound or meaning
to interest, to claim her wild imagination. Instead she would comment,
"I know beauty when I see it." She was a dedicated quiltmaker—
gifted, skillful, playful in her art, making quilts for more than seventy
years, even after her "hands got tired" and her eyesight was "quitting."
It is hard to give up the work of a lifetime, and yet she stopped making
quilts in the years before her dying. Almost ninety, she stopped quilting. Yet she continued to talk about her work with any interested listener. Fascinated by the work of her hands, I wanted to know more,
and she was eager to teach and instruct, to show me how one comes
to know beauty and give oneself over to it. To her, quiltmaking was a
spiritual process where one learned surrender. It was a form of meditation where the self was let go. This was the way she had learned to
approach quiltmaking from her mother. To her it was an art of stillness
and concentration, a work which renewed the spirit.

Fundamentally in Baba's mind quiltmaking was women's work,
an activity that gave harmony and balance to the psyche. According to
her, it was that aspect of a country woman's work which enabled her
to cease attending to the needs of others and "come back to herself." It
was indeed "rest for the mind." I learned these ideas from her as a

child inquiring about how and why she began to quilt; even then her answer surprised me. Primarily she saw herself as a child of the outdoors. Her passions were fishing, digging for worms, planting vegetable and flower gardens, plowing, tending chickens, hunting. She had as she put it "a renegade nature," wild and untamed. Today in black vernacular speech we might say she was "out of control." Bell Blair Hooks, her mother, chose quiltmaking as that exercise that would give the young Sarah a quiet time, a space to calm down and come back to herself. A serious quiltmaker, Bell Hooks shared this skill with her daughter. She began by first talking about quiltmaking as a way of stillness, as a process by which a "woman learns patience." These rural black women knew nothing of female passivity. Constantly active, they were workers—black women with sharp tongues, strong arms, heavy hands, with too much labor and too little time. There was always work to be done, space had to be made for stillness, for quiet and concentration. Quilting was a way to "calm the heart" and "ease the mind."

From the nineteenth century until the present day, quiltmakers have, each in their own way, talked about quilting as meditative practice. Highlighting the connection between quilting and the search for inner peace, the editors of *Artists in Aprons: Folk Art by American Women* remind readers that:

> Quiltmaking, along with other needle arts, was often an outlet
> not only for creative energy but also for the release of a woman's
> pent-up frustrations. One writer observed that "a woman made
> utility quilts as fast as she could so her family wouldn't freeze,
> and she made them as beautiful as she could so her heart
> wouldn't break." Women's thoughts, feelings, their very lives
> were inextricably bound into the designs just as surely as the
> cloth layers were bound with thread.

In the household of her mother, Baba learned the aesthetics of quiltmaking. She learned it as meditative practice (not unlike the Japanese Tea Ceremony), learning to hold her arms, the needles—just so—learning the proper body posture, then learning how to make her work beautiful, pleasing to the mind and heart. These aesthetic considerations were as crucial as the material necessity that required poor rural black women to make quilts. Often in contemporary capitalist society, where "folk art" is an expensive commodity in the marketplace, many art historians, curators, and collectors still assume that the folk who created this work did not fully understand and appreciate its "aesthetic value." Yet the oral testimony of black women quiltmakers from

the nineteenth century and early twentieth century, so rarely documented (yet our mothers did talk with their mothers' mothers and had
a sense of how these women saw their labor), indicates keen awareness of aesthetic dimensions. Harriet Powers, one of the few black
women quiltmakers whose work is recognized by art historians, understood that her elaborate appliquéd quilts were unique and exqui-
site. She understood that folk who made their own quilts wanted to
purchase her work because it was different and special. Economic
hardship often compelled the selling of work, yet Powers did so reluc-
tantly precisely because she understood its value—not solely as regards skill, time, and labor but as the unique expression of her
imaginative vision. Her story quilts with their inventive pictorial narra-
tions were a wonder to behold. Baba's sense of the aesthetic value of
quilting was taught to her by a mother who insisted that work be re-
done if the sewing and the choice of a piece of fabric were not "just
right." She came into womanhood understanding and appreciating the
way one's creative imagination could find expression in quiltmaking.

The work of black women quiltmakers needs special feminist
critical commentary which considers the impact of race, sex, and class.
Many black women quilted despite oppressive economic and social
circumstances which often demanded exercising creative imagination
in ways radically different from those of white female counterparts, especially women of privilege who had greater access to material and
time. Often black slave women quilted as part of their labor in white
households. The work of Mahulda Mize, a black woman slave, is discussed in *Kentucky Quilts 1800-1900*. Her elaborate quilt "Princess
Feathers with Oak Leave," made of silk and other fine fibers, was completed in 1850 when she was eighteen. Preserved by the white family
who owned her labor, this work was passed down from generation to
generation. Much contemporary writing on quiltmaking fails to discuss
this art form from a standpoint which considers the impact of race and
class. Challenging conventional assumptions in her essay "Quilting:
Out of the Scrapbag of History," Cynthia Redick suggests that the crazy
quilt with its irregular design was not the initial and most common approach to quiltmaking, asserting, "An expert seamstress would not
have wasted her time fitting together odd shapes." Redick continues,
"The fad for crazy quilts in the late nineteenth century was a time con-
suming pastime for ladies of leisure." Feminist scholarly studies of
black female experience as quiltmakers would require revision of
Redick's assertions. Given that black women slaves sewed quilts for
white owners and were allowed now and then to keep scraps, or as

we learn from slave narratives occasionally took them, they had access to creating only one type of work for themselves—a crazy quilt.

Writing about Mahulda Mize's fancy quilt, white male art historian John Finley's comments on her work made reference to limitations imposed by race and class: "No doubt the quilt was made for her owners, for a slave girl would not have had the money to buy such fabrics. It also is not likely that she would have been granted the leisure and the freedom to create such a thing for her own use." Of course there are no recorded documents revealing whether or not she was allowed to keep the fancy scraps. Yet, were that the case, she could only have made from them a crazy quilt. It is possible that black slave women were among the first, if not the first group of females, to make crazy quilts, and that it later became a fad for privileged white women.

Baba spent a lifetime making quilts, and the vast majority of her early works were crazy quilts. When I was a young girl she did not work outside her home, even though she at one time worked for white people, cleaning their houses. For much of her life as a rural black woman she controlled her own time, and quilting was part of her daily work. Her quilts were made from reused scraps because she had access to such material from the items given her by white folks in place of wages, or from the worn clothes of her children. It was only when her children were adults faring better economically that she began to make quilts from patterns and from fabric that was not re-used scraps. Before then she created patterns from her imagination. My mother, Rosa Bell, remembers writing away for the first quilt patterns. The place these quilts had in daily life was decorative. Utility quilts, crazy quilts were for constant everyday use. They served as bed coverings and as padding under the soft cotton mattresses filled with feathers. During times of financial hardship which were prolonged and ongoing, quilts were made from scraps left over from dressmaking and then again after the dresses had been worn. Baba would show a quilt and point to the same fabric lighter in color to show a "fresh" scrap (one left over from initial dressmaking) from one that was being reused after a dress was no longer wearable.

When her sons went away to fight in wars, they sent their mother money to add rooms to her house. It is a testament to the seriousness of Baba's quiltmaking that one of the first rooms she added was a workplace, a space for sewing and quiltmaking. I have vivid memories of this room because it was so unusual. It was filled with baskets and sacks full of scraps, hatboxes, material pieced together that was lying on the backs of chairs. There was never really any place to sit in that room unless one first removed fabric. This workplace was constructed like any artist's studio, yet it would not be until I was a young woman and Baba was dead that I would enter a "real" artist's studio and see the connection. Before this workplace was built, quilting frames were set up in the spacious living room in front of the fire. In her workplace quilts were stored in chests and under mattresses. Quilts that were not for use, fancy quilts (which were placed at the foot of beds when company came), were stored in old-fashioned chests with beautiful twisted pieces of tobacco leaves that were used to keep insects away. Baba lived all her life in Kentucky—tobacco country. It was there and accessible. It had many uses.

Although she did not make story quilts, Baba believed that each quilt had its own narrative—a story that began from the moment she considered making a particular quilt. The story was rooted in the quilt's history, why it was made, why a particular pattern was chosen. In her collection there were the few quilts made for bringing into marriage. Baba talked often of making quilts as preparation for married life. After marriage most of her quilts were utility quilts, necessary bed covering. It was later in life, and in the age of modernity, that she focused on making quilts for creative pleasure. Initially she made fancy quilts by memorizing patterns seen in the houses of the white people she worked for. Later she bought patterns. Working through generations, her quiltmaking reflected both changes in the economic circumstances of rural black people and changes in the textile industry.

As fabric became more accessible, as grown children began to tire of clothing before it was truly worn, she found herself with a wide variety of material to work with, making quilts with particular motifs. There were "britches quilts" made from bought woolen men's pants, heavy quilts to be used in cold rooms without heat. There was a quilt made from silk neckties. Changes in clothing style also provided new material. Clothes which could not be made over into new styles would be used in the making of quilts. There was a quilt made from our grandfather's suits, which spanned many years of this seventy-year marriage. Significantly, Baba would show her quilts and tell their stories, giving the history (the concept behind the quilt) and the relation of chosen fabrics to individual lives. Although she never completed it, she began to piece a quilt of little stars from scraps of cotton dresses worn by her daughters. Together we would examine this work and she would tell me about the particulars, about what my mother and her sisters were doing when they wore a particular dress. She would describe clothing styles and choice of particular colors. To her mind these quilts were maps charting the course of our lives. They were history as life lived.

To share the story of a given quilt was central to Baba's creative self-expression, as family historian, storyteller, exhibiting the work of her hands. She was not particularly fond of crazy quilts because they were a reflection of work motivated by material necessity. She liked organized design and fancy quilts. They expressed a quiltmaker's seriousness. Her patterned quilts, "The Star of David," "The Tree of Life," were made for decorative purposes, to be displayed at family reunions. They indicated that quiltmaking was an expression of skill and artistry. These quilts were not to be used; they were to be admired. My favorite quilts were those for everyday use. I was especially fond of the work associated with my mother's girlhood. When given a choice of quilts, I selected one made of cotton dresses in cool deep pastels. Baba could not understand when I chose that pieced fabric of little stars made from my mother's and sister's cotton dresses over more fancy quilts. Yet those bits and pieces of mama's life, held and contained there, remain precious to me.

In her comments on quiltmaking, Faith Ringgold has expressed fascination with that link between the creative artistry of quilts and their fundamental tie to daily life. The magic of quilts for her, as art and artifice, resides in that space where art and life come together. Emphasizing the usefulness of a quilt, she reminds us: "It covers people. It has the possibility of being a part of someone forever." Reading her words, I thought about the quilt I covered myself with in childhood and then again as a young woman. I remembered mama did not understand my need to take that "nasty, ragged" quilt all the way to college. Yet it was symbolic of my connection to rural black folk life— to home. This quilt is made of scraps. Though originally handsewn, it has been "gone over" (as Baba called it) on the sewing machine so that it would better endure prolonged everyday use. Sharing this quilt, the story I tell focuses on the legacy of commitment to one's "art" Baba gave me. Since my creative work is writing, I proudly point to ink stains on this quilt which mark my struggle to emerge as a disciplined writer. Growing up with five sisters, it was difficult to find private space; the bed was often my workplace. This quilt (which I intend to hold onto for the rest of my life) reminds me of who I am and where I have come from. Symbolically identifying a tradition of black female artistry, it challenges the notion that creative black women are rare exceptions. We are deeply, passionately connected to black women whose sense of aesthetics, whose commitment to ongoing creative work, inspires and sustains. We reclaim their history, call their names, state their particulars, to gather and remember, to share our inheritance.

13

CULTURE TO CULTURE

ethnography and cultural studies
as critical intervention

Through the "talk story" and the telling of aphorisms, Sarah Oldham, my mother's mother, communicated her philosophy of being and living. One of her favorite sayings was "play with a puppy he'll lick you in the mouth." Usually this pronouncement prefaced a long lecture that began with declarations like, "I ain't no puppy, I'm a big dog, that don't like mess." These lectures were intended to emphasize the important of distance, of not allowing folks to get close enough "to get up in your face." It was also about the danger of falsely assuming familiarity, about presuming to have knowledge of matters that had not been revealed. Sometimes the lectures were about putting yourself on the same level as someone who was different and then being surprised that they took certain liberties, even, say, that they treated you with contempt. Often these lectures focused on the notion of "difference" and "otherness."

If it happened that white folks were the subject and the talk was about the feasibility of bonding with them across racial boundaries, they were the puppy. I remember these talks often happened after white folks came to visit (usually they wanted something). You have to understand that in the racially segregated South it was unusual for white folks to visit black folks. Most of the white visitors called my grandmama Aunt Sarah, a more dignified version of the word "auntie" used by whites to address black women in slavery, reconstruction, and the apartheid period known as Jim Crow. Baba never called these visitors by their first names irrespective of the number of years that they had been dropping by. Anyhow these white folks would sit in her living room and talk for hours. Some of these conversations led to the making of ties which lasted lifetimes. Though this contact appeared intimate, Baba never forgot slavery, white supremacy, and the experience of Jim Crow. There was never any bond between her and a white person strong enough to counter that memory. In her mind, to be safe one had to "keep a distance."

I remember these lectures as I read new work in literary and cultural studies focusing on race, noting how often contemporary white scholars writing about black people assume positions of familiarity, as though their work were not coming into being in a cultural context of white supremacy, as though it were in no way shaped and informed by that context. And therefore as though no need exists for them to overtly articulate a response to this political reality as part of their critical enterprise. White scholars can write about black culture or black people without fully interrogating their work to see if it employs white western intellectual traditions to re-inscribe white supremacy, to perpetuate racist domination. Within academic and intellectual climates that are striving to respond to the reality of cultural pluralism, there should be room for discussions of racism that promote and encourage critical interrogation. It should be possible for scholars, especially those who are members of groups who dominate, exploit, and oppress others, to explore the political implications of their work without fear or guilt.

Cultural studies has emerged as that contemporary location in the academy that most invites and encourages such analysis. This seems appropriate since much of the new critical work by white scholars and non-white people focusing on issues of "otherness" and "difference" is informed by the recent emphasis on culture and by academic concern with the question of race and post-colonial discourse. Feminist movement played a major role in generating academic focus on these concerns. Significantly, feminist academic and/or intellectual focus on race began with critical contestation about racism, thereby bringing to the academic context a revitalized focus on race as a political issue, assertively linking anti-racist radical politics with scholarly work. This only happened within feminist studies because of the powerful critical intervention of black women/women of color. It must be remembered that black studies programs have explored issues of race and culture from the moment of their inception. To black scholars who are exploring these subjects in programs that are not shrouded in contemporary radical "chic," programs that are definitely not administered by white men, it can be disheartening when new programs focusing on similar issues receive a prestige and acclaim denied black studies. Cultural studies programs are definitely in this category. They are most always administered by white men and are quickly gaining a legitimacy long denied African-American and Third World studies. At some campuses cultural studies programs are seen as potential replacements for black studies and women's studies. By making this observation I in no way want to denigrate cultural studies. It is exciting to have a new arena for the validation and proliferation of inter-disciplinary work. Working and writing, as I do, across disciplines, with English, women's studies, and black studies as starting points for work that is focused on contemporary culture, I am as at "home" in cultural studies as I am in these more familiar locations where issues of difference and otherness have long been a part of the discourse.

Cultural studies is an exciting and compelling addition, as it makes a space for dialogue between intellectuals, critical thinkers, etc. who may in the past have stayed within narrow disciplinary concerns. It calls attention to race and similar issues and gives them renewed academic legitimacy. And it is rapidly becoming one of the few locations in the academy where there is the possibility of inter-racial and cross-cultural discussion. Usually scholars in the academy resist engagement in dialogues with diverse groups where there may be critical contestation, interrogation, and confrontation. Cultural studies can serve as an intervention, making a space for forms of intellectual discourse to emerge that have not been traditionally welcomed in the academy. It cannot achieve this end if it remains solely a privileged "chic" domain where, as Cornel West writes in his essay "Black Culture and Postmodernism," scholars engage in debates which "highlight notions of difference, marginality, and otherness in such a way that it further marginalizes actual people of difference and otherness." When this happens, cultural studies re-inscribes patterns of colonial domination, where the "Other" is always made object, appropriated, interpreted, taken over by those in power, by those who dominate.

Participants in contemporary discussions of culture highlighting difference and otherness who have not interrogated their perspectives, the location from which they write in a culture of domination, can easily make of this potentially radical discipline a new ethnographic terrain, a field of study where old practices are simultaneously critiqued, re-enacted and sustained. In their introduction to the collection of essays *Writing Culture: The Poetics and Politics of Ethnography* editors James Clifford and George Marcus present a critical background against which we can consider work that breaks with the past, to some extent work that redefines ethnography:

Ethnography is actively situated between powerful systems of
meaning. It poses its questions at the boundaries of civilizations,
cultures, classes, races, and genders. Ethnography decodes and
recodes, telling the grounds of collective order and diversity,
inclusion and exclusion. It describes processes of innovation and
structuration, and is itself part of these processes. Ethnography
is an emergent interdisciplinary phenomenon. Its authority and
rhetoric have spread to many fields where "culture" is a newly
problematic object of description and critique...

This book includes many compelling essays which break new ground
in the field of ethnography. I was particularly excited by the essay by
Michael M.J. Fischer, "Ethnicity and the Post-Modern Arts of Memory."

Despite the new and different directions charted in this collection, it was disappointing that black people were still being "talked
about," that we remain an absent presence without voice. The editors
state at the end of their introduction that "the book gives relatively little attention to new ethnographic possibilities emerging from non-
Western experience and from feminist theory and politics." They also
give no attention, no "play" as we would say in black vernacular
speech, to the anthropologists/ethnographers in the United States who
are black, who have either been "indigenous ethnographers" or who
entered cultures where they resemble the people they are studying
and writing about. Can we believe that no one has considered and/or
explored the possibility that the experiences of these non-white scholars may have always been radically different in ways from their white
counterparts and that they possibly had experiences which
deconstructed much old-school ethnographic practice, perhaps reaching conclusions similar to those being "discovered" by contemporary
white scholars writing on the new ethnography? Their voices cannot
be heard in this collection. It in no way challenges the assumption that
the image/identity of the ethnographer is white and male. The gap that
is explained and apologized for in this text is the lack of feminist input.

The construction of the anthology, its presentation, compelled
me to think about race, gender, and ethnography. I was drawn again
and again to the cover of this book. It is the reproduction of a photograph (Stephen Tyler doing fieldwork in India). One sees in this image
a white male sitting at a distance from darker-skinned people, located
behind him; he is writing. Initially fascinated by the entire picture, I
begin to focus my attention on specific details. Ultimately I fix my attention on the piece of cloth that is attached to the writer's glasses,
presumably to block out the sun; it also blocks out a particular field of

vision. This "blindspot," artificially created, is a powerful visual metaphor for the ethnographic enterprise as it has been in the past and as it is being rewritten. As a script, this cover does not present any radical challenge to past constructions. It blatantly calls attention to two ideas that are quite fresh in the racist imagination: the notion of the white male as writer/authority, presented in the photograph actively producing, and the idea of the passive brown/black man who is doing nothing, merely looking on.

After I completed this essay I read a similar critique of this photograph by Deborah Gordon in her essay "Writing Culture, Writing Feminism: The Poetics and Politics of Experimental Ethnography." Gordon writes that, "The authority of the white male is present but not unambiguous—it is now watched, and we watch it being watched." Unlike Gordon, I see nothing active or critical about the watcher; if anything he is curiously fascinated, possibly admiring. To simply be an "observer" does not imply the displacement or subversion of the white "authorial presence." The brown male gaze can be read as consensual look of homoerotic bonding and longing, particularly since he is visually separated from family, kin, community, his gaze turned away from them. The photo implies however subtly that this brown man may indeed desire the authorial, "phallocentric power" of the white man. Significantly, we cannot discuss the brown female gaze because her look is veiled by the graphics of the cover; a black line drawn across her face. Why does this cover doubly annihilate the value of brown female gaze, first by the choice of picture where the dark woman is in the shadows, and secondly by a demarcating line? In *Writing Culture* Paul Rabinow's essay "Representations are Social Fact: Modernity and Postmodernity in Anthropology" suggest that the politics of culture, and here he draws on the work of Pierre Bourdieu, "Has taught us to ask in what field of power, and from what position in that field, any given author writes." Added to that might be the question of what politics of representation are enacted by images. Is it possible that an image, a cover can undermine radical writing—can reinscribe the colonizing anthropology/ethnography that is vigilantly critiqued in *Writing Culture?* Describing this image in his introduction, James Clifford writes, "The ethnographer hovers at the edge of the frame—faceless, almost extraterrestrial, a hand that writes." As an onlooker, conscious of the politics of race and imperialism, looking at this frontispiece I am most conscious of the concrete whiteness and maleness. To my gaze it is anything but extraterrestrial.

Another aspect of this cover strikes me as powerful commentary. The face of the brown/black woman is covered up, written over by the graphics which tell readers the title of the book and its authors. Anyone who glances at this cover notes that the most visible body and face, the one that does not have to be searched for, is the white male image. Perhaps to the observer trained in ethnography and anthropology this cover documents a very different history and vision from the one I see. I look at it and I see visual metaphors of colonialism, of domination, of racism. Surely it is important as we attempt to rethink cultural practice, to re-examine and remake ethnography, to create ways to look at and talk about or study diverse cultures and peoples in ways that do not perpetuate exploitation and domination. Starting from such a perspective one would have to consider intentionality and visual impact when choosing a cover like the one I have been discussing. One would need to consider the possibility that people who might never actually read this book might look at the cover and think that it illustrates something about the information inside. Surely the cover as representation has value and meaning that are not subverted when one reads the content. Inside, black/brown people remain in the shadows. When I look at this cover, I want to know who is the audience for this book.

Linking this question to the development of cultural studies, we must also ask: who are the subjects this discipline addresses its discourse and practice. To consider that we write about "culture," for only those of us who are intellectuals, critical thinkers, is a continuation of a hierarchical idea of knowledge that falsifies and maintains structures of domination. In the introduction to *Writing Culture,* the authors explain their exclusion of certain voices in this way, speaking here about feminism:

> Feminism clearly has contributed to anthropological theory. And various feminist ethnographers, like Annette Weimer (1976), are actively rewriting the masculinist canon. But feminist ethnography has focused either on setting the record straight about women or on revising anthropological categories (for example the nature/culture opposition). It has not produced either unconventional forms of writing or a developed reflection on ethnographic textuality as such.

Similar assumptions have been stated about scholarship by black academics of both genders. After making this statement, the authors of *Writing Culture* emphasize the relevance of exploring "the exclusion and inclusion of different experiences in the anthropological archives, the rewriting of established traditions," declaring, "This is where feminist and non-Western writing have made their greatest impact." To many feminists, especially women of color, the current scholarly trend of encouraging radical rethinking of the idea of "difference" has its roots in anti-racist black liberation efforts and resistance struggles globally. Many new trends in cultural studies and ethnography seem to be piggybacking on these efforts.

It is particularly disturbing to read work that is informed and shaped by the intellectual labor of women of color, particularly black women, which erases or de-emphasizes the importance of that contribution. Often this work is subtly devalued by the evocation of conventional academic standards of judgment that deem work that is not written in a particular manner less important. Clifford writes in a footnote to the statement quoted in the last paragraph:

> It may be generally true that groups long excluded from
> positions of institutional power, like women or people of color,
> have less concrete freedom to indulge in textual
> experimentation. To write in an unorthodox way, Paul Rabinow
> suggests in this volume, one must first have tenure. In specific
> contexts a preoccupation with self-reflexivity and style may be
> an index of privileged estheticism. For if one does not have to
> worry about the exclusion or true representation of one's
> experience, one is freer to undermine ways of telling, to focus on
> form over content. But I am uneasy with a general notion that
> privileged discourse indulges in esthetic or epistemological
> subtleties whereas marginal discourse "tells it like it is." The
> reverse is too often the case.

Like Clifford, I am suspicious of any suggestion that marginalized groups lack the freedom and opportunity to engage in textual experimentation.

Marginalized groups may lack the inclination to engage in certain ways of thinking and writing because we learn early that such work may not be recognized or valued. Many of us experiment only to find that such work receives absolutely no attention. Or we are told by gatekeepers, usually white, often male, that it will be better for us to write and think in a more conventional way. A distinction must be made between our freedom to think and write in multiple ways and the choice to write in accepted ways because we want particular rewards. My struggle over form, content, etc., has been informed by a desire to convey knowledge in ways that make it accessible to a wide range of readers. It is not a reflection of a longing to work in ways that will enable me to have institutional power or support. This is simply not the only form of power available to writers and thinkers. There is power in having a public audience for one's work that may not be particularly academic, power that comes from writing in ways that enable people to think critically about everyday life. When I do write in a manner that is experimental, abstract, etc., I find the most resistance to my choosing that style comes from white people who believe it is less "authentic." Their need to control how I and other black people write seems to be linked to the fear that black folks writing in ways that show a preoccupation with self-reflexivity and style is a sign that they no longer "possess" this form of power. Of course work exists by black folks/people of color which indicates a preoccupation with textuality and style. Here the work of academic and writer Nathaniel Mackey comes to mind. Such work may be an index of privileged aestheticism and a reflection of a concrete need to rethink and rewrite the conventional ways of exploring black experience, as well as the desire to re-vision the nature of our resistance struggle. It may very well be that certain efforts at black liberation failed because they were strategies that did not include space for different forms of self-reflexive critique.

One exciting dimension to cultural studies is the critique of essentialist notions of difference. Yet this critique should not become a means to dismiss differences or an excuse for ignoring the authority of experience. It is often evoked in a manner which suggests that all the ways black people think of ourselves as "different" from whites are really essentialist, and therefore without concrete grounding. This way of thinking threatens the very foundations that make resistance to domination possible. It is precisely the power to represent and make certain knowledge available that is revealed in the collection *Writing Culture*. Despite much that is radically new and intellectually engaging in this work, it is disappointing that the authors did not work to have a more inclusive perspective or make a space for including other voices (even if that meant reconceptualizing the work). Their partial explanations for exclusions are inadequate. Progressive scholars in cultural studies are eager to have work that does not simply suggest new theoretical directions but that implements change. Surely those in power are best positioned to take certain risks. What would have happened had the editors and/or authors in *Writing Culture,* or those among us who are in similar positions, taken the necessary steps to include perspectives, voices, etc. that they tell us are missing, even as they tell us they consider this a lack? Many of us are suspicious of explanations that justify exclusions, especially as this seems to be "the" historical moment when shifting certain paradigms is possible. If white male scholars support, encourage, and even initiate theoretical interventions without opening the space of interrogation so that it is inclusive, their gestures of change appear to be ways of holding onto positions of power and authority in a manner that maintains structures of domination based on race, gender, and class.

The recent academic focus on "culture," epitomized by the formation of cultural studies, has led many white students to explore subjects where they must grapple with issues of race and domination. The courses I teach on black women writers and Third World literature are overcrowded, with large waiting lists. Enthusiasm for these courses is ongoing. To some extent student interest in areas of study that allow for discussion of otherness and difference is changing faculty preoccupations. Professors who were never drawn to these subjects in the past are exploring them, using material in classrooms that they might have considered unsuitable at another time. These shifts in direction transform the academy only if they are informed by non-racist perspective, only if these subjects are approached from a standpoint that interrogates issues of domination and power. A white woman professor teaching a novel by a black woman writer (Toni Morrison's *Sula*) who never acknowledges the "race" of the characters is not including works by "different" writers in a manner that challenges ways we have been traditionally taught as English majors to look at literature. The political standpoint of any professor engaged with the development of cultural studies will determine whether issues of difference and otherness will be discussed in new ways or in ways that reinforce domination.

Those cultural studies programs emphasizing post-colonial discourse bring a global perspective that is often sorely lacking in many traditional disciplines. Within the academy, concern with global perspectives and global issues has been a re-vitalizing response to the crisis in western civilization and western thought. It is both ironic and tragic when conservative academic politics lead to the co-optation of these concerns, pitting Third World scholars and African-American scholars against one another. We not only compete for jobs, we compete for recognition. Anyone who has attended a conference on African-American studies recently knows that there are growing numbers of Third World nationals who are, for diverse reasons, engaged in scholarship on African-American culture. They may be non-white, but they may not necessarily have a radical politic or be at all concerned about challenging racial hierarchies. They may choose instead to exploit the privileged location already allotted them in the existing structure. In such situations all the necessary elements exist for the re-enactment of a paradigm of colonial domination where non-western brown/black-skinned folks are placed in positions where they act as intermediaries between the white power structure and indigenous people of color, usually black folks.

These negative dimensions are countered only by the radical political actions of individual professors and their allies. When conservative forces combine to privilege only certain kinds of discourse and particular areas of study, the expansive invitation to engage in multiple discourses from diverse perspectives that is a core concept of cultural studies is threatened. These days when I enter classrooms to teach about people of color and the students present are nearly all white, I recognize this to be a risky situation. I may be serving as a collaborator with a racist structure that is gradually making it much more difficult for students of color, particularly black students, from impoverished and in some cases privileged backgrounds to participate in undergraduate or graduate study. Their absence can be easily ignored when the subjects studied focus on non-whites, just as their absence in the professorial role can be ignored when white professors are addressing issues of difference. In such circumstances I must interrogate my role as educator. Am I teaching white students to become contemporary "interpreters" of black experience? Am I educating the colonizer/oppressor class so that they can better exert control? An East Indian colleague of mine, Anu Needham, says that we can only respond to this circumstance by assuming a radical standpoint and radicalizing these students so that they learn to think critically, so that they do not perpetuate domination, so that they do not support colonialism and imperialism, but do understand the meaning of resistance. This challenge then confronts everyone who participates in cultural studies and in other inter-disciplinary programs like women's studies, black studies, anthropology, etc. If we do not interrogate our motives, the direction of our work, continually, we risk furthering a discourse on difference and otherness that not only marginalizes people of color but actively eliminates the need for our presence.

Similarly, unless progressive scholars actively pushing for further institutionalization of cultural studies remain ever mindful of the way discursive practices and the production of knowledge are easily appropriated by existing systems of domination, cultural studies cannot and will not serve as critical intervention disrupting the academic status quo. Concurrently, as individual critical thinkers, those of us whose work is marginalized, as well as those whose work successfully walks that elusive tightrope with one foot on the radical edge and one foot firmly rooted on acceptable academic ground, must be ever vigilant, guarding against the social technology of control that is ever ready to co-opt any transformative vision and practice.

If the recent international conference Cultural Studies Now and in the Future is any sign of the discipline's direction, it is evident that grave tensions exist between those who would have cultural studies be that discipline which radically questions and transforms the academy and those who would make it (as one concerned white male put it) "the latest hip racism," where every culture and everybody being talked about is "colored" but those doing the talking and writing are white, with few exceptions. Furthermore, it was noted by the same white male participant that "the most extended discussions of African-American culture and politics came from people outside the United States." When individual black scholars made similar public critiques, their words were dismissed as mad ravings. Given the context of white supremacy, we must always interrogate institutional structures which give voice to people of color from other countries while systematically suppressing and/or censoring the radical speech of indigenous folks of color. While black Americans have every political reason to recognize our place in the African diaspora, our solidarity and cultural connections with people of African descent globally, and while we do appreciate cross-cultural exchange, we must not abdicate intellectual responsibility for promoting a cultural studies that will enhance our ability to speak specifically about our culture and gain a hearing. As a radical critical intervention, cultural studies "now and in the future" can be a site of meaningful contestation and constructive confrontation. To achieve this end, it must be committed to a "politics of difference" that recognizes the importance of making space where critical dialogues can take place between individuals who have not traditionally been compelled by politicized intellectual practice to speak with one another. Of course, we must enter this new discursive field recognizing from the onset that our speech will be "troubled," that there exists no ready-made "common language." Drawing from a new ethnography, we are challenged to celebrate the polyphonic nature of critical discourse, to—as it happens in traditional African-American religious experience—hear one another "speak in tongues," bear witness, and patiently wait for revelation.

14

SAVING BLACK FOLK CULTURE

Zora Neale Hurston as anthropologist and writer

Anthropology, once defined as the "study of alien beings," captured the imagination of Zora Neale Hurston when she was seeking a course of academic study that would be compatible with her longing to write. Like many promising writers, Hurston found the classroom structure a confining place even as she found the academic environment one that stretched and expanded her intellectual horizons. Her roots were in the Southern black folk culture of Eatonville, Florida. As a young writer, she drew from that experience to create stories. Coming to anthropology, she was to discover an academic course of study wherein she could express her passion for black culture, where it could be acknowledged, legitimated scholarship worthy of further exploration.

Unlike many black graduate students today, Hurston quickly found a mentor. The celebrated anthropologist Franz Boas became her guiding spirit. Present at that historical moment when the field of ethnography was changing, Boas helped institutionalize the study of anthropology. Though by no means a radical according to contemporary standards, he did bring to anthropology an oppositional perspective. He did not see the unknown culture to be studied as a world of "alien beings." His perceptions about the nature of anthropological work had been challenged by practical experience doing field work among the Inuit, and his paradigms shifted. He wrote:

> After long and intimate intercourse with the Eskimo, it was with
> feelings of sorrow and regret that I parted from my Arctic friends.
> I had seen that they enjoyed life, as we do, that nature is also

beautiful to them, that feelings of friendship also root in the
Eskimo heart; that, although the character of their life is so rude
compared to civilized life, the Eskimo is a man as we are, his
feelings, his virtues, and his shortcomings are based on human
nature like ours.

This statement indicated the way Boas's initial approach to the
study of other cultures had been informed by colonialism, the sense of
cultural superiority that shaped the field work of his predecessors. As
biased as this paragraph may seem now, it was a radical shift for Boas
to assert that he found himself mirrored in "the Other." Ultimately, he
worked to make anthropology a discipline that would not serve the interest of white cultural imperialism, seeing it instead as a field that
might stand in opposition, trying to correct false proclamations of the
superiority of one culture, one way of life, over another.

Had he not begun to critically interrogate his own approach to
ethnography, Boas might not have been prepared for his encounter
with Hurston. His willingness to challenge racist theories made it possible for him to be more than a mentor for Hurston; he was also an
ally. Perhaps it was working with Boas that initially enabled Hurston to
approach anthropology without consciously critiquing the colonialism,
the cultural imperialism, the racism shaping the discipline. The notion
of "objectivity" and the idea that cultures to be studied were necessarily vanishing, dying out, were two perspectives informed by white cultural imperialism. Rather than question these assumptions, Hurston
adopted them, accepting the idea that "objectivity" was both a perspective one could acquire and a necessary vantage point for the re-
searcher. Anthropology addressed her fears that Southern black folk
culture was a vanishing way of life. Claiming to be "weighed down by
this thought, that practically nothing had been done in Negro folklore
when the greatest cultural wealth of the continent was disappearing
without the world ever realizing that it had ever been," Hurston envi-
sioned her anthropological work as a means of preserving black folk
culture. Yet she never directly states for whom she wished to preserve
the culture, whether for black folks, that we may be ever mindful of
the rich imaginative folkways that are our tradition and legacy, or for
white folks, that they may laugh at the quaint dialect and amusing stories as they voyeuristically peep into the private inner world of poor
Southern black people.

Naively absorbing the dominant white culture's perspective on
anthropological research, Hurston (as a Barnard College trained anthropologist in the making) approached field work with the "objectiv-

ity" that she had learned was a necessary component of academic work. In *Dust Tracks on the Road,* she tells readers:

> My first six months were disappointing. I found out later that it was not because I had no talents for research, but because I did not have the right approach. The glamor of Barnard College was still upon me. I dwelt in marble halls. I knew where the material was all right. But I went about asking, in carefully accented Barnardese, "Pardon me, but do you know any folk-tales or folk-songs?" The men and women who had whole treasures of material just seeping through their pores looked at me and shook their heads. No, they had never heard of anything like that around there...

Failure to accomplish all she hoped for from this attempt at gathering material forced Hurston to critically evaluate the methodology she had learned from academic study. Although she suggests in her introduction to *Mules and Men* that the college training was necessary because it enabled her to "see myself like somebody else and stand off and look at my garments," her approach to field work changed. Rather than placing distance between herself and the people from whom she hoped to glean information, Hurston worked to establish intimate ties with them. She followed a pattern of participant observation that would inform all her anthropological work.

Retrospectively, the introduction to *Mules and Men* can be seen as testimony, bearing witness to the "fictive" scholar/anthropologist Hurston created for the sake of her work and the sake of her narrative. She does not tell readers that her initial attempts to gather material failed because she approached folks as though her training set her apart, maybe even above them, and that as a consequence she changed that approach. Instead, Hurston's introduction suggests that she always behaved as though she was one of the community returning home, rather than a visiting scholar coming to exploit the resources of the community for her own academic ends. This introduction is one of the many narratives which expose and reveal Hurston's tendency to distort the truth to serve her own ends. She employs the same strategy she used in field work to construct her introduction. By presenting herself as "just plain folks," she enables the uninformed non-academic reader to feel less distanced from the process of anthropological work. Hurston wanted her collection of folklore to sell. However, in order to demystify anthropology as a discipline, to make it more accessible, Hurston has to project an image of herself that is not fully accurate. Her opening declaration, "I was glad when somebody told me, you may go and collect Negro folk-lore," is a fine example of the way she masked the scope of her intellectual commitment and analytical skills. She employs this strategy throughout *Mules and Men*. This stance did not convey to readers the extent to which Hurston played a crucial interventionist role in the academy by compelling her academic mentors and peers to support the study of African-American folklore. Hurston's declaration implies that she was merely following orders; in actuality she had defined the terrain.

This declaration can also be read as Hurston's attempt to place herself at the center of the African-American story-telling tradition, letting the aware reader in on the irony of this statement—that anyone would have to command her to gather folk material. Hurston had a treasure house of folk material stored in her mind and heart. Many of the stories she used in *Mules and Men* had appeared in earlier writing. She needed no one, least of all a white person, to tell her the value and significance of this material. Yet Hurston understood the colonizer and knew that it was best to appear as though she was following orders and not operating from an autonomous sense of agency and power.

The seemingly self-effacing posture she assumes at the beginning of the introduction is reiterated in its conclusion. Paying homage to the white patron who had helped finance her field work, Hurston writes:

> Before I enter the township, I wish to make acknowledgements
> to Mrs. R. Osgood Mason of New York City. She backed my
> calling in a hearty way, in a spiritual way, and in addition,
> financed the whole expedition in the manner of the Great Soul
> that she is. The world's most gallant woman.

Without a doubt the last sentence of this paragraph makes use of the hyperbolic language that was a common feature of the black folk story-telling tradition, a language often used when the intent is to ridicule or mock, or to couch one's dislike in flattery that subtly lets the truth be known. It is difficult to believe that Hurston was blind to the cultural imperialism, the white supremacy of her sponsor, Mrs. Mason. This "world's most gallant woman" had compelled Hurston to sign a legal agreement which specified that all material she gathered would be the legal property of her patron and that Hurston could use such material only when granted permission.

According to Hurston's biographer, Robert Hemenway, it was evident to all involved parties that Mason's financing of Hurston's work was not motivated by generosity but by a colonizing greed, made especially manifest in her efforts to control both the nature of the work and its presentation. Hemenway comments:

> Hurston was to collect African-American folklore because Mrs. Mason was "unable because of the pressure of other matters to undertake the collecting of this information in person."
> Hurston was employed as "an independent agent" to "collect all information possible, both written and oral, concerning the music, poetry, folklore, literature, hoodoo, conjure, manifestations of art and kindred subjects relating to and existing among the North American negroes.
> Hurston was forbidden "to make known to any other person, except one designated in writing by said first party [Mrs. Mason], any of said data or information."

Motivated to sign such an agreement because she needed financial support, Hurston may initially have even been amused by the idea that African-American folklore, which was communal property that belonged to no individual, could be bought and the dissemination of it controlled by a rich white lady living in New York. Hurston may have been so bold as to believe she was "scamming" (putting one over on Mrs. Mason) in the same way that the folk figure "High John" outwits and outsmarts ole Massa.

Still, it must have occurred to Hurston when Mason refused to support her effort to acquire a doctorate in anthropology that her patron not only did not want her to be self-sufficient but also did not respect Hurston's intellectual ability. Of course she did not want Hurston to receive full credit for her work or be able to work independently. Even after all financial arrangements with Mrs. Mason were terminated, Hurston never publicly critiqued the motives of her white patron. She never publicly discussed her paternalism, her racism. Any reading of Hurston that suggests she was blind to Mason's white supremacist standpoint or that she endorsed it is too simplistic. Again it must be re-emphasized that Hurston perceived herself always as knowing how to "work" white people, i.e. manipulate them for her own ends. Often she did this by playing the role of faithful caring darky, all the while believing in her power to subvert the situation without ever being found out. Hence the possibly tongue-in-cheek acknowledgement at the end of the introduction, the ironic folktale told at the end of the book, which is about the inversion of conventional power dynamics, and the last declarative sentence of the work.

Mason, though seemingly liberal because she associated with black folks, epitomized the colonizer who masks her desire to control by assuming the role of caretaker. Though she believed that she behaved in a non-racist manner by working to support black writers and artists, she used their labor in the same manner as the plantation owner. Her approach to anthropology was informed by colonialism. She believed that Hurston's use of folklore in fiction and drama devalued and de-legitimized it as work having scientific, anthropological, academic merit. When Hurston took the material she had meticulously gathered in her field work and chose not to turn it into an academic scholarly presentation (her essays in the *Journal of American Folklore* had shown that she was able to write in a scholarly manner), she was going against the designs of her patron, doing with the material what Zora Neale Hurston wanted to do with it.

Without aggressively challenging Mason and thereby possibly cutting off an avenue for future support, Hurston presented material in a manner and style that in no way corresponded with Mason's expectations. Although she justified her actions in a letter to Boas by suggesting that she was compelled by publishers to make her work more accessible, this was a course of action that appealed to her love for popular culture. It enabled her to shape *Mules and Men* in such a way that it both introduced African-American folklore to a wider audience and called attention to the creative genius of Hurston. Corresponding with Boas about whether or not he would write the introduction, Hurston informed him that the publisher, Lippincott, wanted "a very readable book that the average reader can understand, at the same time one that will have value as a reference book." She expressed to him her hope that the "unscientific manner that must be there for the sake of the average reader will not keep you from writing the introduction." Whether or not it was the publisher or Hurston who made the initial decision that *Mules and Men* should be accessible to a mass audience, it was an approach that enabled Hurston, "the writer," to place her anthropological work in a story-telling framework. Choosing to publish her work in a style that countered Mason's orders and Boas's emphasis on scientific presentation of data was an act of defiance that shows Hurston did not see herself as the mere puppet of white benefactors. However, she knew that she needed the introduction from Boas to lend an aura of legitimacy and therefore make her work marketable to both an academic audience and the larger reading public. Here again Hurston manipulated circumstance to serve her own ends.

Placing the data gleaned from field work in a story-telling frame-work made the book both a presentation of Southern black folklore and folkways and a narrative of Hurston's adventures. *Mules and Men* becomes, then, both documentation of Hurston's anthropological research and an autobiographical portrait of Hurston as anthropologist. From her standpoint as writer, Hurston examines herself as field worker. Just as her university experience enabled her to look at black folk culture from a new vantage point, her return to the Eatonville community of her childhood allows her to look at Hurston, the anthropologist in the making, from a different perspective. Her return "home" to do field work was on one level a gesture of self-recovery; Hurston was returning to that self she had been forced to leave behind in order to survive in the public world of a huge Northern city. Up there, Hurston was always playing the role of country darky. In *Mules and Men* she does not need to represent herself as a flamboyant exhibitionist striving always to be the center of attention.

Returning South, especially to Eatonville, Hurston no longer needed to be the focus of everyone's gaze to feel her presence acknowledged or valued. Contemporary critical writing about Hurston emphasizes her flamboyance, seeing it as indication of her unique style and sensibility. It was also, however, a response to alienation. Coming from a communal rural-based culture where her existence was daily affirmed by others, Hurston found city life awesome, developing strategies to ensure her survival. Back in Eatonville she could experience herself both as autonomous individual and as someone connected in a deeply emotional and spiritual way to the life of the community. The return home had such an impact on Hurston's psyche that she could not simply transcribe the material uncovered there as though it were only scientific data. It was vividly connected in her mind to habits of being and a way of life.

Hurston's attitude toward anthropological work was profoundly altered as she endeavored to find the best possible approach to gathering material. After her initial experience doing field work, Hurston began to raise questions with Boas and other colleagues about whether or not academic publications were the best place to share information about African-American folk culture. Hurston's critical reflection led her to the conclusion that the way to ensure that black folk culture would not disappear or vanish was to share that culture with a mass audience. Rather than write about black folk culture in a detached academic style, she chose the style of the folk. After completing her research, Hurston made the comment:

> I needed my Barnard education to help me see my people as
> they really are. But I found that it did not do to be too detached
> as I stepped aside to study them. I had to go back, dress as they
> did, talk as they did, live their life, so that I could get into my
> stories the worlds that I knew as a child.

The Barnard experience had given Hurston an academic framework that allowed her to critically assess the past; after taking that assessment it was necessary for her to bridge the distance. Despite her
attempt to present the Barnard experience as the catalyst for all her research endeavors, she was looking to use anthropological material to
enhance her writing prior to becoming a student.

With *Mules and Men* Hurston re-established her connection to
Southern black folk culture, forging a new basis for that interaction.
Most importantly, her intellectual work renewed her spirit. As narrator,
as story-teller setting the stage for widespread dissemination of folk-
tales, aphorisms and folk beliefs, Hurston placed herself on an equal
footing with her informants. She continually reminded readers that she
was doing this academic stuff, but the bottom line is that she was also
a story-teller. Using an anthropological standpoint from which to
gather material and to some extent processing it scientifically, Hurston
could never fully accept the role of anthropologist if it meant negation
of her writer identity. It was Zora the writer, the great all-time story-
teller who shaped *Mules and Men* into a compelling narrative, the autobiographical account of her adventures, the documentation of
Southern black folkways.

Writing *Mules and Men* enabled Hurston to reconnect fragments
of her self, to bring together writer and anthropologist, and to allow
the writer identity to take precedence over the anthropological standpoint. Hemenway suggests that "the intimacy of *Mules and Men* is an
obtained effect, an example of Hurston's narrative skill." Yet such an
interpretation ignores the way the text conveys, reveals even,
Hurston's intimate engagement in the life of the community. That intimacy was not merely a pose; Hurston's personal grounding was restored by this contact. Among the black folk with whom she shared
history, she was not an object, an exotic Other, a "new negro." She
was not playing the role of happy darky—faithful worshipper at the
throne of whiteness. All these were ways she had been objectified by
her city experience, in personal relationships, and in her academic
study. In Eatonville, Hurston was a subject in the community speaking
with, and to, other subjects with mutual pleasure and exchange.

Implicit in this approach was the deconstruction of the subject/object relationship that characterized the anthropological work she had studied. After successfully gathering material, Hurston could write of her research:

> I enjoyed collecting the folk-tales and I believe the people from
> whom I collected them enjoyed the telling of them, just as much
> as I did the hearing.

This reciprocal relationship of telling and hearing is communicated in *Mules and Men*. Throughout the work Hurston conveys her pleasure and the pleasure of her comrades, who find power and beauty in the act and art of story-telling.

Hurston's attempts to de-emphasize academic training in the field of anthropology have been successful. Despite the great revival of literary interest in her work promoted and encouraged by feminist movement and feminist readers, there has been little attention given her status as scholar. This may be a reflection of the fact that she never received a graduate degree. Be that as it may, *Mules and Men* remains a powerful work, conveying much more about the milieu from which African-American folklore emerges than later, academic studies. It is an invaluable resource for students of African-American history and folklore. Contemporary writings on ethnography and anthropology that seek to talk about the discipline and its history never mention Zora Neale Hurston. Yet she has earned the right to be named in these works. For example, an essay on Hurston would have been a valuable addition to the collection *Writing Culture,* edited by James Clifford and George Marcus, which claims to be a new critical discussion of "The Poetics and Politics of Ethnography." In many ways Hurston was at the cutting edge of new movement in ethnography and anthropology that has only recently been actualized. When Hurston was alive, there was no term like "cultural critic" to encourage and validate her work, no new takes on ethnography that would move away from disparaging conceptions of the "indigenous ethnographer." It seems all the more necessary, then, that there be some contemporary re-evaluation and discussion of the importance of her work, of the way she broke new ground by pushing anthropological work across boundaries, giving it a place in mass culture, taking it back to the same space from which African-American folklore had emerged.

15

CHOOSING THE MARGIN
AS A SPACE OF RADICAL OPENNESS

As a radical standpoint, perspective, position, "the politics of location" necessarily calls those of us who would participate in the formation of counter-hegemonic cultural practice to identify the spaces where we begin the process of re-vision. When asked, "What does it mean to enjoy reading *Beloved*, admire *Schooldaze*, and have a theoretical interest in post-structuralist theory?" (one of the "wild" questions posed by the Third World Cinema Focus Forum), I located my answer concretely in the realm of oppositional political struggle. Such diverse pleasures can be experienced, enjoyed even, because one transgresses, moves "out of one's place." For many of us, that movement requires pushing against oppressive boundaries set by race, sex, and class domination. Initially, then, it is a defiant political gesture. Moving, we confront the realities of choice and location. Within complex and ever shifting realms of power relations, do we position ourselves on the side of colonizing mentality? Or do we continue to stand in political resistance with the oppressed, ready to offer our ways of seeing and theorizing, of making culture, towards that revolutionary effort which seeks to create space where there is unlimited access to the pleasure and power of knowing, where transformation is possible? This choice is crucial. It shapes and determines our response to existing cultural practice and our capacity to envision new, alternative, oppositional aesthetic acts. It informs the way we speak about these issues, the language we choose. Language is also a place of struggle.

To me, the effort to speak about issues of "space and location" evoked pain. The questions raised compelled difficult explorations of "silences"—unaddressed places within my personal political and artistic evolution. Before I could consider answers, I had to face ways these issues were intimately connected to intense personal emotional upheaval regarding place, identity, desire. In an intense all-night-long conversation with Eddie George (member of Black Audio Film Collective) talking about the struggle of oppressed people to come to voice, he made the very "down" comment that "ours is a broken voice." My response was simply that when you hear the broken voice you also hear the pain contained within that brokenness—a speech of suffering; often it's that sound nobody wants to hear. Stuart Hall talks about the need for a "politics of articulation." He and Eddie have engaged in dialogue with me in a deeply soulful way, hearing my struggle for words. It is this dialogue between comrades that is a gesture of love; I am grateful.

I have been working to change the way I speak and write, to incorporate in the manner of telling a sense of place, of not just who I am in the present but where I am coming from, the multiple voices within me. I have confronted silence, inarticulateness. When I say, then, that these words emerge from suffering, I refer to that personal struggle to name that location from which I come to voice—that space of my theorizing.

Often when the radical voice speaks about domination we are speaking to those who dominate. Their presence changes the nature and direction of our words. Language is also a place of struggle. I was just a girl coming slowly into womanhood when I read Adrienne Rich's words, "This is the oppressor's language, yet I need it to talk to you." This language that enabled me to attend graduate school, to write a dissertation, to speak at job interviews, carries the scent of oppression. Language is also a place of struggle. The Australian aborigines say "that smell of the white man is killing us." I remember the smells of my childhood, hot water corn bread, turnip greens, fried pies. I remember the way we talked to one another, our words thickly accented black Southern speech. Language is also a place of struggle. We are wedded in language, have our being in words. Language is also a place of struggle. Dare I speak to oppressed and oppressor in the same voice? Dare I speak to you in a language that will move beyond the boundaries of domination—a language that will not bind you, fence you in, or hold you? Language is also a place of struggle. The oppressed struggle in language to recover ourselves, to reconcile, to reunite, to renew. Our words are not without meaning, they are an action, a resistance. Language is also a place of struggle.

It is no easy task to find ways to include our multiple voices within the various texts we create—in film, poetry, feminist theory. Those are sounds and images that mainstream consumers find difficult to understand. Sounds and scenes which cannot be appropriated are often that sign everyone questions, wants to erase, to "wipe out." I feel it even now, writing this piece when I gave it talking and reading, talking spontaneously, using familiar academic speech now and then, "talking the talk"—using black vernacular speech, the intimate sounds and gestures I normally save for family and loved ones. Private speech in public discourse, intimate intervention, making another text, a space that enables me to recover all that I am in language, I find so many gaps, absences in this written text. To cite them at least is to let the reader know something has been missed, or remains there hinted at by words—there in the deep structure.

Throughout *Freedom Charter,* a work which traces aspects of the movement against racial apartheid in South Africa, this statement is constantly repeated: *our struggle is also a struggle of memory against forgetting.* In much new, exciting cultural practice, cultural texts—in film, black literature, critical theory—there is an effort to remember that is expressive of the need to create spaces where one is able to re-deem and reclaim the past, legacies of pain, suffering, and triumph in ways that transform present reality. Fragments of memory are not sim-ply represented as flat documentary but constructed to give a "new take" on the old, constructed to move us into a different mode of artic-ulation. We see this in films like *Dreaming Rivers* and *Illusions,* and in books like *Mama Day* by Gloria Naylor. Thinking again about space and location, I heard the statement "our struggle is also a struggle of memory against forgetting"; a politicization of memory that dis-tinguishes nostalgia, that longing for something to be as once it was, a kind of useless act, from that remembering that serves to illuminate and transform the present.

I have needed to remember, as part of a self-critical process where one pauses to reconsider choices and location, tracing my jour-ney from small town Southern black life, from folk traditions, and church experience to cities, to the university, to neighborhoods that are not racially segregated, to places where I see for the first time inde-pendent cinema, where I read critical theory, where I write theory. Along that trajectory, I vividly recall efforts to silence my coming to voice. In my public presentation I was able to tell stories, to share memories. Here again I only hint at them. The opening essay in my book, *Talking Back,* describes my effort to emerge as critical thinker, artist, and writer in a context of repression. I talk about punishment, about mama and daddy aggressively silencing me, about the censorship of black communities. I had no choice. I had to struggle and resist to emerge from that context and then from other locations with mind intact, with an open heart. I had to leave that space I called home to move beyond boundaries, yet I needed also to return there. We sing a song in the black church tradition that says, "I'm going up the rough side of the mountain on my way home." Indeed the very meaning of "home" changes with experience of decolonization, of radicalization. At times, home is nowhere. At times, one knows only extreme estrangement and alienation. Then home is no longer just one place. It is locations. Home is that place which enables and promotes varied and everchanging perspectives, a place where one discovers new ways of seeing reality, frontiers of difference. One confronts and accepts dispersal and fragmentation as part of the construction of a new world order that reveals more fully where we are, who we can become, an order that does not demand forgetting. "Our struggle is also a struggle of memory against forgetting."

This experience of space and location is not the same for black folks who have always been privileged, or for black folks who desire only to move from underclass status to points of privilege; not the same for those of us from poor backgrounds who have had to continually engage in actual political struggle both within and outside black communities to assert an aesthetic and critical presence. Black folks coming from poor, underclass communities, who enter universities or privileged cultural settings unwilling to surrender every vestige of who we were before we were there, all "sign" of our class and cultural "difference," who are unwilling to play the role of "exotic Other," must create spaces within that culture of domination if we are to survive whole, our souls intact. Our very presence is a disruption. We are often as much an "Other," a threat to black people from privileged class backgrounds who do not understand or share our perspectives, as we are to uninformed white folks. Everywhere we go there is pressure to silence our voices, to co-opt and undermine them. Mostly, of course, we are not there. We never "arrive" or "can't stay." Back in those spaces where we come from, we kill ourselves in despair, drowning in nihilism, caught in poverty, in addiction, in every postmodern mode of dying that can be named. Yet when we few remain in that "other" space, we are often too isolated, too alone. We die there, too. Those of us who live, who "make it," passionately holding on to aspects of that "downhome" life we do not intend to lose while simultaneously seeking new knowledge and experience, invent spaces of radical openness. Without such spaces we would not survive. Our living depends on our ability to conceptualize alternatives, often improvised. Theorizing about this experience aesthetically, critically is an agenda for radical cultural practice.

For me this space of radical openness is a margin—a profound edge. Locating oneself there is difficult yet necessary. It is not a "safe" place. One is always at risk. One needs a community of resistance.

In the preface to *Feminist Theory: From Margin to Center,* I expressed these thoughts on marginality:

> To be in the margin is to be part of the whole but outside the main body. As black Americans living in a small Kentucky town, the railroad tracks were a daily reminder of our marginality. Across those tracks were paved streets, stores we could not enter, restaurants we could not eat in, and people we could not look directly in the face. Across those tracks was a world we could work in as maids, as janitors, as prostitutes, as long as it was in a service capacity. We could enter that world but we could not live there. We had always to return to the margin, to cross the tracks to shacks and abandoned houses on the edge of town.
>
> There were laws to ensure our return. Not to return was to risk being punished. Living as we did—on the edge—we developed a particular way of seeing reality. We looked both from the outside in and from the inside out. We focused our attention on the center as well as on the margin. We understood both. This mode of seeing reminded us of the existence of a whole universe, a main body made up of both margin and center. Our survival depended on an ongoing public awareness of the separation between margin and center and an ongoing private acknowledgement that we were a necessary, vital part of that whole.
>
> This sense of wholeness, impressed upon our consciousness by the structure of our daily lives, provided us with an oppositional world-view—a mode of seeing unknown to most of our oppressors, that sustained us, aided us in our struggle to transcend poverty and despair, strengthened our sense of self and our solidarity.

Though incomplete, these statements identify marginality as much more than a site of deprivation; in fact I was saying just the opposite, that it is also the site of radical possibility, a space of resistance. It was this marginality that I was naming as a central location for the production of a counter-hegemonic discourse that is not just found in words but in habits of being and the way one lives. As such, I was not speaking of a marginality one wishes to lose—to give up or surrender as part of moving into the center—but rather of a site one stays in, clings to even, because it nourishes one's capacity to resist. It offers to one the possibility of radical perspective from which to see and create, to imagine alternatives, new worlds.

This is not a mythic notion of marginality. It comes from lived experience. Yet I want to talk about what it means to struggle to maintain that marginality even as one works, produces, lives, if you will, at the center. I no longer live in that segregated world across the tracks. Central to life in that world was the ongoing awareness of the necessity of opposition. When Bob Marley sings, "We refuse to be what you want us to be, we are what we are, and that's the way it's going to be," that space of refusal, where one can say no to the colonizer, no to the downpressor, is located in the margins. And one can only say no, speak the voice of resistance, because there exists a counter-language. While it may resemble the colonizer's tongue, it has undergone a transformation, it has been irrevocably changed. When I left that concrete space in the margins, I kept alive in my heart ways of knowing reality which affirm continually not only the primacy of resistance but the necessity of a resistance that is sustained by remembrance of the past, which includes recollections of broken tongues giving us ways to speak that decolonize our minds, our very beings. Once mama said to me as I was about to go again to the predominantly white university, "You can take what the white people have to offer, but you do not have to love them." Now understanding her cultural codes, I know that she was not saying to me not to love people of other races. She was speaking about colonization and the reality of what it means to be taught in a culture of domination by those who dominate. She was insisting on my power to be able to separate useful knowledge that I might get from the dominating group from participation in ways of knowing that would lead to estrangement, alienation, and worse—assimilation and co-optation. She was saying that it is not necessary to give yourself over to them to learn. Not having been in those institutions, she knew that I might be faced again and again with situations where I would be "tried," made to feel as though a central requirement of my being accepted would mean participation in this system of exchange to ensure my success, my "making it." She was reminding me of the necessity of opposition and simultaneously encouraging me not to lose that radical perspective shaped and formed by marginality.

Understanding marginality as position and place of resistance is crucial for oppressed, exploited, colonized people. If we only view the margin as sign marking the despair, a deep nihilism penetrates in a destructive way the very ground of our being. It is there in that space of collective despair that one's creativity, one's imagination is at risk, there that one's mind is fully colonized, there that the freedom one longs for as lost. Truly the mind that resists colonization struggles for freedom one longs for as lost. Truly the mind that resists colonization struggles for freedom of expression. The struggle may not even begin with the colonizer; it may begin within one's segregated, colonized community and family. So I want to note that I am not trying to romantically re-inscribe the notion of that space of marginality where the oppressed live apart from their oppressors as "pure." I want to say that these margins have been both sites of repression and sites of resistance. And since we are well able to name the nature of that repression we know better the margin as site of deprivation. We are more silent when it comes to speaking of the margin as site of resistance. We are more often silenced when it comes to speaking of the margin as site of resistance.

Silenced. During my graduate years I heard myself speaking often in the voice of resistance. I cannot say that my speech was welcomed. I cannot say that my speech was heard in such a way that it altered relations between colonizer and colonized. Yet what I have noticed is that those scholars, most especially those who name themselves radical critical thinkers, feminist thinkers, now fully participate in the construction of a discourse about the "Other." I was made "Other" there in that space with them. In that space in the margins, that lived-in segregated world of my past and present. They did not meet me there in that space. They met me at the center. They greeted me as colonizers. I am waiting to learn from them the path of their resistance, of how it came to be that they were able to surrender the power to act as colonizers. I am waiting for them to bear witness, to give testimony. They say that the discourse on marginality, on difference has moved beyond a discussion of "us and them." They do not speak of how this movement has taken place. This is a response from the radical space of my marginality. It is a space of resistance. It is a space I choose.

I am waiting for them to stop talking about the "Other," to stop even describing how important it is to be able to speak about difference. It is not just important what we speak about, but how and why we speak. Often this speech about the "Other" is also a mask, an oppressive talk hiding gaps, absences, that space where our words would be if we were speaking, if there were silence, if we were there. This "we" is that "us" in the margins, that "we" who inhabit marginal space that is not a site of domination but a place of resistance. Enter that space. Often this speech about the "Other" annihilates, erases: "No need to hear your voice when I can talk about you better than you can speak about yourself. No need to hear your voice. Only tell me about your pain. I want to know your story. And then I will tell it back to you in a new way. Tell it back to you in such a way that it has become mine, my own. Re-writing you, I write myself anew. I am still author, authority. I am still the colonizer, the speaking subject, and you are now at the center of my talk." Stop. We greet you as liberators. This "we" is that "us" in the margins, that "we" who inhabit marginal space that is not a site of domination but a place of resistance. Enter that space. This is an intervention. I am writing to you. I am speaking from a place in the margins where I am different, where I see things differently. I am talking about what I see.

Speaking from margins. Speaking in resistance. I open a book. There are words on the back cover, *Never in the Shadows Again*. A book which suggests the possibility of speaking as liberators. Only who is speaking and who is silent. Only who stands in the shadows— the shadow in a doorway, the space where images of black women are represented voiceless, the space where our words are invoked to serve and support, the space of our absence. Only small echoes of protest. We are re-written. We are "Other." We are the margin. Who is speaking and to whom. Where do we locate ourselves and comrades.

Silenced. We fear those who speak about us, who do not speak to us and with us. We know what it is like to be silenced. We know that the forces that silence us, because they never want us to speak, differ from the forces that say speak, tell me your story. Only do not speak in a voice of resistance. Only speak from that space in the margin that is a sign of deprivation, a wound, an unfulfilled longing. Only speak your pain.

This is an intervention. A message from that space in the margin that is a site of creativity and power, that inclusive space where we recover ourselves, where we move in solidarity to erase the category colonized/colonizer. Marginality as site of resistance. Enter that space. Let us meet there. Enter that space. We greet you as liberators.

Spaces can be real and imagined. Spaces can tell stories and unfold histories. Spaces can be interrupted, appropriated, and transformed through artistic and literary practice.

As Pratibha Parma notes, "The appropriation and use of space are political acts."

To speak about that location from which work emerges, I choose familiar politicized language, old codes, words like "struggle, marginality, resistance." I choose these words knowing that they are no longer popular or "cool"—hold onto them and the political legacies they evoke and affirm, even as I work to change what they say, to give them renewed and different meaning.

I am located in the margin. I make a definite distinction between that marginality which is imposed by oppressive structures and that marginality one chooses as site of resistance—as location of radical openness and possibility. This site of resistance is continually formed in that segregated culture of opposition that is our critical response to domination. We come to this space through suffering and pain, through struggle. We know struggle to be that which pleasures, delights, and fulfills desire. We are transformed, individually, collectively, as we make radical creative space which affirms and sustains our subjectivity, which gives us a new location from which to articulate our sense of the world.

16

STYLISH NIHILISM

race, sex, and class at the movies

C olonization made of us the colonized—participants in daily rituals of power where we, in strict sado-masochistic fashion, find pleasure in ways of being and thinking, ways of looking at the world that reinforce and maintain our positions as the dominated. Any coming to critical consciousness simply heightens the reality of contradictions. We are often silent about how we cope with those contradictions. To focus on them is to expose our complicity, to expose the reality that even the most politically aware among us are often compelled by circumstances we do not control to submit, to collude. Certainly in the space of popular media culture black people in the U.S. and black people globally often look at ourselves through images, through eyes that are unable to truly recognize us, so that we are not represented as ourselves but seen through the lens of the oppressor, or of the radicalized rebel who has broken ideologically from the oppressor group but still envisions the colonized through biases and stereotypes not yet understood or relinquished. Nowhere is this more evident than in contemporary filmmaking. More than ever before, white filmmakers are working to include images and stories of black people in their work. In this one sense the film version of Alice Walker's *The Color Purple* was groundbreaking and especially threatening and dangerous. Yet it also stands as an expression of the liberal white filmmaker's willingness to exploit the culture of blackness as he or she might exploit any subject matter. This act was culturally hegemonic and signified how little radical politics regarding race have really altered the way we as black people are seen by white people and the way our labor is appropriated. It also blurs our ability to clearly know and define the oppressor.

The white supremacist racist patriarch who looms large as an agent of racial oppression does not make films about us. Yet this does not mean the liberal white filmmaker who places black images in films will not be either consciously or unconsciously creating a film perspective that reinforces and perpetuates racial domination. To talk about such films we must expand our critical discourse so that we are not simply putting a film, or a filmmaker, down as racist, but rather that we talk about the complexity of what is taking place. I am particularly interested in contemporary films like *Brother From Another Planet, Choose Me, Mona Lisa, Little Shop of Horrors,* where screen images of black people function in a variety of ways—at times to reinforce domination through extensive use of negative stereotypes, at other times working to radicalize and challenge pre-conceived notions.

The film I saw most recently that challenged in this manner was the Stephen Frears/Hanif Kureishi production of *Sammy and Rosie Get Laid.* I place these names on an equal footing because the two films that have most brought Stephen Frears to the attention of audiences in this country, and to the attention of non-white viewers, have been films done with screenplays by Hanif Kureishi. Together they did *My Beautiful Laundrette.* They make a rather formidable pair; the white man with power to produce and direct—the man of color who provides the fascinating vision, who sees ethnicity, race relations, the politics of difference and diversity that is so much the content of these films. In the case of *Sammy and Rosie,* we as brown and black people are first imaged in the mind of one who is us, but not completely so because he is the child of an English mother and a South Asian father (somehow this mixture seems to dictate his urge to understand both sides, to find middle ground). In his autobiographical statement, *The Rainbow Sign,* Kureishi expresses his concern with politics of racial separatism, advocating what he sees as a more realistic model of constructive engagement. What charmed many viewers about the two films Frears and Kureishi have produced together is that we see people of color on center stage, and the tensions of race and racism, particularly as they intersect with sex and sexuality, as well as class struggle, portrayed in ways that convey the complexity of our concerns, the contradictions, the efforts to resist, to live in resistance so that we respond critically, actively, and not passively to the world around us.

Sammy and Rosie Get Laid, as cultural representation of our contemporary fascination with difference, especially as it becomes increasingly the "in" subject matter for art and hip theoretical discourse, is a useful text for any discussion that speaks about the dangers, the risks involved when one produces an art that is meant to challenge and subvert politics of domination, an art that is meant to resist. I want to speak about these dangers in terms of the politics of inclusion and appropriation, both of which seem to me to be territorial acts taking place in this film. Inclusion is expressed as that effort to create cultural representations that reflect life in a plural culture, racial diversity, the varieties of our experience. As a new breed of artists and cultural critics who are not caught within the conservative racism and sexism of the dominant culture, some of us, and Kureishi is a fine example, want to give expression to life as we have lived it, calling attention to our participation in a social context where white is not always what is at the center, where the central concern may be subversion of the status quo—where we may see ourselves as actively engaged in ongoing resistance to politics of domination. Kureishi works in his plays and autobiographical writing to expose oppressive aspects of the dominant white heterosexist culture, as well as the ways the cultures of brown and black people are transformed as we internalize the colonizing mentality, acting in complicity with forces that oppress and exploit, and finally mapping the terrain of our resistance. Since one of the deepest expressions of our internalization of the colonizer's mentality has been self-censorship, reluctance to speak about aspects of our reality that do not further assimilation or racial and/or ethnic uplift, Kureishi's daring is refreshing and exciting. He expresses in his autobiographical work a commitment and a determination to be open and frank about his take on reality, which means that he shows us not just those neat little politically correct areas of his vision but also those murky, shadowy, confused places; they are there in the film. His is a politics of inclusion, and he is not unaware of the way in which liberal and radical white folks engage in the process of appropriation, particularly as it relates to the current cultural production of artistic works that focus on differences of race, sex, and class. He also appropriates. The problematic issue is, to what ends.

In *Sammy and Rosie Get Laid* and other contemporary films by white directors that focus on black characters or people of color in general, the experiences of the oppressed black people, specifically dark-skinned black people, are appropriated as colorful exciting backdrop, included in a way that stimulates interest (just seeing all the different black people on the screen is definitely new), yet often their reality is submerged, obscured, deflected away from, so that we will focus our attention even more intensely on the characters whose reality really matters. In *Sammy and Rosie*, Kureishi based the first scene on an actual incident in which Cherry Groce, a black woman, was paralyzed when accidentally shot during a police raid. While his intent may have been to expose viewers to the cruelty and indifference of white police as they raid this building where mostly black people live, the scene is shot in such a way that it undermines this concern. In the opening scene, a black woman is shown slinging the hot oil in which she is cooking french fries at the white police. This undercuts the idea that she is being shot accidentally, suggesting instead that, however violent the police may be, they are responding to a perceived threat. This is a very subtle filmic moment, one that happens so quickly it is easy to miss, shot as though the filmmaker could not simply depict white police shooting the woman at her stove without provocation. We watch this very violent death of a black woman, which sets off racial rioting—all of which becomes backdrop for the drama of Sammy and Rosie. If there was any intent to depict the pain of oppression and systematic violence in the lives of Britain's black underclass, it is undercut not only by the "spectacular," thrilling, fast paced movement of the scenes, but also by the way they are portrayed as mere farce. The realism embedded in such imagining is lost, and what lingers is solely the quality of entertaining, violent spectacle.

It is the actions of the white people, their responses, that most holds one's attention (well, cinematically, this is certainly nothing new). The indifference of white people who are not oppressed yet see themselves as politically correct, who witness the pain of the oppressed, who sympathize and then ignore, is mirrored in the lighter-skinned brown people who are almost white. This is the deep satirical message of the film, when it comes across as satire, its social critique—for it says that the cool white people, and even perhaps the cool non-whites, who supposedly "understand" what is happening with the oppressed, really don't care in a way that counts, especially when counting means surrendering center stage, or privilege. This is best highlighted in two marvelous scenes, one where Sammy wanks off, eats his cheeseburger, listens to music, and does a little coke, while the riot goes on, and the scene where Rosie strolls right through the violent action, pausing for a moment of picture taking. Rather than these "cool" white people appropriating the labor of black servants to build empires, they appropriate the pain and passion of the oppressed to build images of themselves as politically correct, as different from oppressive white people who do not lead a more diverse, colorful, intense life, who do not "get down." While audiences laughed at these contradictions, it was obvious from the comments white students from Yale were making during these scenes that they laughed heartily because they identified with Sammy's indifference, his narcissism, yet not in a critical or subversive way. Sammy's father, Rafi, as patriarchal non-white adult, again and again exposes the superficial responses of his "children" to real oppression. Yet he too succumbs to narcissism and, worse, despair.

Given the farcical elements in the film, one never knows quite when a scene should be viewed seriously. Writing about the filming of *My Beautiful Laundrette,* Kureishi comments:

> We decided the film was to have gangster and thrilling elements, since the gangster film is the form that corresponds most closely to the city, with its gangs and violence. And the film was to be an amusement despite its references to racism, unemployment and Thatcherism. Irony is the modern mode, a way of commenting on bleakness and cruelty without falling into dourness and didacticism.

These comments apply as well to the strategy in *Sammy and Rosie Get Laid,* which, even more than the first film, "amuses" as it juxtaposes the lives of those on the periphery who are against domination with those who do not know where they stand. Kureishi's irony is not always conveyed. At times he seems to be suggesting in the film that resistance to racism, sexism, and other forms of domination assumes the quality of spectacle and farce because the forces to be overcome are all-powerful, a rather despairing take. It is not surprising that some audiences miss the irony and think that the message is that one should focus on personal pleasure to have any satisfaction in life, since the oppression does not end.

I spoke with a black male in his twenties, born in Britain, who saw the movie twice with white companions who just "loved" it. He felt it was impossible to express to them why he disliked the film. When he spoke he said, "Never have I seen a film which made me feel so powerless. All the while watching I was angry with the way black people were used." We both talked about the images of black and brown women in the film; they were portrayed in very negative and, at times, stereotypical ways. In his film diary Kureishi talks about a white woman reading the script and asking him, "Why have you developed the black women, Vinia and Rani?" He does not tell whether he answered; he just registers his annoyance that she was asking. Had I been there, I would have wanted to know why, as in *My Beautiful*

Laundrette, the South Asian woman character who has radical political beliefs is portrayed as "hysterical," one might even say as monstrous. She and her black woman lover are "into" confrontation; they want to hold Rafi responsible for his actions. They are portrayed as uptight and uncool, as in that scene where Sammy tells her that she is a prick. Not only is there never even the slightest hint of bonding between Sammy, Vinia, and Rani, black women continually appear on the screen and are disposed of, like props taken away as soon as they have fulfilled their function. The black woman "mother" murdered at the beginning of the film and the absent black mother of the black male child that Danny (Rosie's black lover) often has with him are two examples. In one scene Rafi meets Danny walking with a black woman and child and invites him to a party. The black woman is not included. He hands the child to her and leaves with Rafi.

Identification with the character of Danny reinforced the sense of powerlessness felt by the black male mentioned earlier. Danny, also known as Victoria—a name which suggests that he can be both male and female, masculine and feminine—tells Rosie that the murdered black woman cared for him as a child, yet he does not know how to respond to her death. He does not participate in the rioting, but neither does he grieve. Instead he seems to be totally distracted by his sexual desire for Rosie. Danny comes on the scene as magnificent outsider, the rebel who observes and processes before he acts. Yet he continually fails to respond to political situations, finding solace in the realm of desire. Danny's desire for Rosie blocks him from engaging in effective political response. When he comes to the scene of the crime, he has eyes only for Rosie. Throughout the film, non-white men are portrayed as lusting after white women. Alice, Rafi's lover, tells him, "The penis has been your life-line," critiquing both his sexism and the way it shapes and informs his sexual desire. Still, she does not refuse him. Like Sammy, Rafi and Danny use sexuality as a way to escape their inability to respond politically. It is as though the impotence these Third World men feel, their powerlessness to stop domination, to be anything but collaborators and perpetrators through either passivity or direct action, renders them incapable of facing reality. Rafi internalizes the values of the white colonizers and aggressively calls Rosie's attention to the reality that the Third World best learned the art of oppression as a means of social control from white imperialists. White women appear in this film as the consolation prize non-white men receive as reward for their betrayal. White female bodies become the site where the non-white man finds solace for his pain.

Rosie is the quintessential white "feminist." When she is not having sex, she is bonding with white women and non-white women to
critique masculinity. Conveniently, this bonding is not disrupted by
sexual competition for men, since the two most visible black women
are lesbians. Sammy's mother is an absent non-white female presence
who was disposed of by Rafi because he considered her "ugly."
Danny's mother is absent. The black male child he often carries has no
visible black mother, and he seems to be the primary nurturer. After
Rosie has sex with him, she is portrayed stroking the black child as
though she has now become the symbol of nurturance and mother-
hood. Well, none of this should have been surprising; let's face it, the
black woman as mother was wiped off the planet in the very first
scene. If black women constitute the garbage to be disposed of, and
black and brown men have no meaningful response to this aggression
and violation (we have no idea how the black woman's son responds
to her death; after all, as backdrop he is also discarded), then the
genocide is complete; culture and people are effectively "appropriated," destroyed, "wiped out."

At one point in the film Danny and Rosie fuck, Sammy and
Annie fuck, Rafi and Alice fuck, to the beat of black male Rastas sing-
ing "My Girl." This was farce and spectacle at its best, highlighted by
the fact that the dudes could sing. As a black female watching this
scene, I was struck by this use of a song which emerged from segregated African-American culture as an expression of possessive love between black female and black male, evoked here to celebrate this
inter-racial spectacle of non-white men with white women. I found
this scene very amusing. It graphically exposed contradictions. However, when I stopped laughing I found its message to be potentially
frightening and even threatening, because it did not overtly promote
critical reflection about the absence of black women, and could easily
be seen as making light of the disposing of women of color, of sexual
and racial violation of women of color by white women and men
(Rosie is visibly sexually turned on when Danny shares with her that
the murdered black woman nursed him as a child). Seen as ironic
comment, this scene is very powerful and becomes very tragic; one
begins in laughter and ends in tears. Talking with many white viewers,
I was not shocked to hear that the irony never registers, that they saw
these scenes as a celebration of sex and desire, as a meeting place
across race and ethnicity. Their responses raise again the issue of
whether irony alone can be used to promote critical consciousness. It
seems to pre-suppose a politically conscious viewer, one who can see
both what is being shown and what is not.

The tragedy of these scenes registered in my consciousness after I enjoyed them as spectacle. Before I could fully register the tragedy, before it could penetrate and lead to insight, the scene changed. Harmony is restored to diversity; imperialist machinery has wiped out the homes of people who live on the periphery, who are multi-racial. Where is the grief for these displaced people, whose worlds are continually destroyed? Are we to grieve when Danny shouts with jubilation, "I'm on my way out"? Are we to see the tragedy behind his cool? Of course, his exit allows for the reunion of Sammy and Rosie. It enables Sammy to act as though he wishes finally to work at establishing a meaningful relationship with his father. Yet it is too late—Rafi hangs himself. This deeply tragic expression of the inability of brown people to reconcile collaboration in the perpetuation of domination, or our failure to make revolution, fails to be a moving moment. Our attention leaves Rafi and is focused again on Sammy and Rosie, who we see in the final scene reunited on the floor in their heterosexual unity, rocking back and forth crying and kissing one another, as though once again desire mediates pain of grief and tragedy. Sammy, as Third World infant, turns for comfort to Mother Rosie, who considers abdicating her maternal role for a brief moment, but then is once again drawn back into the familial fold. This ending suggests that the cool, politically correct, (dare I say it?) "feminist" white woman, who identifies with blacks and lesbians alike, wants to have a relationship with the Third World in which she dominates as nurturing mother, duplicating in a slightly inverted form the white male, imperialist, paternal position. At first the film seemed to subtly critique Rosie, exposing her appropriation of the pain of Third World people, our issues, and our sexuality, but the traditionally romantic ending affirms her. All along, Sammy has been complicit in this appropriation, both welcoming and inviting it, yet Rosie as dominating figure bears the weight, takes the heat. I was reminded of Wertmuller's film *Swept Away*, where the white woman is also symbol of domination. In both films the white male is curiously absent, there most vividly in the first scenes, and then as distant oppressor in the shadows.

When I left the film, tightly clutching my ticket stub, I felt wound up, tight inside, disturbed. I noticed that the ticket simply said "Rosie." And I thought it was finally Rosie's film, a comment on the nature of her politics and her desire. Despite the primacy of Rafi's presence, the compelling nature of the story, even that is undercut by the focus on Rosie. In his film diary, Kureishi states that he based the character of Rosie on Sarah, a white woman friend, revealing in his playfully self-critical way that she called the film "Hanif Gets Paid, Sarah Gets Exploited," a title which very pointedly evokes the absent white male power behind the scenes that produces and directs, that pays. Two men (one brown, one white) create yet another patriarchal text, where a woman, in this case a white woman, and all the brown and black people who act as colorful backdrop, are powerless stars—a text wherein the two men playfully point to the failure of the dominated, and those radicals who would act in solidarity, to engage in meaningful resistance. Rosie is a symbol of failed modern radicalism. She does not stand alone. She embodies the helplessness, the powerlessness, that overwhelms many politically aware, cool people. She is stylishly nihilistic! When Rosie speaks with Danny of her past, she names herself the victim of paternal violence and abuse. Her attempt to mother Sammy, and her feeble effort to cease mothering, mask the fact that she too cannot grow up, cannot face reality. This is the profoundly despairing comment in the film, a message which neither subverts nor liberates. The title *Sammy and Rosie Get Laid* can be read finally as a statement not about what they do with their bodies, not about desire, but about what is done to them. They are both fucked up and fucked over by political systems that they do not effectively challenge or change. They hide in desire, in that narcissistic space of longing where difference—rather than becoming the new site for resistance and revolution, for ending domination—becomes the setting for high spectacle, the alternative playground.

17

REPRESENTING WHITENESS

seeing wings of desire

W im Wenders's 1988 film *Wings of Desire* received much critical acclaim and was loved by movie goers everywhere, yet I found the film very stylized, so intent to impress its seriousness upon the audience that there were moments when I just wanted to laugh, and there were tedious moments when I was just plain bored. Arriving at the cinema early, I took a seat which allowed me to watch folks coming to see this much talked-about film. Seated around me were viewers who had seen the film many times. They were praising Wenders even as they munched popcorn and searched for seats. As is often the case at this type of artsy film, there were few black viewers (three of us). I was curious to know how the two black women saw the film but did not dare ask (after all, they might not "see" themselves as black).

Seeing the film with a politically aware white feminist friend who loved it and was seeing it a second time, I could not resist teasing her by saying, "How come you love this film when all the male stars are angels and the female star is a trapeze artist? I mean, isn't this every straight male's fantasy?" She didn't get it. I said, "You know, the woman who can twist her body into any position, like those Modigliani paintings." Later I said, "So why didn't you tell me this was a film about white German angst?" She didn't get it. "You know," I declared, "It's another in a series where postmodern white culture looks at itself somewhat critically, revising here and there, then falling in love with itself all over again." She didn't get it. I gave up and began to speak English, that is to say, to speak a language she could understand (no more subaltern black codes).

Seriously, this film made me think deeply about white culture, though not simply in terms of skin color—rather whiteness as a concept underlying racism, colonization, and cultural imperialism. Wenders's earlier film *Paris, Texas* (a work I find interesting and problematic) did not raise whiteness as an issue. *Wings of Desire* evoked images of that imperialist colonizing whiteness that has dominated much of the planet. This image was reinforced by the use of nonwhite people as colorful backdrop in the film, a gesture that was in no way subversive and undermining in that much of the film was an attempt to represent white culture in a new light. Encountering white friends raving about the magic of this film, I would respond by saying it was just "too white." They would give me that frustrated "no racism again, please" look that is so popular these days and explain to me that, after all, Berlin is a white city. Of course I had to remind them about those black and brown people in the background—none of whom were either angels or trapeze artists. And that no, Berlin is not exclusively a "white city."

Talking to serious black movie goers who also could not get into this film, I was relieved. There was one exception, a fellow black woman "cultural terrorist" (a name we jokingly call ourselves) who liked the film's focus on history and memory. I could not see how she missed linking those concerns to white culture. I was surprised that she did not ponder the basic question of why all the angels were white. Her response was to ask me if I "could really imagine black angels." I thought immediately of the black angels (handmade dolls) hanging in my kitchen. I was surprised that she had never seen the brown-faced angels in Ethiopian talismanic art, work much older than figurative drawing.

"Why," I exclaimed, "I have one of those angels painted on a scroll in my living room! I see black angels every day." We continued to talk about the film, about the way in which ethnicity does or does not shape our viewing sensibility. We even tried to explore whether I had experienced some racist trauma the day I saw the film which might have made me more acutely aware of the issue. My insistence was that the issue was there in the work.

Filmmaker Wim Wenders does place this work in a decidedly white European context with an underlying focus on western civilization and history. In an interview with *Cineaste,* Wenders discusses the importance of not forgetting history, relating it to the film: "If there is any response to my parents' generation or to the one before it, it is the way they treated history after 1945. They tend to make everyone forget, which made it impossible to deal with."

Incorporating footage of war-torn Berlin and Nazism, Wenders compels audiences to remember. If, as he suggests, the angels are "a metaphor for history, a particular memory," we would all have seen these angels differently had they not been predominantly male and all white. In many ways, the film attempts to create a space of otherness, where white masculinity can be reconceptualized and white patriarchal imperialist history critiqued. Such a project raises questions about whether the alternative narrative Wenders constructs actually subverts or challenges the old. Wenders's work represents a trend in white avant-garde aesthetic circles toward re-visioning old narratives of opposition. *Wings of Desire* does not fulfill this promise. It does not tell a new story.

Homer, the aged writer/story-teller, asserts his longing for another narrative even as we witness his nostalgia for sentimental aspects of the old. He recovers himself through memory, through the act of story-telling. Interviewed in *Film Quarterly,* Wenders talks about his fascination and renewed interest in story-telling: "It is one of the most reassuring things. It seems its very basis is that it reassures you that there is a sense to things. Like the fact that children want to hear stories when they go to sleep. I mean not so much that they want to know this or that, but that they want it as it gives them a security. The story creates a form and the form reassures them so that you can almost tell them any story—which you can actually do. So there is something very powerful in stories, something that gives you security and a sense of identity and meaning."

To many audiences watching *Wings of Desire,* the reassuring story may be that narrative which promises the possibility of radical change in European history, in white culture. It's important, then, that the primary signifier of that change is the rejection by white males (the old story-tellers, the main angels Damiel and Cassiel) of destructive violence symbolized by war and genocidal holocaust. Imperialist masculinity is negated, and the new vision evoked by angelic style is of a world wherein the visionary white men exude divine presence and regard life as sacred. They do so as angels. They do so as men. Peter Falk (playing himself), in Berlin to make a detective movie, bonds with Damiel, sharing that he had once been an angel. His retention of the capacity to recognize divine presence links the insight of angels to that of mortals. Through much of the film, male angels use their bodies in ways that subvert traditional masculine physicality; their movements suggest tenderness and gentleness, never aggressiveness or brutality. However, the film's implied critique of oppressive masculinity is undercut by the re-inscription of sexist male bonding as regards sexual desire.

Only the male angels repudiate this form of bonding. Capable of compassionate empathy and abundant generosity, Damiel and Cassiel move about the city making connections with sensitive mortals, with hurt individuals who need healing. We witness their caring gestures, the way they appear to understand one another's longings, their bond expressed in deep penetrating glances at one another. At times they gaze at one another sensually, evoking an aura of angelic homoerotic bonding. However, their friendship changes as Damiel pursues Marion, the desired "mortal" female. Toward the end of *Wings of Desire,* Damiel meets Marion for the first time at a rock concert. Cassiel appears to be anguished by the pending separation from his friend. There is a powerful moment when he turns towards the wall, hands covering his face as though deeply wounded. On the other side of the wall the erotic bond between Marion and Damiel is forming. The loss of meaningful connection between the angels suggests that homosocial bonding, however innocent, must become secondary to the fulfillment of heterosexual desire.

In essence, the relationship between Damiel and Marion is a romantic reassertion of the primacy of heterosexual love. Ironically, despite his angelic past, Damiel approaches heterosexual desire in ways that are too familiar. His desire for Marion is first expressed via the objectifying gaze; she is the object of his look. Watching him watch her, I was reminded of that often quoted statement of John Berger in *Ways of Seeing:*

> Men act and women appear. Men look at women. Women watch themselves being looked at. This determines not only most relations between men and women but also the relation of women to themselves. The surveyor of woman in herself is male; the surveyed female. Thus she turns herself into an object of vision: a sight.

Wenders certainly does not re-write this script. He graphically dramatizes it. The audience first sees Marion working as a trapeze artist, every movement of her body watched by males. Their voyeuristic gaze is upon her and so is ours. She is scantily clothed; they are fully dressed. We in the onlooking audience are fully dressed. Since her movements on the trapeze are difficult exertions of physical skill, we are all the more mesmerized. Her attire and the men watching deflect attention away from physical effort and her body movements are sexualized.

Berger's comments on male presence suggest that it is defined by power, by what "he is capable of doing to you or for you." Throughout much of the film we are impressed by the way Damiel carries himself, by what he does. We watch his actions. His repeated touching of bodies is not sexualized. In contrast, Marion's every movement on stage or off is sexualized. As Berger suggests, her female presence is determined by attitude: "A woman must continually watch herself. She is almost continually accompanied by her own image of herself...From earliest childhood she has been taught and persuaded to survey herself continually." When Marion stops working and returns to her trailer, we watch as she surveys herself, as she examines her face in the mirror. We are placed in the position of voyeurs as is the angelic Damiel. His watching her (unidentified and unseen) in her private space can be seen as benevolent since he is an angel. In this scene he can be viewed as guardian, as protector. This is one way to look at it. Another is that the embedded message here is that the angelic cloak is a disguise marking the potential reality of his gaze, especially as we later witness that gaze turn into an intense lustful stare. Constructing a male angel who both protects and ultimately desires the innocent unsuspecting female is a gesture more fundamentally linked to patriarchal valuation of dissimulation than a radical rethinking of coercive masculinity.

Casting the men as angels without wings is not an unambiguous gesture. We watch them knowing they are to be seen as figures of innocence though we simultaneously recognize their embodiment as men. Every time their hands were placed on people's bodies, I contrasted that caring touch with the reality of white male disregard and violation of other people's body space. Throughout the film, viewers are to believe that angelic status diffuses their power so it is in no way harmful. Yet it is difficult to see subversive content in this imagery when white male agencies like the FBI and CIA as well as their Berlin counterparts would have us believe that their surveillance of the planet is for our own good. How can this imagery be trusted when the male gaze which begins as benevolent ends as a self-interested stare, expressed as longing for sexual possession? When the potential lovers finally meet at the bar, Marion wants to talk and Damiel wants to physically consume her (he is all over her). His acquiescence to her demands is not a gesture that transforms the dominating positioning of his desire. Much of the film centers on his enthrallment with her, which is so intense he surrenders being an angel to make contact.

Yet Wenders can say in *Film Quarterly* that he thought "it would be fatal for the film if she had been the object of his desire." It is disturbing that he is convinced that the film represents a change in his treatment of female subjectivity, that he can claim that Marion is "the leading character." Even the title *Wings of Desire* emphasizes the primacy of Damiel's character. His desire is central. Marion's sexuality is never fulfilled. Contrary to critics who interpret the voice-over where she expresses her point of view as a declaration of subjectivity, it is solely an expression of her ideas about love distinct from sexual desire. Again an old script is rewritten—women want love, men want sex.

Both *Wings of Desire* and Wenders's earlier film *Paris, Texas* explore male erotic fantasy, portraying male inability to acknowledge the subjectivity of women. Though scenes in *Paris, Texas* moved me deeply, from a feminist perspective it was a problematic film. The film was groundbreaking in that it portrayed a male character coming to understand the degrees to which clinging to male domination and coercive control damages his primary love relationship. Yet that understanding is undercut when expressed in the context of a scene which re-inscribes structures of domination. During the "peepshow" scene, which is the climactic point in the film, the male character tells the story of his sexist abuse and exploitation of his young wife, speaking to her. She is working in the booth. He watches her; she cannot see him. He knows her identity; she cannot recognize him until he identifies himself (sound familiar?—we could be speaking about Damiel and Marion). While naming coercive male control as destructive, he does not surrender control, only the coercive element. However touching this confession and her ultimate recognition, it is not a scene of female empowerment; just as the scene where Marion speaks to Damiel does not change the dominating power of his presence. *Wings of Desire* ends with a scene where Marion performs, the object of Damiel's gaze. Despite her earlier insistence on will, knowledge, and choice, nothing has changed their physical placement in the film. The visual image that remains is of a woman performing for male pleasure. Presumably her non-erotic desire has been satisfied, her longing to be touched by "a wave of love that stirs."

That this "love story," like *Cinderella, Sleeping Beauty,* and many others, satisfies and reassures is no cause for celebration. Perhaps it is dangerous that Wenders and the white male who interviewed him in *Film Quarterly* were so congratulatory and confident that this film had a "feminist" message, though they do not use that word. And even more dangerous, they do not question their vantage point. Are they so well informed about feminist thinking that they are able to determine whether Marion is portrayed as subject or object? It is as though the stage of acquiring the feminist standpoint that would be a basis for constructing different images of women and critically examining that construction, though unnamed, is presumed to have occurred; the same might be said of race. Representations of both gender and race in the film suggest otherwise. Current trends in avant-garde cultural production by white people which presume to challenge the status quo regarding race and gender are ethically and politically problematic. While it is exciting to witness a pluralism that enables everyone to have access to the use of certain imagery, we must not ignore the consequences when images are manipulated to appear "different" while reinforcing stereotypes and oppressive structures of domination.

In *Wings of Desire,* the library as storehouse of knowledge is the meeting place of angelic visionaries. It is only white people who are angels, only white men who dialogue with one another, only white men who interpret and revise old scripts (benevolently reading people's minds, touching them in their intimate body space). Wenders's imaginative offering of an alternative to destructive white masculinity is appealing, yet he does not fulfill the promise of his own creative assertions.

White avant-garde artists must be willing to openly interrogate work which they or critics cast as liberatory or oppositional. That means they must consider the role whiteness plays in the construction of their identity and aesthetic visions, as well as the way it determines reception of their work. Coco Fusco explains the importance of such awareness in her essay "Fantasies of Oppositionality," published in *Afterimage:* "Racial identities are not only black, Latino, Asian, Native American, and so on; they are also white. To ignore white ethnicity is to redouble its hegemony by naturalizing it. Without specifically addressing white ethnicity, there can be no critical evaluation of the construction of the other."

If the current fascination with otherness is an authentic expression of our desire to see the world anew, then we must be willing to explore the cultural blindness of the many people who saw *Wings of Desire* and who did not see whiteness represented there as sign and symbol.

18

COUNTER-HEGEMONIC ART

do the right thing

Talking about how the white public might respond to his latest film, *Do The Right Thing,* Spike Lee asserts in a rather cocky manner: "Listen, if white America has to squirm for two hours, if they're really uncomfortable watching this film, that's just too fucking bad. Because that's the way it is all the time for black people." Such bravado shocks and amuses. Presenting an "us and them" dichotomy, this comment rules out the possibility that black folks might find this film difficult to watch, that the portrayal of racism might wound and depress our spirits. Reading Lee's comment, I thought about all the smug, self-satisfied white folks in theaters everywhere watching *Do The Right Thing,* not squirming at all, just enjoying themselves watching a familiar (albeit exaggerated) spectacle, everybody letting their prejudices hang out, eruptions of racialized violence, culminating in the death of a young black man. So what else is new? We could be watching any cop show on television or catching a glimpse of the evening news anywhere and see this drama. Mass media in the United States exploit this representation of race and racialized contact in various ways daily: angry black folks doing violence, somebody—usually a young black man—dying. It happens so frequently on television screens, viewers hardly notice; they are too busy waiting to see what the hero (most often a white man) is going to do next.

Black males are usually portrayed as villains on television and in films. Spike Lee's film makes no radical break with this tradition. Even though he tries to subvert the "villain" role so that young black men are not seen as "the enemy," and viewers will understand this to be a mislabeling, his strategy does not work, as it is based on the assumption that to witness wrongdoing makes it clear who is right or wrong. Given the conservative thrust of this society, many viewers do not see the death of Radio Raheem as a brutal murder. It is rarely mentioned when the film is discussed. His character was not sympathetic. Certainly many underclass blacks, especially young men, who saw the film were deeply moved when they witnessed his fate, as it could possibly in real life be their own. Yet this is not an indication that the film was powerful, only that individuals identify with characters like themselves.

White radicals and liberals could and did identify with Mookie, the critical-thinking individualist in the film, concerned primarily with his own comfort (hustling women and hustling on the job, trying to get as much "play" as he can without giving much emotional commitment). Mookie is the hero of this film. Articulate, aware, shrewd, he has the freedom and power to make choices. Even his throwing the garbage can through the pizzeria window, the act which sets off the violence, does not emerge from spontaneous rage but is rather, a carefully considered response. He acts; he does not react. This gesture sets him apart from the other black folks in the neighborhood. He is one of them, yet "different." Just before he enters the conflict he is sitting at a distance, looking at the crowd, contemplative, united with his sister, who is also an onlooker. They sit apart, bonded as a family. It is at this point in the film that Mookie ceases to run interference between the black underclass and the white entrepreneur Sal.

Mookie's character has particular fascination for viewers who realize that he is both a character in the film and the filmmaker. Part of the new wave of avant-garde, up and coming young black university-educated filmmakers and artists who constitute an elite group (even though many of them came from underprivileged class backgrounds or were raised in poor black neighborhoods), Lee brings to film a self-consciously Afrocentric aesthetic. He reveals the ins and outs of life in an urban underclass black neighborhood. Skillfully, he never lets the audience forget that it is just that—an interpretation, not a documentary, even though he often shoots in this genre. Little details remind us that this is fiction (the always-clean designer clothes worn throughout the film by most characters irrespective of their role, the often noted absence of drugs, etc.). An aura of posturing and studied representation pervades this film. Rather than inviting the audience to escape, it compels them to stay at a distance like Mookie, to observe, to be nonparticipatory. Brilliant cinematography and great music create an intimacy that the narrative does not allow. Inviting the audience to maintain distance keeps separate the events shown on the screen and the viewer's daily life.

Do The Right Thing does not evoke a visceral response. That any observer seeing this film could have thought it might incite black violence seems ludicrous. White critics who imagine that this might be the black public's response clearly do not understand black experience. It is highly unlikely that black people in this society who have been subjected to colonizing brainwashing designed to keep us in our place and to teach us how to submit to all manner of racist assault and injustice would see a film that merely hints at the intensity and pain of this experience and feel compelled to respond with rage. Folks of all ethnicities come away from it talking about how much they enjoyed this film, as though it were just another adventure story.

What is so enjoyable about a film that culminates in the brutal killing of a young black man? Who are the viewers that sat in theaters feeling fear and pain as they watched violence ravaging a black neighborhood? Who wept and grieved as Radio Raheem's body was carried away? Where are their voices? Why is it that most of the folks talking and writing about this film focus little attention on Raheem's death, if any at all?

White audiences may enjoy this film because they watch it the same way they approach many television shows with black characters, searching for reassurance that they need not fear that black folks will infringe on their turf. The white owner of the pizzeria suffers because he is out of his place, trying to make it on someone else's turf. One scary, conservative idea voiced over and over again in this film is that everybody is safest in their "own" neighborhood, that it is best if we remain with people like ourselves.

There are masses of people who believe this, who live in ways that uphold the values of racial separatism even if they do not publicly articulate this stance. Often white folks claim that one of the major reasons they do not want black folks in their neighborhoods is the fear that our presence will cause violence. In a fascinating essay, "Deride and Conquer," Mark Miller contends that white people are reassured when they watch television shows that "negate the possibility of black violence with lunatic fantasies of containment." Separate neighborhoods are seen as a way to contain undesirables. Spike Lee's film offers a different version of the same theme. Containment occurs when people maintain boundaries. *Do The Right Thing* reassures white viewers that the "lunatic" violence erupting in "segregated" black communities finally hurts black people more than anyone else. Despite the burning of the pizzeria, it is a black community and relations among black people that are wrecked and ravaged.

A distressingly nihilistic ritual of disempowerment is enacted when a large crowd of black people watch as a "few" policemen brutally murder a young black man. Such a scene delivers a powerful message in a white supremacist society. The message is not about police brutality and how outraged citizens should be that the law does not protect black people deemed dangerous; it is instead that the white supremacist system of policing and control is intact and black people are powerless to assert any meaningful resistance. The crowd symbolically re-enacts the lynching mob, only with black victims as spectators. It is difficult to imagine the many white folks who have praised this film uncritically celebrating this work if it had been Sal who was killed, or one of his sons. The white "father" lives; only his shop is burned. His losses can be recovered. When the spirit of black rebellion and resistance is quelled by Raheem's death, suppressed and silenced, the questioning of white domination that has preceded this tragedy appears foolish and misguided. Watching Smiley pin portraits of Martin Luther King and Malcolm X on the charred and burned-out walls of the pizzeria can offer only a false sense of victory. This gesture implies that black folks have no substantive understanding of revolutionary liberation struggle that moves beyond the question of representation.

Few critics have seen *Do The Right Thing* as a serious indictment of contemporary black liberation struggle. Yet the black male characters who are most allied with black nationalism in the film lack a cogent program for struggle. They are either inarticulate or individuals who talk a good rap but when the shit hits the fan are unable to provide necessary leadership. There has been little discussion of the political implications of these images. Given continued critical emphasis on the issue of black representation, a discussion which has focused on the issue of good and bad images of black men, either in films like *The Color Purple* or in the writings of contemporary black women writers, Spike Lee's portraits of black masculinity have aroused no spirited debate. There seems to be tacit assumption that because he is a black man his images are "purer" and therefore not subject to the same rigorous critique that, say, a Spielberg, or any other white filmmaker exploiting black subject matter, merits.

Lee uses many conventional stereotypical and archetypal figures (the "wino," the wise "matriarchal" black woman, the "hound dog" who is obsessed with sexuality, etc.). While he provides many characters, they have no complexity. All the black male characters seem "lightweight," tragically flawed in ways that keep them from assuming full responsibility for their lives. This dimension of the film is overshadowed by heavy-handed focus on racial prejudice. The narrative suggests that the impotency that circumscribes and determines the fate of black men is solely due to racist oppression. Gender and class are not evoked as forces which shape the construction of racial identity. This seems highly ironic, since Spike Lee's film journals reveal that he is acutely aware of class and gender politics. Strategically, the film denies the problematical nature of identity and offers a simplistic view that would have skin color be all-encompassing. Such a narrative does not challenge conventional thinking about the "meaning" of race and its relation to identity formation. Contemporary progressive discussion of race in literary studies and in critical theory works against this simplistic analysis, attempting to chart radical and subversive directions for dialogues about race and strategies for resistance. Analyzed from this perspective, the film is regressive and lacking in critical insight.

Significantly, dynamic production and marketing strategies promoted the labeling of this film as "radical" and shaped public response. In actuality, it is the film's blatant "conservatism" (shaping the way racism is presented) that gives it wide appeal, crossing class boundaries and political affiliations. Like all good capitalist products, there is something for everyone.

Privileged elite white folks can be reassured that they are not "racist" since they do not espouse the crude racism expressed by Sal and his sons. Yet the film (via these same white men) can also legitimate racist folks by providing a public space where suppressed racist slurs and verbal assaults can be voiced and heard. No one seemed to worry that the film would offer white folks license to verbalize racist aggression.

Bourgeois black folks can watch *Do The Right Thing* and be reassured that they have made it, because the conditions of their lives are not like those portrayed on the screen. Yet they can still feel connected to their "roots" because they enjoy the same music as the black underclass or have the same approach to "style." The film also displays designer clothing, emphasizing style and personal representation. At times, it seems like a two-hour runway where the current trends in ethno-fashions are on display (the use of African kente cloth in expensive leisure clothes, etc.). Folks with money can check out the outfits and appropriate the style, buying the clothes, the look, the experience. (Note the long list of designers and brand names at the end of the movie.) Poor folks can look and long.

Underclass urban black people watching this film may feel momentarily empowered because their experience is deemed worthy subject matter, is represented and therefore affirmed, a response which can blot out the way that experience is appropriated and used.

Traditionally, the black middle class or a privileged intellectual elite has drawn on the life experience of lower-class black people to make aesthetic products which do not challenge the racist system of domination that creates oppressive economic circumstances exploiting essentialist notions of an authentic black experience that is colorful, sensuous, lively, etc., images that obscure the reality of pain and deprivation. Just because a black artist evokes a nationalist aesthetic may not mean that their work actually serves the collective interest of black people.

Neo-nationalism provides the ideological groundwork for Lee's mixture of aesthetics, politics, and economics. Unlike the narrow black capitalism that informed the 1960s black power movement, Lee's production and marketing strategies offer an approach where one can "stay in one's place," i.e., hang out with people who are just like you, celebrating the old "us and them" dichotomy, yet package your product to reach a crossover audience. Unfortunately, such an audience may need to see familiar stereotypes and archetypes to feel comfortable. Practically every character in *Do The Right Thing* has already been "seen," translated, interpreted, somewhere before, on television sitcoms, evening news, etc. Even the nationalism expressed in the film or in Lee's interviews has been stripped of its political relevance and given a chi-chi stance as mere cultural preference.

In a powerful discussion of the way nationalism is evoked in Lee's new film, Michael Dyson (in *Tikkun*) calls attention to the limitations of a black aesthetic that relies so heavily on the reconstruction of archetypes:

> Lee is unable to meet his two ambitions—to present the breadth
> of Black humanity while proclaiming a Black neo-nationalist
> aesthetic. His attempt to present a Black universe is admirable,
> but that universe must be one in which people genuinely act and
> do not respond as mere archetypal constructions. Because the
> characters carry such weighty symbolic significance (resonant
> though it might be), they must act like symbols, not like humans.
> As a result, their story seems predetermined, and they are denied
> agency within a complicated configuration of social, personal,
> and political choice.

The denial of agency is most apparent in the characterizations of black men. It is bitterly ironic that the two black male leaders, Martin Luther King and Malcolm X, whose images are sold in the community were highly educated, articulate critical thinkers, yet the person who attempts to keep their memory alive, Smiley, is inarticulate, unable to verbally convey the power of their message.

Surely if Alice Walker had created this cast of characters, critics would have suggested that it was meant to symbolically strip black men of agency. The articulate black men in the movie, the wise elders, are all addicts (drunks). The trio of middle-aged men, Sweet Dick Willie, ML, and Coconut Sid dialogue with one another with their back literally against the wall. It is not a speech of resistance. An elaborate circular discourse, however entertaining and colorful, it serves to signify again and again their powerlessness, their inability to assert agency. Then there is Da Mayor, wise drunk par excellence, the isolated ineffectual thinker whose constant good spirits belie the tragedy of his circumstance. Are these the "positive" images of black masculinity black men have been demanding, images that fail to convey the true plight of black males in a white supremacist capitalist patriarchy?

While none of Lee's male characters are portrayed as violent brutes (with the possible exception of Raheem, who also has a gentle side), they are depicted solely as victims. Their ability to laugh, joke, and hang together in the face of harsh reality is admirable, but it is not an oppositional stance. Again the portraits of black men conform to popular stereotypes in the white racist imagination. Rather than threaten white audiences, they assuage their fear.

By showing a young black male, Radio Raheem, instigating violence, Spike Lee uses the same image to symbolically stand for that which "threatens" maintenance of law and order that the New Right and other conservatives use. Conservative folks do not leave this film with the idea deconstructed or challenged that young black men are a menace and a threat. At a historical moment when so much racial violence is perpetrated by young white males, it is disturbing to see yet another media construction which suggests young black men are "the problem." Notice that as black folks in the movie, mainly black men, are disrupting the peace, being violent, the two young white males who have shown themselves to be just as "into" violence are suddenly passive. Lee's attempt to challenge the construction of young black men as violent menace by portraying the more deadly police brutality does not work. Raheem's death is predictable. Anticipated, the pathos which should surround his murder is seriously undercut.

Neo-nationalism as projected in the film is coupled with an un-critical acceptance of sexist notions of masculinity that involve the appearance of stoicism and "cool." This agenda does not enable full exploration of black male pain. Richard Majors suggests in his essay "Cool Pose: The Proud Signature of Black Survival" that "cool" is a form of self-expression black men use to suppress and mask feelings:

> Cool Pose, manifested by the expressive lifestyle, is also an aggressive assertion of masculinity. It emphatically says, "White man, this is my turf, you can't match me here." Though he may be impotent in the political and corporate world, the black man demonstrates his potency in athletic competition, entertainment and the pulpit with a verve that borders on the spectacular. Through the virtuosity of a performance, he tips the socially balanced scales in his favor. "See me, touch me, hear me, but, white man you can't copy me." This is the subliminal message which black males signify in their oftentimes flamboyant performances. Cool Pose, then, becomes the cultural signature for such black men.

Black men in *Do The Right Thing* are cool. Buggin' Out personifies this expressive style, competing only with Mookie, who has his own particular brand of cool. Indeed, Spike Lee, as self-invented charismatic figure both in and out of the film, resonates with this cultural signature; he is "too" cool, posturing and posing all over the place. Check out the place of "poses" in the film. Since many of us, black folks and the rest of y'all, enjoy manifestations of cool as aesthetic style and as subversive response to adversity, we can easily overlook the danger of cool when it is linked to destructive notions of masculinity. According to Majors:

> In many situations a black man won't allow himself to express or show any form of weakness or fear or other feelings and emotions. He assumes a facade of strength, held at all costs, rather than "blow his front," and thus his cool. Perhaps black men have become so conditioned to keeping up their guard against oppression from the dominant white society that this particular attitude and behavior represents for them their best safeguard against further mental or physical abuse. However, this same behavior makes it very difficult for these males to let their guard down and show affection, even for people that they actually care for, or for people that may really care about them.

This negative dimension of cool is on display throughout *Do The Right Thing*. Shrouded in the aura of a revised black nationalism linked with black capitalism, the film and the hype surrounding it manage to reinvoke outmoded sexist constructions of black masculinity that were a central dynamic in the 1960s black power movement without suffering harsh critique. Perhaps sympathetic viewers, especially all those folks who manage to write about the film without calling attention to the construction of gender, sexism, or misogyny, "overlook" these elements because they want to continue promoting the erroneous assumption that the perpetuation of racism is not linked to the perpetuation of sexism, or the more dangerous notion that focus on sexism or gender undermines one's capacity to struggle against racist oppression.

Do The Right Thing echoes that strand of black nationalism promoting the exclusion of black women and their role in liberation struggle. During a recent protest against racism at a Connecticut college, black females concerned about gender and racism were told by their black male neo-nationalist leadership, "This is a race thing, this is not about women." Spike Lee's movie delivers a similar message. The long beginning sequence of the film (rarely mentioned by critics) highlighting an unidentified black woman dancing in a manner that is usually a male performance is a comment on gender and role playing. Positively, she has "mastered" an art form associated primarily with male performance. Yet to do so, she must stretch and distort her body in ways that make her appear grotesque, ugly, and at times monstrous. That she is attempting to appropriate a male style (we can see the "female" version of this dance in the Neneeh Cherry video "Kisses On the Wind") is emphasized by her donning the uniform for boxing, a sport most commonly associated solely with males, even though there are a few black female boxers. By evoking the boxing metaphor, this scene echoes Ishmael Reed's new book of essays, *Writin' is Fightin'*, with its exclusive focus on black males, associating the pain of racism primarily with its impact on that group. Alone, isolated, and doing a male thing, this solitary dancer symbolically suggests that the black female becomes "ugly" or "distorted" when she assumes a role designated for males. Yet simultaneously the onlooker, placed in a voyeuristic position, can only be impressed by how well she assumes this role, by her assertive physicality.

This image is not mediated by the discovery as the film progresses that the dancer is a black Puerto Rican who has parented a child with Mookie and who wishes to continue their romantic involvement. She is portrayed in the film as verbally strong, a "talk shit, take none, fussing black woman," constantly "reading" Mookie and calling him out. Her skill at this, like her dancing, can easily persuade viewers that she is empowered, even though she is powerless. Completely objectified and victimized by Mookie (tricked by him into performing as sex object, acting out his fantasies), she is ultimately seduced in a manner that recalls the sado-masochistic sex scenes in the movie 9½ Weeks. Tina is unable to negotiate her relationship with Mookie. Manipulating in an attempt to fulfill her desires, she is consistently outmaneuvered. The somnolent child who lies between them (looking like an advertisement for undernourishment) is indeed emotionally deprived, a symbol of their ineffectual bonding.

Many of the scenes highlighting the presence of black women in the film appear spliced into the central drama (various conflicts between men) like commercials. They take the heat off and replace it with erotic play. Every relationship between black females and males in this film has a sexualized dimension. Every black female in the film, whether she be mother, daughter, or sister, is constructed at some point as sex object. The most glaring example of this manipulation of the female image and the female body occurs when the solitary dance ends and the camera focuses on Mookie lying in bed with his sister, Jade. Initially, the onlooker has no clue that this couple is brother and sister, as they appear to be waking up together. Mookie touches Jade's body in a manner that is familiar, conveying an intimacy that could easily have an erotic dimension. Puzzled by this scenario, many viewers passed it off as Lee being clever. Yet it is crucial commentary indicating the way black female bodies will be treated in this film; their privacy will be invaded, they will be manipulated by black men. They will be portrayed as needing (as in the case of Jade) black men to "teach" them that white males objectify them sexually in a degrading manner. Give us a break! The casual treatment of a symbolic incest scene (which can be read as "signifying" on all those works by black women which seek to expose the horror and pain of incest) sets the tone for the type of destructive sexuality that emerges in this film. Few critics have regarded this subject as a topic for critical response.

Spike Lee may think that he is simply putting it out there the way it is, but he is doing much more. By portraying the subtle and not-so-subtle, sexist humiliation of black females by black men in ways that depict it as cute, cool, heavy, he re-inscribes those paradigms. The one young black woman who "hangs" with the boys in the film is introduced in a scene where she is tricked, manipulated, and humiliated. Passive acceptance of this role seems to be the rite of initiation enabling her to be in the group. When the violence erupts, we suddenly see her in a traditionally sexist-defined female role, hovering on a corner hysterically crying and in a later scene pleading with the "men" to stop. Perhaps the devaluation of black womanhood in this film passes unnoticed because it fits so easily with the sexism pervasive in the culture. If the meaningful critique of racism surfacing strongly now and then in the film should alienate viewers, the sexism seduces them back into the film, provides the satisfaction denied in the other narrative. Tina, Mookie's woman friend, appears tough when the film begins, but when it ends she is trapped into that old movie frame where the woman is "seduced and abandoned," gaslighted again and again.

Despite the sexist exploitation of the female image in the film, the covert allusion to pornographic scenarios (that pose of the nude female body standing, hovering over the prostrate male), it is a black female who delivers one of the more powerful messages in the film, even though it is undercut by the reality that no one, especially the heroic male, is listening to her voice. Jade declares, with more autonomy than she has shown throughout the movie, that she is "down for something positive in the community." This "something positive," translated to mean meaningful resistance to racism and other forces of domination, does not occur. Folks who watched but did not "enjoy" this film, who sat in their seats feeling depressed by what they had just witnessed, remembering Jade's declaration felt a sense of powerlessness and defeat, stunned by the film's inability to articulate that "something positive."

Despite Spike Lee's courageous attempt to mix politics and art, to use film as a vehicle for exploring racism, and a popular film genre at that, the movie graphically portrays the racism we know without suggesting what can be done to bring about change. The film does not challenge conventional understandings of racism; it reiterates old notions. Racism is not simply prejudice. It does not always take the form of overt discrimination. Often subtle and covert forms of racist domination determine the contemporary lot of black people. To understand and resist our present predicament we cannot examine racism through a narrowly focused neo-nationalist lens that turns it into an issue of "us and them." As Dyson asserts: those who "strive to resist new-style racism must dedicate themselves to pointing out the slippery attitudes and ambiguous actions that signal the presence of racism without appearing to do so."

Combating racism and other forms of domination will require that black people develop solidarity with folks unlike ourselves who share similar political commitments. Racism does not cease to exist when white folks vacate black neighborhoods. It is not erased when

we control the production of goods and services in various black communities, or infuse our art with an Afrocentric perspective. Nostalgia
for expressions of black style that are less and less accessible to black
folks who no longer live in predominantly black communities may
color our critical response to *Do The Right Thing*.

Spike Lee's power as self-conscious artist and filmmaker lies in
his willingness to acknowledge that art is political, that it does express
political perspectives, that it can be a medium to chart new political
agendas without aesthetic compromise. Generating much discussion,
his film shows that art can serve as a force shaping and transforming
the political climate. Overwhelmingly positive reception to *Do The
Right Thing* highlights the urgent need for more intense, powerful
public discussion about racism, the need for a rejuvenated visionary
black liberation struggle. Aesthetically and politically, Spike Lee's film
has opened another cultural space for dialogue, but it is a space which
is not intrinsically counter-hegemonic. Only through progressive radical political practice will it become a location for cultural resistance.

19

A CALL FOR MILITANT RESISTANCE

In 1988 I was invited by the Malcolm, Rodney, Biko Collective in Toronto to come and speak on August 9 at an event commemorating the day black South African women assembled en masse in Pretoria to protest against pass laws, to protest against apartheid. Though I was honored by the invitation (it was one of the rare times radical black men on the left have organized a feminist lecture and urged black women to speak), I expressed uncertainty about whether I was the right person for the occasion. I felt that I did not know enough about the history of apartheid in South Africa or the particular circumstances of black women there. Even after I confessed my limitations, they urged me, "Sister, come and speak, we need your words." I agreed to come, saying that what I had to offer was a message from the heart of solidarity in struggle, from African-American women to black South African women. After reading intensively about the situation of black women in South Africa, I chose to talk about the way sexism informs the system of apartheid, the gendered nature of the assault on black people, particularly about the disruption of family life, about black women working as domestics in white homes. My talk was called "We Know How Our Sisters Suffer." It did not begin with South Africa but with my memories of growing up in the apartheid black American South, memories of black women leaving the racially segregated spaces of our community to work in white homes. As I spoke these memories, repeating often a line that runs through *Freedom Charter,* a work documenting aspects of black liberation movement in South Africa—"Our struggle is also a struggle of memory against forgetting"—black South African women in the audience responded. They knew firsthand what I was describing. They heard in my words a commonality of experience—a link between the African-American past and the contemporary struggle against white supremacy which unites us.

A piece I wrote for *Z Magazine* in January 1988 on white supremacy began with a declaration of solidarity between black Americans and black South Africans, stating that we share a common struggle rooted in resistance—the fight to end racism and white supremacist domination of black people globally. After my article was published, several white left academic colleagues let me know that it was misguided—that they did not agree with the idea that the United States is a white supremacist society. These colleagues have made their academic fame writing about race—interpreting black folks, our history, our culture. They no longer supported my intellectual efforts after the publication of this piece. For me it was a militant piece, voicing ideas many black folks hold but dare not express lest we terrify and alienate the white folks we encounter daily. White and black folks alike told me this piece was "too extreme." Whatever its form, black militancy is always too extreme in the white supremacist context, too out-of-order, too dangerous. Looking back at the history of black liberation struggle in the United States one can see that many glorious moments, when our plight was most recognized and transformed, when individuals black and white sacrificed—put their lives on the line in the quest for freedom and justice—happened because folks dared to be militant, to resist with passionate commitment. I often tell students who have no memory of this time to look at footage of civil rights struggle, at those old photographs (remember the ones of the young black and white women and men sitting at the Woolworth counter?) and they will see the sacrifice and the suffering endured.

Confronting the profound, life-threatening nihilism that has a choke-hold on masses of black people today, strangling us so that we cannot engage in effective protest and resistance, I ponder not so much where that spirit of militancy has gone, but the way in which it sustained and nurtured our capacity to struggle. Some folks may have heard resignation in that prophetic sermon when Martin Luther King declared that he had been to the mountaintop and received a vision—for many of us it was a militant message. We heard him testify that he had found reconciliation on that mountaintop, the understanding that black liberation struggle was worth the sacrifice, that he was ready to give his life. Though not heard by many, playwright Lorraine Hansberry echoed this militancy when she wrote in 1962, "The condition of our people dictates what can only be called revolutionary attitudes." Countering white criticisms of "black power" and militant opposition to racism, Hansberry declared: "...Negroes must concern themselves with every single means of struggle: legal, illegal, passive, active, violent and nonviolent. They must harass, debate, petition, give money to court struggles, sit-in, lie-down, strike, boycott, sing hymns, pray on steps—and shoot from their windows when the racists come cruising through their communities."

The statement she makes that has most urged me on in moments when I feel too tired to struggle is the militant reminder that: "The acceptance of our present condition is the only form of extremism which discredits us before our children." Hansberry was one of the many black artists, writers, thinkers, and intellectuals of her day who were not ashamed to link art and revolutionary politics, who were not afraid to speak out publicly against white imperialism in Africa.

A similar militancy can be seen in Euzan Palcy's anti-apartheid film *A Dry White Season*. It is a work which explores the emergence of critical consciousness from the standpoint of black folks engaged in militant resistance to apartheid and a white liberal father and son who become radicalized struggling on behalf of the oppressed. The film's focus on a white family disturbed many progressive viewers who did not want to see another film about a white man becoming radical, particularly one made by a black woman filmmaker. As clichéd and boring as this representation may be for some folks, it is certainly a representation of whiteness that disrupts that status quo, one that challenges the white spectator to interrogate racism and liberalism in a far more progressive way than is normally seen in mainstream cinema. How many films show white men acting in solidarity with the oppressed to resist white racist domination? Why is it that so many reviews saw this representation as uninteresting, as though it is a common sight? Talking about "cold war liberalism" in a 1960s forum on "The Black Revolution and the White Backlash," Hansberry stressed:

> Radicalism is not alien to this country, neither black nor white.
> We have a great tradition of white radicalism in the United
> States—and I never heard Negroes boo the name of John Brown.
> Some of the first people who have died so far in this struggle
> have been white men.... I don't think we can decide ultimately
> on the basis of color. The passion that we express should be
> understood, I think, in that context. We want total identification.
> It's not a question of reading anybody out; it's a merger...but it
> has to be a merger on the basis of true and genuine equality.
> And if we think that it isn't going to be painful, we're mistaken.

Palcy's film is the cinematic exploration of a white liberal's real-ization of what authentic solidarity with the oppressed demands, yet this powerful dimension of the film has received little attention. The reality that the continued racism of Hollywood and the culture of white supremacy dictates that masses of people are more likely to watch a film about South Africa that has a compelling story line cen-tralizing white folks does not diminish the radical subversive element in the film. And one of those features is the complex representation of "whiteness." The story of a white liberal acquiring a radical conscious-ness is a needed representation for many indifferent or uncertain white folks who do not know that they have a role to play in the struggle to end racism.

Yet liberals are not all alike in this film. As the cynical lawyer who has presumably been through what Ben du Toit is going through, Marlon Brando offers us another perspective, and the radical white fe-male journalist and her supportive father give us yet another take. Concurrently, what contemporary film has depicted white female com-plicity in the perpetuation of white supremacy as clearly as Palcy's film? White supremacy is a family affair, not a mere spectacle of patri-archy.

Even though Palcy faced constraints that undoubtedly forced her to deradicalize her vision, *A Dry White Season* has many subversive cinematic moments. Again and again whiteness is interrogated, ex-posed, problematized in groundbreaking ways. One such moment happens when Ben transgresses the boundaries of white supremacy by the seemingly unimportant gesture of publicly embracing Emily, the black wife of the murdered gardener, Gordon. Right then the film poses critical questions about the intersection of race and gender, about sexuality and power, that are rarely addressed in cinema. Palcy explores the question of whether a white male who chooses to give up his privilege and work on behalf of the oppressed who struggle against racism does not as a consequence challenge the system of pa-triarchal male power. Ben du Toit must turn his back on the patriar-chal birthright that is the husband's legacy, offered him as a necessary initiation rite. It is this gesture that proves he is worthy of black solidar-ity. To use Adrienne Rich's phrase, he must be "disloyal to civilization," and thus Palcy, whether consciously or unconsciously, links the strug-gle to end racism with feminist struggle, suggesting that any authentic white male challenge to white supremacy threatens the structure of white patriarchy. Few white feminists have acknowledged that the struggle to end racism challenges and disrupts white supremacist patri-archy, even though it is now commonplace for feminists to acknowledge the importance of race. Privileged phallocentric white women in Palcy's film want to keep intact their luxurious lifestyles and actively support white supremacist patriarchy. Representations of white womanhood in the film do not allow the viewer to overlook race and class and see these characters as "just women."

Again and again in *A Dry White Season* Palcy suggests that it is not one's race, gender, class, or circumstance that determines whether or not one will have a radical political standpoint. Exploited black people are as reluctant to participate in resistance struggle as paralyzed whites like Ben du Toit. Like him, they must choose radical political commitments, and the power of that choice will be indicated by the sacrifices and risks taken to fulfill those commitments.

Though black people in the film share a common plight, they do not share a common understanding of their situation. They are not all radicalized. Palcy shows radical critical consciousness to be a learned standpoint, emerging from awareness of the nature of power and domination that is confirmed experientially. That is why the black children assume a primary role, questioning their parents, resisting the status quo. Many viewers allowed their dissatisfaction with the focus on white people to blind them to the powerful representations of black militancy. When has a Hollywood film shown black characters fiercely resisting white supremacy? What recent films by black filmmakers, Hollywood movies or independent productions, explore meaningful black resistance to white supremacy? Perhaps it is this cinematic standpoint that caused the public's lukewarm reception to *A Dry White Season*. Coming out of a theater in the Midwest, I heard white folks telling other people in line not to see the film because it was "too violent." Did too violent mean that the good white hero dies and the revolutionary black male hero lives?

It is not just the leading characters who are militant in the film. The most powerful dramatization of black militancy involves minor characters who are rarely mentioned in reviews. Yet their actions disrupt the idea that black liberation struggle can only take place if there is an inspired individual messianic (preferably male) leader. Two memorable scenes challenge this assumption. One occurs with the dramatization of the Soweto demonstration, where black school children were brutally murdered by police. Sophie Tema, a black woman journalist, gave the world the first eyewitness account of this event. Palcy re-enacts this gesture through her re-telling. Audiences watch as two black girls run from the police. The little one is brutally shot and her older sister stands facing her oppressors saying, "You killed my sister, kill me too!" This scene is utterly subversive, one of the most radi-

cal cinematic representations of black militancy. The direct gaze she
gives the camera and her oppressors lets us know that she is not a victim. She stands in the midst of slaughter, not silent, but able to bear
witness through speech, able to talk back. What young black girl
watching this scene would not be awed and inspired by the courage
on the older sister's face? Even though her little sister has been murdered as sacrifice, she lives to bear witness and to go forward in struggle. She remembers. This scene may have had little impact on viewers
in this society who pay no attention to the affairs of little black girls,
yet I wanted every black girl struggling to resist racism to see it—to be
able to hold it in the mind's eye, placing it alongside all the passive
sexist/racist portraits of black girlhood which abound in the mass
media.

Another unpredictably subversive scene takes place in the court-
room. There, it is not Marlon Brando's performance that grips the audience but that of the black male messenger who takes the witness stand
ostensibly to provide testimony that will cover up the evils of white supremacy, that will deny the torture and violence against black people.
When he rebels, audiences are not only surprised, they are overwhelmed. It is scenes like this one that make *A Dry White Season* a
successful thriller. But I was thrilled by the portrayal of resistance.
Again, it was a resistance that demanded sacrifice. Militant rebellion
has its price. The scene is no less powerful because it is utopian. Perhaps in these less than militant times we need to imagine the possibility of resistance anew; for what we cannot imagine will never happen.
The messenger's actions are a call for militant resistance.

That spirit of militant resistance is most personified in the character of Stanley, played by South African Zakes Mokae. I first saw Zakes
in a Fugard play. Talking with him about his performance, about the
situation in South Africa, I was struck by the aura of calm that ema-
nates from him. It is this calmness in the face of struggle that the character Stanley consistently conveys. Throughout the film he is the
rational revolutionary strategist. We see his emotional vulnerability
only when Emily dies, a scene which suggests that even the most militant spirit can be broken. Stanley can only achieve his revolutionary
goals with collective support. It is Ben's support which sustains him
during that difficult moment. Who can argue with the film's message
that white people should assume a major role in the fight against racism and white supremacy and that black people should militantly resist?

It took Palcy five years to make this film. With this film she dares
viewers to confront the current situation in South Africa. This is the ful-

fillment of the radical promise of the film, that it will both awaken and renew interest in the struggle against apartheid, that it will make us remember—"Our struggle is also a struggle of memory against forgetting." Anyone who does not hear the call for militant participation in black liberation struggle that this film conveys has missed its most important message.

After my talk in Toronto, I met with black South Africans to eat and dialogue. Sitting near me was Mangi, a young black male. I was impressed by his knowledge of black liberation struggles globally and his sophisticated understanding of feminist politics. I saw reflected in him the hope of a decolonized, liberated black mind. That night he talked of life in exile away from his mother and sister. In exile he is safe, alive, well, and critically conscious. Yet I hear in his voice the longing for an intimacy and family and community that are lost. The black family and community are torn asunder in *A Dry White Season*. That is the reality for most black families in South Africa. African-Americans share this plight. Our families and communities are in crisis. Can we face that crisis with militancy, with the passionate will to resist and commitment to struggle that will lead to transformation in our lives and in society? Sick and dying, Lorraine Hansberry continued to interrogate her political commitment, asking: "Do I remain a revolutionary? Intellectually—without a doubt. But am I prepared to give my body to the struggle or even my comforts?" Palcy's film also poses that question. Who will answer?

20

SEDUCTIVE SEXUALITIES

representing blackness in poetry and on screen

Written in a familiar jocular tone, Langston Hughes's poem "Old Walt" tells readers that Walt Whitman was a man who "went finding and seeking, finding less than sought, seeking more than found." These lines are mysterious. The reader never really knows what it is Whitman searches for or the nature of his longing. Remembering him as one of the first closeted gay poets of America whose poems spoke openly of male homoeroticism, one can hear in Hughes's salute to Whitman a praisesong for his willingness to explore transgressive desire. Hughes's work conveys admiration, recognition, and shared sensibility. The poem suggests intimacy, familiarity, as though Whitman and the speaker are comrades. The lines that delight me in this poem are the ones that tell readers Whitman was "pleasured equally in seeking and in finding." It is this evocation of pleasure that is seductive, that suggests the poem is about sexuality and desire.

A devout reader of Langston Hughes's poetry for more than twenty years (learning to recite it from childhood on, then teaching it, or reading it silently to myself in the shadows of lonely nights), I imagine always that I am reading the Hughes most folks don't want to know, the sensual poet obsessed with desire. Much of his work speaks about erotic longing, tormenting desire, unfulfillment, romantic abandonment, relationships between black men and women that don't work, that end in pain, bitterness, that leave folks overwhelmed by sorrow, deep in despair, longing for death. No, this is not the Langston Hughes most folks read or remember. They do not hear the poet who in "Lament over Love" writes: "I hope my child'll never love a man. I

193

say I hope my child'll never love a man. Love can hurt you mo'n any-thing else can."

In Hughes's work romantic desire is a maddening, tormenting passion. Often in his poems the speaker is a lovesick anguished black woman. Comfortable with this fictive transvestism, Hughes appropri-ates female voices, making them synonymous with sexual vulnerabil-ity. Who is this black woman who longs, who opens herself to love and is betrayed, always hurt, never satisfied? Hughes's poems paint graphic portraits of sexual vulnerability, of sexual sado-masochism. The eroticism he speaks again and again in his poems is bound, caught in a litany of loss, abandonment, and broken promises: desire is a wound.

It is this Langston Hughes I find passionately represented in Isaac Julien's moving film *Looking for Langston*. Unlike critics who see this film and come away thinking "it ain't about Langston Hughes," I came away stunned by how brilliantly and vividly the film evoked an inti-mate dimension of Hughes's poetic reality, the attitudes towards sex-ual longing and erotic despair expressed in his poems. Writing in *Art Forum*, critic Greg Tate says that "what Julien has called a film medita-tion on the poet and writer Langston Hughes is really more a collage about the historical conditions of being black, gay, silenced, and in-comprehensible." Certainly *Looking for Langston* makes one of the most powerful statements about these concerns. The film also chal-lenges viewers to acknowledge this broader reality without oversha-dowing the specific meditative focus on Hughes. Much of the dramatic tension in the film emerges as Julien cinematically attempts (as he puts it in an interview with Essex Hemphill in *Black Film Review*) to "have desire exist in the construction of images and for the story-telling to ac-tually construct a narrative that would enable audiences to meditate and to think, rather than be told." Some viewers may leave this film seeing it solely as a visual documentation of black gay reality. They may leave it pondering their confrontation with images never seen be-fore and in no way connect them with Langston Hughes or the multi-dimensional meditative exploration that occurs on the screen.

Watching *Looking for Langston,* I felt an edginess, a tension, a tightness in my body, experienced usually only when I am watching a thriller, anticipating the unexpected. These sensations were aroused because the film is about transgression, movement into unknown mys-terious undefined territory. It both portrays transgressive desire and is itself the embodiment and re-enactment of a transgression we witness and watch. It speaks that which, in this visual genre, has been silent, unspoken. And even its very production and construction are informed by forces of repression and denial, by the efforts of the Hughes estate to control representation, to set boundaries and contain. We bear witness to this tension in the film. Wanting more of Hughes's words, his poems, we accept less even as we must interrogate the absence, the forces that silence, that create this lack.

Looking for Langston crosses boundaries and flaunts its transgression. Audiences are startled by the dramatic unveiling of black gay identity, the direct bold-faced portraits of black male artists, the outspoken homosexuality of James Baldwin, Bruce Nugent, and others, not because their preferences were not known but because they are not represented isolated and alone. The power of these images resides in their collective presence. Against this backdrop of openness falls the shadow of Hughes's closeted unnamed sexual practice. At the very onset the film names itself as searching with the camera eye for that hidden repressed sexuality that is alluded to but never directly addressed, both in Hughes's work and in much of the critical writing about that work. Since any attempt to reconstruct that sexuality is always a reminder of what is lost, it is fitting that the film opens with the scenes of mourning.

Death and desire are linked in *Looking for Langston*. Mourners are arranged beautifully—seductively even. Their stance suggests that not to share in the mourning of this death is to miss something precious, to be outside the collectivity of black experience. Black women and men stand side-by-side in this scene, experiencing a shared grief that someone, undoubtedly a loved one, is gone. Only he is not named. And when the image of the filmmaker appears represented as deceased, the film acts to document presence, to resurrect and bring back to life what has been lost; it identifies and names. These early funeral scenes are powerfully romantic and nostalgic. Loss exists alongside beauty which, though life affirming, cannot render death powerless.

Death claims center stage at the beginning of *Looking for Langston*. Imaginatively constructing an aesthetic universe where beauty merges with death and decay, where they seem inseparable, Julien's work—like the novels of Japanese writer Yukio Mishima, who was obsessed with homoerotic desires—suggests that this is an irrevocable bond. Rather than diminishing desire, the possibility of death only makes it more intense. In his biography of Mishima, Peter Worlge correctly surmises that in Mishima's world view "anything of value exists in close proximity to death." The funeral ceremony as ritual of remembrance at the beginning of *Looking for Langston,* with its serene elegance and pomp, wordlessly lets us know that this passing is precious and should not be forgotten. In a world terrified by the on-slaught of incurable diseases, one where the threat of AIDS links death to sexuality, all forms of transgressive sexuality are represented as both horrific and deadly. In such a cultural context, homosexual desire is often made to appear ugly, unromantic, undesirable. Julien's film criti-cally disrupts and subverts this representation. Here the homoerotic, homosexual desire that, like all sexual passions, culminates in recogni-tion of the possibility of loss, of dying, is both tragic and full of won-der. Death is no longer nightmare; it is an elegant transformative ritual, an occasion that demands, requires even, meaningful recognition and remembrance. During the funeral scene, the beloved one who has been excluded, outcast, is collectively embraced, held in the arms of memory. The opening scenes in *Looking for Langston* are a welcom-ing, a homecoming. As the audience we are present to witness both death and resurrection. From the grave emerges the mutilated image of Langston Hughes, the distorted representation, the hidden sexual practice. It is resurrected as symbol of desired and desirable black male body and being, of homoerotic, homosexual, sex radical, trans-gressive subject.

The new anthology *Hidden From History: Reclaiming the Gay and Lesbian Past* edited by Martin Bauml Duberman, Martha Vicinus, and George Chauncey, Jr. includes an essay by Eric Garber, "A Specta-cle In Color: The Lesbian and Gay Subculture of Jazz Age Harlem," documenting that "homosexuality was clearly part of this world" but also that the open expression of this desire was part of a larger frame-work of sexually diverse and transgressive practices. The atmosphere of the times was such that sexuality could not be seen as expressed simply by the binary opposition of gay and straight but by varied forms of sexual practice. It was a time when black gays who dared could be "out" and it was equally a time of sexual fluidity. Thus the singer of "Sissy Man Blues" could demand, "If you can't bring me a woman, bring me a sissy man." The sexuality these lyrics playfully evoke is complex. They do not suggest a sexuality structured on the foundation of consensual agreement between two adults but one that is multi-layered and multi-dimensional, one that is informed by exist-ing hierarchies and power structures. When Langston Hughes's sexual-ity is considered with this cultural context in mind, there are many ways to approach an interpretation and understanding of his sexual practice. Garber writes of him that the "exact nature of Hughes's sexu-ality remains uncertain." It is this tantalizing gap between fact and pos-sibility that made all attempts to document, in some exclusive way, Hughes's sexual practice a potential erasure. Hughes's biography suggests that he enjoyed the element of mystery. Transgressive sexual practice is rooted in mystery, the flirtation between secrecy and disclosure. Repression and containment, though painful, may also intensify desire. There may yet be no cultural context that allows us to understand that desire which does not wish to be named, not out of fear (Hughes's open exploration of sexuality in his work indicates he was not afraid to address sexual issues) but out of perverse regard. Mishima believed that the most meaningful sustained passion remained undeclared, even if acted out. Perhaps Hughes had a similar erotic ethos. Julien's film links Hughes to homosexual practice without letting go of this element of mystery. The film toys with it, makes it the stuff of exciting sexual intrigue and quest.

Looking for Langston re-constructs and invents a history of black gay sexuality while simultaneously problematizing the notion of secrecy and repression. The representation of a closeted hidden "location" for black gay sexual desire during the jazz age, the Harlem Renaissance is depicted as a space that contains even as it becomes the site of unique sub-cultural expression. There is always an aura of mystery in the film. Desire remains shadowy and unclear, and the possibility of fulfillment uncertain. Longing for open recognition is juxtaposed with the rareified intensity of desire emerging in the context of repression. Images in the film pose questions: what does desire look and feel like in the repressive context? What form does desire take in that space where full recognition is dangerous and denied? Julien's work suggests that within this location the eye, rather than the penis, becomes the primary signifier. In the unexplored terrain of black male homosexual desire, of black men looking at one another, then, it is the gaze that makes visible that which could pass unseen. Just as Hughes suggests in "Old Walt" that there is pleasure in seeking, Julien cinematically constructs a world where seduction begins with the look, with eyes that speak one's desire even when one has no voice. Passionate longing for that erotic fulfillment that is also recognition is expressed in the film as black men of all shades, hues, and body types glance, stare, look at one another. This is not a documentation of reality; it is an imaginative evocation of what is desired.

Reality is fraught with contradictions. The presence of white gay men in the film reminds the viewers that race, racism, and the politics of white supremacy inform the construction of black sexual identity, of black gayness. Desire for recognition that liberates is contrasted with the cannibalistic commodification of black male sexuality, vividly evoked in inter-racial encounters in the film. The white males appear ghoulish, strange, and out of place. Yet "whiteness" calls attention to their presence, centralizes, stands out in the dark. Symbolically, they represent that longing which dismembers black flesh. They evoke the reality of homosexual desire in a culture of white supremacy, a history where black bodies—the younger, the better—will be bartered, sold, "worked" by the highest bidder, and made to serve. The gaze of the white male as it appears in the film is colonizing; it does not liberate. What desire is expressed when the only frontal nudity seen in the film appears as secondhand image—the pictures of naked black men taken by wealthy white photographer Robert Mapplethorpe? Who owns these images and to whom do they belong? In them it is the erect penis and not the eye that personifies black homoerotic maleness. These images lose meaning and power in the context of the film. They are subsumed by the filmmaker's eye critically intervening, challenging without suppressing or denying the legitimacy of this representation. Though acknowledged, Mapplethorpe's vision is simply not compelling when it is displayed within a framework where the prevailing image is that of the black male body defining itself as subject, not as object.

Much of the visual power in this film derives from its confrontation with stereotypical images of black male bodies, sexuality, and the production of an intervening counter-aesthetic. Viewers are compelled to see dark skin, thick lips—all those features of blackness and maleness that have been portrayed in racist/sexist culture as the epitome of all that is not beautiful—from an affirming perspective, one that challenges the negative stereotype and transforms the image. Watching this film may be the first instance for many people to look at black maleness with visual pleasure, not with a sense of threat or danger. Contrary to popular stereotype, in *Looking for Langston* black men appear vulnerable, shed the protective shield of hardened masculinity they are in real life expected to wear like a mask.

Within the artistry of Julien's vision, black men can meet and know one another in the fullness of an encounter that allows varied expressions of identity and selfhood even as it celebrates in a fundamental way erotic display of mutual passion between black men. That passion is intensely evoked by the poetry of Essex Hemphill. In poetic voice-overs that boisterously and loudly declare the pleasure and pain of black homoeroticism, homosexuality, Hemphill's words break the silence, claim a gayness that is not afraid of being *over*-heard, that assumes a presence in history. There is a tension throughout the film between this outspoken black gay erotic voice and the silence of uncertainty, unknowing, that contains and closets Hughes's sexuality. Hemphill's voice seems to say that if Hughes's repressed sexuality could speak this is what it would say. This gesture threatens to over-shadow the way in which the silenced sexuality of Hughes, of his generation, speaks in the very images Julien gathers. Footage of the Harlem Renaissance, of the jazz age, of blues singers gives voice to the past. And what those images say has more to do with the forms desire takes when it is not openly and directly declared, or when its declarations are mediated by the pain of internalized racism, shame about skin color, oppressive color caste hierarchies, and the inability of many black men then and now to mutually give each other the recognition that would be truly liberating—the fulfillment of desire. *Looking for Langston* exposes the depth of this longing, the need for a history that will name and affirm black gay identity. The poetic voice in the film passionately states, "I long for my past." A longing that is reiterated when we are told, "It's not wrong for the boy to be looking for his gay black fathers." Such testimony speaks about the connection between recognition and self-actualization.

In *Bonds of Love,* Jessica Benjamin's discussion of feminism, psychoanalysis, and domination, she suggests that it is the recognition given the child by the parent figure which allows the development of a distinct self: "Recognition is that response from the other which makes meaningful the feelings, intentions, and actions of the self. It allows the self to realize its agency and authorship in a tangible way." The attempt to uncover and resurrect a black gay past is rooted in the acknowledgement that the restoration of this history enriches the present. *Looking for Langston* problematizes the quest for black gay history, acknowledging the need to claim forefathers, to rescue them from nameless burial, even as it also suggests that this quest cannot always be fully realized, especially when necessary documentation cannot be found (as in the case of Hughes). This does not mean that one ceases to search. It means that the pain that this gap of unknowing causes must be understood as a crucial dynamic in the formation of black gay identity and sensibility.

The possibility that desired recognition will remain elusive is vividly evoked by the scene in that field of dreams where the fully clothed black male meets the naked, desired Other that is both his mate and reflection of himself, only to be told yet again to wait. The seeker must confront a desire that has no end, that leads him to situations where he is acknowledged and abandoned, yet he must continue to search. At that moment his gaze is tragic and painful. We voyeuristically watch these possible lovers who meet only to part, who never find the desired fulfillment. Shrouded in a background of romance and beauty, the pain of this moment can easily remain unseen by the audi-

ence since there is no verbal narration. There is so much elegance and
beauty in the film that it has the quality of both spectacle and mas-
querade, all of which can obscure the ways this beauty has tragic dimensions, elements of longing and loss, that lead to depression and
despair. These negative elements are suggested by the focus on commodification of black male bodies, the ways black gay identity and
sexual practice are informed by the demands of material survival. In
Hughes's work sexual passion is always mediated by issues of materiality, class position, poverty. Whether he is speaking clearly about heterosexual relationships or in ambiguous language that could refer to
same-sex encounters, in his poems black male sexual performance is
always overdetermined by material circumstances. This is especially
true for the black underclass. The connection between poverty and
sexual potency is repeatedly made in the collection of poems "Mon-
tage of a Dream Deferred." Expressions of sexual longing are contrasted with the inability of folks to sustain erotic passion. In "Same in
Blues" Hughes suggests that a psyche that is depressed by poverty, by
the loss of dreams, cannot maintain a productive sexuality. This loss of
sexual potency is repeated in various stanzas but painfully evoked
when the seductive declaration "daddy, daddy, daddy, all I want is
you" is made, and the response is "you can have me, baby, but my
lovin' days is through" and the narrator's refrain, "a certain amount of
impotence in a dream deferred." Despair disrupts, perverts, and distorts sexuality, in Hughes's poems, in Julien's film. It is primarily in the
realm of erotic fantasy that dreams of sexual healing, sexual satisfaction can be realized, where the fragmented, broken-hearted self can
be recovered and restored to wholeness. The black gay men who are
"falling angels" are represented in dreamlike states where they recover
the means to fly, where they once again regain a sense of mission.
They guard, protect, and offer the healing touch that makes self-recovery possible. Speaking with Hemphill about the way in which the
search for black gay history is rooted in the longing for wholeness, Julien asserts: "If you are talking about black gay identity, you're talking
about identities which are never whole in the sense that there is always a desire to make them whole, but in real life, experiences are always fragmentary and contradictory."

Looking for Langston gathers these fragments, offers an imaginative configuration that gives a sense of wholeness that satisfies even as
it remains incomplete, without neat narrative closure. The need to uncover, restore, and even invent black gay history is ongoing. It includes the search for a narrative that will enable us to understand the
complex closeted eroticism of Langston Hughes. Like the poem "Old

Walt," Julien's film celebrates the seeking. It is both gesture of fulfillment and promise.

21

BLACK WOMEN AND MEN: PARTNERSHIP
IN THE 1990s

a dialogue between bell hooks and Cornel West
presented at Yale University's African-American
Cultural Center

b.h. I requested that Charles sing "Precious Lord" because the conditions that led Thomas Dorsey to write this song always make me think about gender issues, issues of black masculinity. Mr. Dorsey wrote this song after his wife died in childbirth. That experience caused him to have a crisis of faith. He did not think he would be able to go on living without her. That sense of unbearable crisis truly expresses the contemporary dilemma of faith. Mr. Dorsey talked about the way he tried to cope with this "crisis of faith." He prayed and prayed for a healing and received the words to this song. This song has helped so many folk when they are feeling low, feeling as if they can't go on. It was my grandmother's favorite song. I remember how we sang it at her funeral. She died when she was almost ninety. And I am moved now as I was then by the knowledge that we can take our pain, work with it, recycle it, and transform it so that it becomes a source of power.

Let me introduce to you my "brother," my comrade Cornel West.

C.W. First I need to just acknowledge the fact that we as black people have come together to reflect on our past, present, and objective future. That, in and of itself, is a sign of hope. I'd like to thank the Yale African-American Cultural Center for bringing us together. bell and I thought it would be best to present in dialogical form a series of reflections on the crisis of black males and females. There is a state of siege raging now in black communities across this nation linked not only to drug addiction but also consolidation of corporate power as we know it, and redistribution of wealth from the bottom to the top, coupled with the ways with which a culture and society centered on the market, preoccupied with consumption, erode structures of feeling, community, tradition. Reclaiming our heritage and sense of history are prerequisites to any serious talk about black freedom and black liberation in the twenty-first century. We want to try to create that kind of community here today, a community that we hope will be a place to promote understanding. Critical understanding is a prerequisite for any serious talk about coming together, sharing, participating, creating bonds of solidarity so that black people and other progressive people can continue to hold up the blood-stained banners that were raised when that song was sung in the civil rights movement. It was one of Dr. Martin Luther King's favorite songs, reaffirming his own struggle and that of many others who have tried to link some sense of faith, religious faith, political faith, to the struggle for freedom. We thought it would be best to have a dialogue to put forth analysis and provide a sense of what form a praxis would take. That praxis will be necessary for us to talk seriously about black power, black liberation in the twenty-first century.

b.h. Let us say a little bit about ourselves. Both Cornel and I come to you as individuals who believe in God. That belief informs our message.

C.W. One of the reasons we believe in God is due to the long tradition of religious faith in the black community. I think, that as a people who have had to deal with the absurdity of being black in America, for many of us it is a question of God and sanity, or God and suicide. And if you are serious about black struggle you know that in many instances you will be stepping out on nothing, hoping to land on something. That is the history of black folks in the past and present, and it continually concerns those of us who are willing to speak out with boldness and a sense of the importance of history and struggle. You speak knowing that you won't be able to do that for too long because America is such a violent culture. Given those conditions you have to ask yourself what links to a tradition will sustain you given the absurdity and insanity we are bombarded with daily. And so the belief in God itself is not to be understood in a noncontextual manner. It is understood in relation to a particular context, to specific circumstances.

b.h. We also come to you as two progressive black people on the left.

C.W. Very much so.

b.h. I will read a few paragraphs to provide a critical framework for our discussion of black power, just in case some of you may not know what black power means. We are gathered to speak with one another about black power in the twenty-first century. In James Boggs's essay, "Black Power: A Scientific Concept Whose Time Has Come," first published in 1968, he called attention to the radical political significance of the black power movement, asserting: "Today the concept of black power expresses the revolutionary social force which must not only struggle against the capitalist but against the workers and all who benefit by and support the system which has oppressed us." We speak of black power in this very different context to remember, reclaim, re-vision, and renew. We remember first that the historical struggle for black liberation was forged by black women and men who were concerned about the collective welfare of black people. Renewing our commitment to this collective struggle should provide a grounding for new direction in contemporary political practice. We speak today of political partnership between black men and women. The late James Baldwin wrote in his autobiographical preface to *Notes of a Native Son:* "I think that the past is all that makes the present coherent and further that the past will remain horrible for as long as we refuse to accept it honestly." Accepting the challenge of this prophetic statement as we look at our contemporary past as black people, the space between the sixties and the nineties, we see a weakening of political solidarity between black men and women. It is crucial for the future of black liberation struggle that we remain ever mindful that ours is a shared struggle, that we are each other's fate.

C.W. I think we can even begin by talking about the kind of existentialist chaos that exists in our own lives and our inability to overcome the sense of alienation and frustration we experience when we try to create bonds of intimacy and solidarity with one another. Now part of this frustration is to be understood again in relation to structures and institutions. In the way in which our culture of consumption has promoted an addiction to stimulation—one that puts a premium on bottled commodified stimulation. The market does this in order to convince us that our consumption keeps oiling the economy in order for it to reproduce itself. But the effect of this addiction to stimulation is an undermining, a waning of our ability for qualitatively rich relationships. It's no accident that crack is the postmodern drug, that it is the highest form of addiction known to humankind, that it provides a feeling ten times more pleasurable than orgasm.

b.h. Addiction is not about relatedness, about relationships. So it comes as no surprise that as addiction becomes more pervasive in black life it undermines our capacity to experience community. Just recently, I was telling someone that I would like to buy a little house next door to my parent's house. This house used to be Mr. Johnson's house but he recently passed away. And they could not understand why I would want to live near my parents. My explanation that my parents were aging did not satisfy. Their inability to understand or appreciate the value of sharing family life inter-generationally was a sign to me of the crisis facing our communities. It's as though as black people we have lost our understanding of the importance of mutual inter-dependency, of communal living. That we no longer recognize as valuable the notion that we collectively shape the terms of our survival is a sign of crisis.

C.W. And when there is crisis in those communities and institutions that have played a fundamental role in transmitting to younger generations our values and sensibility, our ways of life and our ways of struggle, we find ourselves distanced, not simply from our predecessors but from the critical project of black liberation. And so more and more we seem to have young black people who are very difficult to understand, because it seems as though they live in two very different worlds. We don't really understand their music. Black adults may not be listening to NWA (Niggers With Attitude) straight out of Compton, California. They may not understand why they are doing what Stetsasonic is doing, what Public Enemy is all about, because young people have been fundamentally shaped by the brutal side of American society. Their sense of reality is shaped on the one hand by a sense of coldness and callousness, and on the other hand by a sense of passion for justice, contradictory impulses which surface simultaneously. Mothers may find it difficult to understand their children. Grandparents may find it difficult to understand us—and it's this slow breakage that has to be restored.

b.h. That sense of breakage, or rupture, is often tragically expressed in gender relations. When I told folks that Cornel West and I were talking about partnership between black women and men, they thought I meant romantic relationships. I replied that it was important for us to examine the multi-relationships between black women and men, how we deal with fathers, with brothers, with sons. We are talking about all our relationships across gender because it is not just the heterosexual love relationships between black women and men that are in trouble. Many of us can't communicate with parents, siblings, etc. I've talked with many of you and asked, "What is it you feel should be addressed?" And many of you responded that you wanted us to talk about black men and how they need to "get it together."

Let's talk about why we see the struggle to assert agency—that is, the ability to act in one's best interest—as a male thing. I mean, black

men are not the only ones among us who need to "get it together."
And if black men collectively refuse to educate themselves for critical
consciousness, to acquire the means to be self-determined, should our
communities suffer, or should we not recognize that both black
women and men must struggle for self-actualization, must learn to "get
it together"? Since the culture we live in continues to equate blackness
with maleness, black awareness of the extent to which our survival depends on mutual partnership between women and men is undermined. In renewed black liberation struggle, we recognize the position
of black men and women, the tremendous role black women played
in every freedom struggle.

Certainly Septima Clark's book *Ready from Within* is necessary
reading for those of us who want to understand the historical development of sexual politics in black liberation struggle. Clark describes her
father's insistence that she not fully engage herself in civil rights struggle because of her gender. Later, she found the source of her defiance
in religion. It was the belief in spiritual community, that no difference
must be made between the role of women and that of men, that enabled her to be "ready within." To Septima Clark, the call to participate
in black liberation struggle was a call from God. Remembering and re-
covering the stories of how black women learned to assert historical
agency in the struggle for self-determination in the context of community and collectivity is important for those of us who struggle to promote black liberation, a movement that has at its core a commitment
to free our communities of sexist domination, exploitation, and oppression. We need to develop a political terminology that will enable
black folks to talk deeply about what we mean when we urge black
women and men to "get it together."

C.W. I think again that we have to keep in mind the larger context of
American society, which has historically expressed contempt for black
men and black women. The very notion that black people are human
beings is a new notion in western civilization and is still not widely accepted in practice. And one of the consequences of this pernicious
idea is that it is very difficult for black men and women to remain attuned to each other's humanity, so when bell talks about black
women's agency and some of the problems black men have when
asked to acknowledge black women's humanity, it must be remembered that this refusal to acknowledge one another's humanity is a reflection of the way we are seen and treated in the larger society. And
it's certainly not true that white folks have a monopoly on human relationships. When we talk about a crisis in western civilization, black
people are a part of that civilization even though we have been be-

neath it, our backs serving as a foundation for the building of that civilization, and we have to understand how it affects us so that we may remain attuned to each other's humanity, so that the partnership that bell talks about can take on real substance and content. I think partnerships between black men and black women can be made when we learn how to be supportive and think in terms of critical affirmation.

b.h. Certainly black people have not talked enough about the importance of constructing patterns of interaction that strengthen our capacity to be affirming.

C.W. We need to affirm one another, support one another, help, enable, equip, and empower one another to deal with the present crisis, but it can't be uncritical, because if it's uncritical then we are again refusing to acknowledge other people's humanity. If we are serious about acknowledging and affirming other people's humanity then we are committed to trusting and believing that they are forever in process. Growth, development, maturation happens in stages. People grow, develop, and mature along the lines in which they are taught. Disenabling critique and contemptuous feedback hinders.

b.h. We need to examine the function of critique in traditional black communities. Often it does not serve as a constructive force. Like we have that popular slang word "dissin' " and we know that "dissin' " refers to a kind of disenabling contempt—when we "read" each other in ways that are so painful, so cruel, that the person can't get up from where you have knocked them down. Other destructive forces in our lives are envy and jealously. These undermine our efforts to work for a collective good. Let me give a minor example. When I came in this morning I saw Cornel's latest book on the table. I immediately wondered why my book was not there and caught myself worrying about whether he was receiving some gesture of respect or recognition denied me. When he heard me say "where's my book," he pointed to another table.

Often when people are suffering a legacy of deprivation, there is a sense that there are never any goodies to go around, so that we must viciously compete with one another. Again this spirit of competition creates conflict and divisiveness. In a larger social context, competition between black women and men has surfaced around the issue of whether black female writers are receiving more attention than black male writers. Rarely does anyone point to the reality that only a small minority of black women writers are receiving public accolades. Yet the myth that black women who succeed are taking something away from black men continues to permeate black psyches and inform how we as black women and men respond to one another. Since capitalism is rooted in unequal distribution of resources, it is not surprising that we as black women and men find ourselves in situations of competition and conflict.

C.W. I think part of the problem is deep down in our psyche we recognize that we live in such a conservative society, a society of business elites, a society in which corporate power influences are assuring that a certain group of people do get up higher.

b.h. Right, including some of you in this room.

C.W. And this is true not only between male and female relations but also black and brown relations and black and Korean, and black and Asian relations. We are struggling over crumbs because we know that the bigger part of lower corporate America is already received. One half of one percent of America owns twenty-two percent of the wealth, one percent owns thirty-two percent, and the bottom forty-five percent of the population has twenty percent of the wealth. So, you end up with this kind of crabs-in-the-barrel mentality. When you see someone moving up you immediately think they'll get a bigger cut in big-loaf corporate America and you think that's something real because we're still shaped by the corporate ideology of the larger context.

b.h. Here at Yale many of us are getting a slice of that mini-loaf and yet are despairing. It was discouraging when I came here to teach and found in many black people a quality of despair which is not unlike that we know is felt in "crack neighborhoods." I wanted to understand the connection between underclass black despair and that of black people here who have immediate and/or potential access to so much material privilege. This despair mirrors the spiritual crisis that is happening in our culture as a whole. Nihilism is everywhere. Some of this despair is rooted in a deep sense of loss. Many black folks who have made it or are making it undergo an identity crisis. This is especially true for individual black people working to assimilate into the "mainstream." Suddenly, they may feel panicked, alarmed by the knowledge that they do not understand their history, that life is without purpose and meaning. These feelings of alienation and estrangement create suffering. The suffering many black people experience today is linked to the suffering of the past, to "historical memory." Attempts by black people to understand that suffering, to come to terms with it, are the conditions which enable a work like Toni Morrison's *Beloved* to receive so much attention. To look back, not just to describe slavery but to try and reconstruct a psycho-social history of its impact has only recently been fully understood as a necessary stage in the process of collective black self recovery.

C.W. The spiritual crisis that has happened, especially among the well-to-do blacks, has taken the form of the quest for therapeutic release. So that you can get very thin, flat, and uni-dimensional forms of spirituality that are simply an attempt to sustain the well-to-do black folks as they engage in their consumerism and privatism. The kind of spirituality we're talking about is not the kind that remains superficial just physically but serves as an opium to help you justify and rationalize your own cynicism vis-à-vis the disadvantaged folk in our community. We could talk about churches and their present role in the crisis of America, religious faith as the American way of life, the gospel of health and wealth, helping the bruised psyches of the black middle class make it through America. That's not the form of spirituality that we're talking about. We're talking about something deeper—you used to call it conversion—so that notions of service and risk and sacrifice once again become fundamental. It's very important, for example, that those of you who remember the days in which black colleges were hegemonic among the black elite remember them critically but also acknowledge that there was something positive going on there. What was going on was that you were told every Sunday, with the important business of chapel, that you had to give service to the race. Now it may have been a petty bourgeois form, but it created a moment of accountability, and with the erosion of the service ethic the very possibility of putting the needs of others alongside of one's own diminishes. In this syndrome, me-ness, selfishness, and egocentricity become more and more prominent, creating a spiritual crisis where you need more psychic opium to get you over.

b.h. We have experienced such a change in that communal ethic of service that was so necessary for survival in traditional black communities. That ethic of service has been altered by shifting class relations. And even those black folks who have little or no class mobility may buy into a bourgeois class sensibility; TV shows like *Dallas* and *Dynasty* teach ruling class ways of thinking and being to underclass poor people. A certain kind of bourgeois individualism of the mind prevails. It does not correspond to actual class reality or circumstances of deprivation. We need to remember the many economic structures and class politics that have led to a shift of priorities for "privileged" blacks. Many privileged black folks obsessed with living out a bourgeois dream of liberal individualistic success no longer feel as though they have any accountability in relation to the black poor and underclass.

C.W. We're not talking about the narrow sense of guilt privileged black people can feel, because guilt usually paralyzes action. What we're talking about is how one uses one's time and energy. We're talking about the ways in which the black middle class, which is relatively privileged vis-à-vis the black working class, working poor, and underclass, needs to acknowledge that along with that privilege goes responsibility. Somewhere I read that for those to whom much is given, much is required. And the question becomes, "How do we exercise that responsibility given our privilege?" I don't think it's a credible notion to believe the black middle class will give up on its material toys. No, the black middle class will act like any other middle class in the human condition; it will attempt to maintain its privilege. There is something seductive about comfort and convenience. The black middle class will not return to the ghetto, especially given the territorial struggles going on with gangs and so forth. Yet, how can we use what power we do have to be sure more resources are available to those who are disadvantaged? So the question becomes "How do we use our responsibility and privilege?" Because, after all, black privilege is a result of black struggle.

I think the point to make here is that there is a new day in black America. It is the best of times and the worst of times in black America. Political consciousness is escalating in black America, among black students, among black workers, organized black workers and trade unions, increasingly we are seeing black leaders with vision. The black church is on the move, black popular music, political themes and motifs are on the move. So don't think in our critique we somehow ask you to succumb to a paralyzing pessimism. There are grounds for hope and when that corner is turned, and we don't know what particular catalytic event will serve as the take-off for it (just like we didn't know December 1955 would be the take-off), but when it occurs we have got be ready. The privileged black folks can play a rather crucial role if we have a service ethic, if we want to get on board, if we want to be part of the progressive, prophetic bandwagon. And that is the question we will have to ask ourselves and each other.

b.h. We also need to remember that there is a joy in struggle. Recently, I was speaking on a panel at a conference with another black woman from a privileged background. She mocked the notion of struggle. When she expressed, "I'm just tired of hearing about the importance of struggle; it doesn't interest me," the audience clapped. She saw struggle solely in negative terms, a perspective which led me to question whether she had ever taken part in any organized resistance movement. For if you have, you know that there is joy in struggle.

Those of us who are old enough to remember segregated schools, the kind of political effort and sacrifice folks were making to ensure we would have full access to educational opportunities, surely remember the sense of fulfillment when goals that we struggled for were achieved. When we sang together "We shall overcome" there was a sense of victory, a sense of power that comes when we strive to be self-determining. When Malcolm X spoke about his journey to Mecca, the awareness he achieved, he gives expression to that joy that comes from struggling to grow. When Martin Luther King talked about having been to the mountain top, he was sharing with us that he arrived at a peak of critical awareness, and it gave him great joy. In our liberatory pedagogy we must teach young black folks to understand that struggle is process, that one moves from circumstances of difficulty and pain to awareness, joy, fulfillment. That the struggle to be critically conscious can be that movement which takes you to another level, that lifts you up, that makes you feel better. You feel good, you feel your life has meaning and purpose.

C.W. A rich life is fundamentally a life of serving others, a life of trying to leave the world a little better than you found it. That rich life comes into being in human relationships. This is true at the personal level. Those of you who have been in love know what I am talking about. It is also true at the organizational and communal level. It's difficult to find joy by yourself even if you have all the right toys. It's difficult. Just ask somebody who has got a lot of material possessions but doesn't have anybody to share them with. Now that's at the personal level. There is a political version of this. It has to do with what you see when you get up in the morning and look in the mirror and ask yourself whether you are simply wasting time on the planet or spending time in an enriching manner. We are talking fundamentally about the meaning of life and the place of struggle. bell talks about the significance of struggle and service. For those of us who are Christians there are certain theological foundations on which our commitment to serve is based. Christian life is understood to be a life of service. Even so, Christians have no monopoly on the joys that come from service and those of you who are part of secular culture can also enjoy this sense of enrichment. Islamic brothers and sisters share in a religious practice which also places emphasis on the importance of service. When we speak of commitment to a life of service we must also talk about the fact that such a commitment goes against the grain, especially the foundations of our society. To talk this way about service and struggle we must also talk about strategies that will enable us to sustain this sensibility, this commitment.

b.h. When we talk about that which will sustain and nurture our spiritual growth as a people, we must once again talk about the importance of community. For one of the most vital ways we sustain ourselves is by building communities of resistance, places where we know we are not alone. In *Prophetic Fragments,* Cornel began his essay on Martin Luther King by quoting the lines of the spiritual, "He promised never to leave me, never to leave me alone." In black spiritual tradition the promise that we will not be alone cannot be heard as an affirmation of passivity. It does not mean we can sit around and wait for God to take care of business. We are not alone when we build community together. Certainly there is a great feeling of community in this room today. And yet when I was here at Yale I felt that my labor was not appreciated. It was not clear that my work was having meaningful impact. Yet I feel that impact today. When I walked into the room a black woman sister let me know how much my teaching and writing had helped her. There's more of the critical affirmation Cornel spoke of. That critical affirmation says, "Sister, what you're doing is uplifting me in some way." Often folk think that those folks who are spreading the message are so "together" that we do not need affirmation, critical dialogue about the impact of all that we teach and write about and how we live in the world.

C.W. It is important to note the degree to which black people in particular, and progressive people in general, are alienated and estranged from communities that would sustain and support us. We are often homeless. Our struggles against a sense of nothingness and attempts to reduce us to nothing are ongoing. We confront regularly the question: "Where can I find a sense of home?" That sense of home can only be found in our construction of those communities of resistance bell talks about and the solidarity we can experience within them. Renewal comes through participating in community. That is the reason so many folks continue to go to church. In religious experience they find a sense of renewal, a sense of home. In community one can feel that we are moving forward, that struggle can be sustained. As we go forward as black progressives, we must remember that community is not about homogeneity. Homogeneity is dogmatic imposition, pushing your way of life, your way of doing things onto somebody else. That is not what we mean by community. Dogmatic insistence that everybody think and act alike causes rifts among us, destroying the possibility of community. That sense of home that we are talking about and searching for is a place where we can find compassion, recognition of difference, of the importance of diversity, of our individual uniqueness.

b.h. When we evoke a sense of home as a place where we can renew ourselves, where we can know love and the sweet communion of shared spirit, I think it's important for us to remember that this location of well-being cannot exist in a context of sexist domination, in a setting where children are the objects of parental domination and abuse. On a fundamental level, when we talk about home, we must speak about the need to transform the African-American home, so that there, in that domestic space, we can experience the renewal of political commitment to the black liberation struggle. So that there in that domestic space we learn to serve and honor one another. If we look again at the civil rights, at the black power movement, folks organized so much in homes. They were the places where folks got together to educate themselves for critical consciousness. That sense of community, cultivated and developed in the home, extended outward into a larger more public context. As we talk about black power in the twenty-first century, about political partnership between black women and men, we must talk about transforming our notions of how and why we bond. In *Beloved,* Toni Morrison offers a paradigm for relationships between black men and women. Sixo describes his love for Thirty-Mile Woman, declaring, "She is a friend of mind. She gather me, man. The pieces I am, she gather them and give them back to me in all the right order. It's good, you know, when you got a woman who is a friend of your mind." In this passage Morrison evokes a notion of bonding that may be rooted in passion, desire, even romantic love, but the point of connection between black women and men is that space of recognition and understanding, where we know one another so well, our histories, that we can take the bits and pieces, the fragments of who we are, and put them back together, re-member them. It is this joy of intellectual bonding, of working together to create liberatory theory and analysis that black women and men can give one another, that Cornel and I give to each other. We are friends of one another's mind. We find a home with one another. It is that joy in community we celebrate and share with you this morning.

22

AN INTERVIEW WITH BELL HOOKS BY GLORIA WATKINS

no, not talking back, just talking to myself, January 1989

GW: Why remember the pain, that's how you began?

bh: Because I am sometimes awed, as in finding something terrifying, when I see how many of the people who are writing about domination and oppression are distanced from the pain, the woundedness, the ugliness. That it's so much of the time just a subject—a "discourse." The person does not believe in a real way that "what I say here, this theory I come up with, may help change the pain in my life or in the lives of other people." I say remember the pain because I believe true resistance begins with people confronting pain, whether it's theirs or somebody else's, and wanting to do something to change it. And it's this pain that so much makes its mark in daily life. Pain as a catalyst for change, for working to change. Sometimes working in the academic place I have found it's my peers not understanding this pain that has made for such a deep sense of isolation. I think that's why everywhere I am, my true comrades are often non-academic workers—who know that pain, who are willing to talk about that pain. That is what connects us—our awareness that we know it, have known it, or will know it again. This is part of black experience that Toni Morrison draws on in *Beloved*.

GW: I thought you were sometimes opposed to using fiction or referring to fiction as a way to talk about concrete black experience?

bh: No, it's not that. I am of course disturbed and rightly so when folks want to read fiction in place of sociology, in place of history. What fiction can do, and do well, is evoke, hint at, so to speak, that which may have been experienced in concrete reality. *Beloved* was so powerful to me, not so much because of the story, which in very Morrison-like fashion one knows very early on, rather it is the anguish of slavery, that lingering emotional suffering that she evokes in the writing. And frankly I do not think there are enough non-fiction books written that try to talk about this anguish—this black people grief that is so profound—it has made us wordless. In very negative reviews of *Beloved* (one written by Ann Snitow, white woman critic and one by Stanley Crouch, black male critic), both reviewers liken it to holocaust literature, specifically to literature of Jewish experience that emerged from the Nazi tragedy. While they see this similarity as negative, I see it as a crucial attempt to impress upon the reader's consciousness that the experience of slavery here was, for African-Americans and their descendants, a holocaust experience—a tragedy of such ongoing magnitude that folk suffer, anguish it today.

GW: Are you saying then that there should be more literature that addresses this trauma and its present day effect on our psyches?

bh: Absolutely, especially literature that addresses the psychological impact. I was in Canada—in Montreal—speaking to a group of filmmakers about many things, but among them making films about groups to which you don't belong, and I met a filmmaker who has done a documentary film, "Dark Lullabies," about Jewish children whose parents survived concentration camps. I saw the film with another black woman, just the two of us in a room. After we finished viewing it, we both talked about how the film made us think about black experience—slavery, reconstruction, apartheid (otherwise known as Jim Crow) and how it hurts us as aware black people to know that there has not been such documentation of the pain and suffering of black people and its debilitating effect on our emotional lives. Irene, the filmmaker, is herself the child of survivors (in fact, much of the film focuses on her journeying to unlock the past). She and I talked about relationships between black folk and Jewish white folk, about the envy that black people have about the way the Jewish experience of holocaust is increasingly documented—the way folks, especially in films, are made mindful and aware not only of this experience, but the terrible damage to the psyches of survivors. Often many aspects of black experience are not documented—not slavery—not Jim Crow (that period when black folks could not try on clothing they wanted to buy, little things—that have tremendous impact on one's emotional life, one's sense of self. Anyhow, I think black women writers and their fictions have tried to document this, to make folk mindful.

GW: Not surprising—and this shifts the subject some—a lot. You use an example that has to do with clothing, with fashion. Why? Why are you so into fashion!

bh: That's really a long discussion—one for another time. But I'll take it up some. I don't see that as so off the subject at all, because the ways we image ourselves, our representation of the self as black folks, have been so important because of oppression, domination. Clothing for us has had so much to do with the nature of underclass exploited reality. For we have pleasure (and the way this pleasure is constituted has been a mediating force between the painful reality, our internalized self-hate, and even our resistance) in clothing. Clothes have functioned politically in black experience. See, that's another aspect of our experience that must be studied, talked about. I am particularly interested in the relationship between style as expressed in clothing and subversion, the way the dominated, exploited peoples use style to express resistance and/or conformity. For the book I am working on now, *Sisters of the Yam: Black Women and Self-Recovery,* I've done a piece on hair (and since I've been talking about films, let me mention here Ayoka Chenzira's short film "Hairpiece," which documents in a funny, deep way our historical thing about hair). Anyhow, for the book I've written a chapter on hair, which talks about how I went around to different places asking black women about our hair, what we do with it, how we feel—the way it expresses us politically in a white supremacist society...

GW: You say this new book is on self-recovery—what do you mean?

bh: This is also related to what I was talking about earlier, about holocaust experience, about ongoing genocide, because a lot of my critical thinking right now is focused on black experience of oppression and how it damages and wounds us. And I am particularly concerned with what we do to heal ourselves, to recover a sense of wholeness. Here in the U.S. self-recovery is a term that is used most often in therapy related to substance abuse, addiction. That's not where I encountered the term; it came into my thinking when I was reading the work of Buddhist monk Thich Nhat Hahn who talks about it in relation to ways people who are oppressed, dominated, or otherwise politically victimized recover themselves, the way colonized people work to resist and throw off the colonizer mentality, for example. Lately I say often that mental health is the important field right now, a central revolutionary frontier for black folks, 'cause you can't effectively resist domination when you are all messed up. The title of this new work, *Sisters of the Yam,* comes from Toni Cade Bambara's novel *The Salt Eaters,* which is a fiction work that deals with self-recovery, with being well. I mean it begins with that marvelous sentence "Are you sure, sweatheart, that you want to be well?"

GW: Much of what you are talking about focuses on black people. Are you calling attention to racism now more so than sexism?

bh: No. You know I feel deeply that black people must focus on the importance of domination and oppression in all its forms in our lives if we are to recover ourselves, if we are to be critically thinking, critically resisting, in a revolutionary way, oppression. And resisting oppression means more than just reacting against one's oppressors, it means envisioning new habits of being, different ways to live in the world. It often makes me tired to think that black women must still defend our concern with eradicating sexism and sexist oppression, with feminist politics, that we must continually deal with folk asking us which is more important, or telling us race is more important. That's why I think it's so crucial to focus on ending oppression and domination, because such a focus is inclusive; it enables us to look at ourselves as a whole people who are affected by sexism and racism and class exploitation. It's thinking about a complex structure of domination that really helps us to get a concrete grip on political issues that we have to confront daily.

GW: Let's return to the issue of self-recovery, to the Buddhist monk—say more, I know you are interested in spirituality. How do you reconcile that concern with radical politics?

bh: For me spiritual life is not an interest, it's a way of life, of being in the world, the foundation of everything.

GW: Could you be more specific about what spiritual life means to you?

bh: Well that's difficult isn't it—difficult to contain in words. I can't say much. There's so much mystery, so much that's not definite, clear. Simply, it has to do with the fundamental belief in divine spirit—in God and in love as a force that enables one to call forth one's godliness and spiritual power. I have been most interested in the mystical dimension of religious experience. And that concern has not been experienced as being in conflict with political concerns, but more as in harmony with them. They are integrated for me, part of a whole. Lately I've been reading Thomas Merton, especially his writings on monastic life, and I can see deep connections between spirituality, the religious experience, and longing to make a space for critical thinking, for contemplation. Part of the appeal of Thich Nhat Hahn for me is his engagement with political concerns. I first read him in *The Raft is not the Shore*—a series of conversations between him and Daniel Berrigan where they talk about religious life, about the Vietnam war (Nhat Hahn is Vietnamese), and the need for resistance and protest. They speak of this in a context where they also acknowledge the primacy of spiritual life—the connection between the two. Spiritual life has much to do with self-realization, the coming into greater awareness not only of who we are but our relationship within community which is so profoundly political.

GW: And is this connected to self-recovery?

bh: Very much so. There is such perfect union between the spiritual quest for awareness, enlightenment, self-realization, and the struggle of oppressed people, colonized people to change our circumstance, to resist—to move from object to subject; much of what has to be restored in us before we can make meaningful organized protest is an integrity of being. In a society such as ours it is in spiritual experience that one finds a ready place to establish such integrity.

GW: Can you focus for a minute on organized protest, on civil rights movement. Do you think we are apathetic?

bh: To me, one of the most powerful, moving resistance struggles in the world is the civil rights movement. I have so much respect for the black people, for all of the people who gave themselves, who gave their lives in the movement. I was giving a talk and during the dialogue, a young black woman student said that when she thought about the civil rights movement she thought of it mainly in terms of black men getting the right to have white female partners. She wanted to know if it had really accomplished anything. Her statement shocked me—appalled me—but it was so true to these ahistorical times. So I reminded her and all of us that the sexism of black men notwithstanding, the civil rights movement made it possible for me to be talking. None of us, that is to say black people, would be here in this room and at this university if it were not for the civil rights movement. I encouraged her to study this movement, to read the words, the reflections of Septima Clark. I think this movement still stands as an important model for protest struggle in the U.S. even though many of us may think there is such apathy, indifference; I find there is really such ignorance, such pervasive feelings of powerlessness which take away our power to protest, to organize.

GW: Where does this feeling of powerlessness come from?

bh: It comes from the real concrete circumstances of exploitation. But much more dangerously, it is also learned through media, through television, because it is through watching TV that many black people learn to adopt the values and the ideology of the ruling class even as they live in circumstances of oppression and deprivation. Shows like "Dynasty" and "Dallas" that focus on rich white men, where much of the colonization of our minds as black people takes place. And most of us, these days, are not watching with a critical eye.

GW: That seems to me to return, once again, to the issue of self-recovery, which I know is fundamentally linked, in your mind, with education for critical consciousness.

bh: See, education and self-recovery go back to organization—to protest. People must know what's happening to them. Many of us can't read. We are not going to learn it in books—where, when, and how—and who—who is going to teach. And that's where we can begin to conceptualize the racial politicization of mental health.

GW: In *Feminist Theory: from margin to center,* you suggested that feminists should go door-to-door telling people about feminist politics. That same approach could apply here. Topics have been shifting, and you have digressed all over the place. Could you speak more about your engagement with feminism? Many black women still do not commit themselves publicly to feminism, although there has been tremendous change.

bh: Deep down I am so passionately committed to feminist politics as a black woman because I feel that so much of our capacity to struggle against oppression, domination, and especially racism is diminished by internal oppression and domination caused by collective support among black people of sexism—and sexist oppression. And I see the struggle to end sexism and sexist oppression as so necessary to our survival as black people, it always seems so tragically ironic to me that anyone could suggest that feminist struggle to end sexism undermines black liberation (of course I fundamentally believe that feminist struggle must be disassociated from white women's rights efforts, which support white supremacy). Recently, talking with seventy young black women about feminism, I continually emphasized that when I think of feminism it is not first symbolized by white women. I think of sexism, and then in an expanded way I think of the struggle to end sexism and sexist oppression. There is a definite separation which has to be made between feminist struggle which can take place in solidarity with white women or apart from them, and seeing ourselves as black women supporting a racist women's rights movement.

GW: This brings up the issue of separate movements.

bh: I believe in the strength of a diverse feminist struggle and movement, one that is oriented toward becoming a mass-based political movement. I do not think that the central focus of contemporary feminist movement has been in this direction, that the movement has had an ongoing radical focus which addresses many people; this is why the reformist concerns of nonradical, privileged white women has been so much in the limelight. As political beings engaged in dialectical struggle, it is our task (and here when I say "our" I mean any of us who are committed to revolutionary feminist movement) to work at challenging and changing the focus, the direction of future feminist movement. That it is our task, to encourage like-minded people to contribute to such effort. When and if these efforts are not successful we must certainly act in separation and isolation. Right now when it comes to black women I am more concerned that we begin to think critically about sexist exploitation and oppression in our lives and envision strategies for resistance, some of which will no doubt be linked to those of white women, and all women, and some which will be expressive of our particular concerns as black women. I think right now what's most important is for us to collectively begin to examine our experience and to look at what must be done to educate black people about feminist struggle.

GW: Finally then, talk about how you see yourself—as a feminist, as a writer. Why did you want to do this, to have a chat with yourself—that kind of splits you in two—bell hooks and Gloria Watkins.

bh: Funny to say "split in two"—when for me these are two parts of a whole self that is composed of many parts. And as you know in much of my life I am such a serious person. To be contemplative in these times is to be seriously serious and I have to take a break now and then to balance things. So I indulge the playful me. That me that in a very childlike way loves play, drama, spectacle. Of course there is a way that play is very serious for me. It is a form of ritual. Which returns me then to how I see me—obsessed with aesthetics. I see me as a writer and thinker—then all else follows. I want to write more—many different things in many different ways.

GW: Has thinking about feminist politics interfered with this?

bh: Yes! Yes! I remember in *Lavender Culture* by Karla Jay and Allen Young there is this piece by a white woman who describes life before she comes out as a lesbian—then after. Suddenly everything she does is focused on that center and other parts of herself, of life, fall away. Till finally she becomes concerned. And I think many women deeply immersed in feminist politics feel the same way. Let me give a small but important example. Before so much feminist thinking I would enter bookstores and look mainly at poetry, art, spiritual writings, etc. Then suddenly deep in feminism I was always there solely in the women's section and not even able to keep up with all the books that were being published. So for a time all of these concerns that express other parts of me have been somewhat neglected—like my poetry and other creative writing, most of which is not published. And I don't work as hard as a I should to publish it because I am so focused on the feminist books which get attention, which have an audience. Right now I'm trying to publish two manuscripts: a crazy, witty detective novel (not your typical detective novel) with, of course, a black woman detective and a memoir of my girlhood. I very much want to establish myself as a creative writer, which is difficult, especially since I've been into this academic thing first finishing a dissertation on Toni Morrison, and now writing more literary criticism. I recently finished a new piece on the *The Bluest Eye,* which is absolutely one of my favorite books.

GW: Seems like you love Toni Morrison's work.

bh: Well I've spent a lot of time with it. I have to live with books to know them. And I live with her books. She is a writer whose artistic vision fascinates me—and I do not find every book she writes equally compelling—but her vision is special as is the vision of Toni Bambara, Bessie Head, and so many more.

GW: Do you mainly read black women writers?

bh: Girl , I wish. I wish there were so many black women writing so many books that every day of my life I could be reading at least one new piece by us—but no. I read everything—all kinds of stuff—and I would not want to change that. Certainly teaching courses on black women writers keeps me more in tune with what we're doing. I like very much experimental—playful texts—the works of Marguerite Duras for example or Natalie Saraute. I think one of the difficulties I have had in terms of finding publishers for my work is that it is different—strange. Of course not to me but strange to the marketplace.

Work by black women just isn't one of those hot commodities in the literary market. We are in danger of that market creating a very fixed, static, objectified notion of who and what a black woman writer is and what she should write about. And that's a hard one. How to create fiction that will be read—but that is one's own. And not just a response to white people, to a white market, to any market.

GW: So do you intend to write more feminist theory books?

bh: I'd like to do something on feminism and black liberation struggle—or on sexuality. But right now it's the *Yam* book that has my attention.

GW: You say the *Talking Back* book was hard to put together.

bh: Hard because it was different for me. Not a whole piece, but a collection. And there is repetition which makes it less exciting. Still, overall it has its place. Writing many different things I've come to understand that every piece of writing doesn't have to do the same thing or have the same effect.

GW-bh: Anyhow writing wise, I'm moving on.

23

A FINAL YEARNING

January 1990

G.W. How do you relate this new book *Yearning* to the interest in self-recovery that you talked about in the earlier interview?

bh. Well, I had intended to finish the *Sisters of the Yam* project, that was to be the book on self-recovery before *Yearning,* but it did not work out that way. I do bits and pieces on the *Yam* book, so it's coming slowly. Still I think that *Yearning* is connected to it, in that cultural production can and does play a healing role in people's lives. It can be a catalyst for them to begin the project of self-recovery. That's how many readers experienced Alice Walker's novel *The Color Purple,* and Toni Morrison's *The Bluest Eye* and/or *Beloved.* Certainly two books that really set me thinking about the ways in which black people can approach the issue of self-recovery are Paule Marshall's *Praisesong For The Widow* and Gloria Naylor's *Mama Day.* Marshall's work fascinates me because the novel really offers a map, charts a journey where people who have lost their way might come back to themselves. Unlike many novels by black women writers, *Praisesong* depicts a heterosexual relationship between Jay and Avey that is really positive, rooted in their shared pleasure in black history and cultural production (all the references to black music, the quotes from black poetry) and yet they lose their connection as Jay becomes obsessed with capitalism and "making it." There is this one passage where Avey, thinking critically about the past, says, "We behaved as though there was nothing about ourselves worth honoring." These lines stayed with me, haunted me. I thought about my life, my one long relationship which I felt was torn asunder by our inability to cope with being two black artists/intellectuals operating simultaneously in a predominantly white context, and in a conventional relationship. Looking back, I think a lot might have been different if we had approached our life recognizing connections between our efforts to make a loving relationship and the struggle to be decolonized black people, the work of political self-recovery.

GW. How does this relate to *Mama Day?* It has received so little critical attention.

bh. *Mama Day* is such an unusual book. It's really a celebration of the wisdom of traditional black folk, of the healing rituals which were part of that life. And Naylor strongly suggests, and I agree with her, that black folks can learn from the past and don't have to give it up to fit into city life. I love the contrast between country and city experience in this work. But mostly I am moved by the "lead, kindly, light" ritual that again, like the passage in *Praisesong,* is about black people putting into place rituals of remembrance that commemorate the past and renew our spirits so we can face the future.

GW. So far you have mentioned only novels. What other kinds of literature would you like to see addressing these issues?

bh. I would like to see the production of a body of work on psychoanalysis and black experience. In my own life, I have been really helped by reading the work of Alice Miller (even though I think it contains elements of mother blame). Her work, in particular, and other work that attempts to understand how the experience of trauma shapes personality and actions from childhood into adult life seem an important contribution for black people that has not been sufficiently explored. Another that comes to mind is *Soul Murder: Persecution in the Family* by Morton Schatzman, which again tries to provide a psychological framework for us to understand the effects of trauma.

GW: What about all those folks who would say this psychoanalytic stuff is white and can't help us to understand anything about black life?

bh. While novels like *Dessa Rose* or *Beloved* evoke the passion of trauma during slavery as it carries over into black life when that institution is long gone, these works don't necessarily chart a healing journey that is immediately applicable to contemporary black life. Certainly in *Black Rage* and other works that appeared in the sixties and seventies, black thinkers were trying to take seriously the way racism and the terrorism of living in the context of white supremacy affect us as black people, but many of those works did not go far enough. Often their interpretations were insufficient and shallow. One of the black students I teach is really into psychoanalysis and we talk endlessly about the fact that we do not need anyone to simply take the white critical texts of psychoanalysis and superficially transpose them onto black life. What we need is the kind of sophisticated explication of these materials that would enable us to take from them what is useful. We also need more black men and women entering the field of psychoanalysis in order to do more research and generate theory which is inclusive, sensitive, and understanding of black history and culture.

GW: You are talking about the production of theoretical material, kinds of work that are not usually read by a mass audience. What process would allow this knowledge to reach a wider audience?

bh: Let me say first that I really believe politicized mental care is the new revolutionary frontier for black people. And certainly Franz Fanon was sharing that fact with us years ago. It worries me that so few black thinkers have built upon his work, or taken up where his work left off. Certainly most of the traditional works which address the psychological issues black people face are sexist, and that makes them very unproductive texts in many ways. There are so many ways to reach a mass black audience with the message of politicized self-recovery. One way is the production of self-help literature. Another is through spreading the word in churches, community centers, houses, etc. Recently, I was talking with black students at a university in Washington state who were describing how divided they are as a community. I asked them if they considered having a series of discussions that would talk about "racial healing."

GW. Say more about you mean, 'cause I immediately thought about Marvin Gaye's "sexual healing."

bh. Again I think they are very connected. Clearly if you read Gaye's biography, *A Divided Soul,* you learn that he really was raised in the context of a dysfunctional family setting that made it impossible for him to construct an identity, a sense of self, outside of this wounded context. And it is clear that the area of his life in which he felt the most wounded was around sexuality. It seems to me that racial healing is really about us as black people realizing that we have to do more than define how racism ravages our spirit (it has certainly been easier for us to name the problem)—we have to construct useful strategies of resistance and change.

GW.Well, how do we do this?

bh. Lately, whenever I'm speaking to a group of black people, I ask us to share knowledge of how we cope with the impact of racism and sexism in daily life. People who feel that they have been able to critically intervene in their lives and the lives of their loved ones in a meaningful way offer insight and concrete strategies for change.

GW. What about your work? Where is it going now?

bh. I suppose it is telling that more than a year has passed since the "no not talking back, just talking to myself" interview and my two completed manuscripts, the novel *Sister Ray* and the memoir of my girlhood *Black is a Woman's Color,* remain unpublished. Which means they have been rejected here and there—that's part of being a writer in this society. Of course since both works are really different kinds of writing, I think it will be harder to find publishers to accept that work. More than ever before I feel acutely aware of the way in which marketing strategies lead publishers to push black writers (and other folks) to develop certain kinds of sellable writing personas and then only accept work which fits that persona. This tactic effectively stifles creative production, particularly for women of color.

GW. How do you respond? If you want to be heard, to get your work out there.

bh. In the Introduction to *Yearning* I talked about trying to place the piece on Issac Julien's film *Looking for Langston* with *Z Magazine.* Later when I spoke with them, I was given this friendly little lecture about how my best work is really that which is autobiographical, more in plain speech, etc. (They told me they considered rejecting the piece but decided to publish it with minor editorial changes. This compromise was acceptable to me at the time. Then when I thought about it later I was "freaked out" thinking about how easily minor changes could change the meaning and spirit of the piece.) I listened to their rap and did not even try to intervene; it's tiring. Individuals who are not writers are not always sensitive to the desire I feel, and I know that other black writers share these sentiments, to write in multiple voices, and not to privilege one voice over another. To me the essay on Issac's film is different from other work that I like just as much. I don't sit around comparing my work to see which voice is better; to me they are different, and precisely because of that difference may appeal to different audiences. That's the joy of being polyphonic, of multi-vocality.

GW. I want you to talk about the oncoming work but first I'm dying to know if you think that *Yearning,* despite its critique of postmodernism, is a postmodern work?

bh. Tanya, my "play-daughter," who works at South End Press and helped edit this book, wanted an answer to this question. To some extent the book could be seen as postmodern in that the very poly-phonic vocality we are talking about emerges from a postmodern so-cial context. There are so many different locations in this book, such journeying. That movement is expressive of those postmodern condi-tions of homelessness, displacement, rootlessness, etc.

GW. Would you please link this discussion to Cornel West's insistence on "pervasive nihilism" in black life.

bh. Since we know that African-Americans are a displaced, exilic peo-ple, it should be understood that we suffer the pain of estrangement and alienation in all its multiple manifestations. And as the conditions of life worsen materially and spiritually within the context of postmodernism, it does not seem surprising that underclass black peo-ple feel more acutely this contemporary anguish and despair. Again, I do not think it useful to simply name this nihilism and let it go at that, to be passively terrorized by it, we have to find and talk about the ways we critically intervene, to provide hope, to offer strategies of transformation. We certainly cannot move black folks in new direc-tions if we are weighed by intense feelings of despair, if our lives are without purpose and meaning. Though I am not at all into the term "role model," I know that having many young black women looking at me, not just at my work, but at how I'm living my life—my habits of being, and seeing me as an example, as someone charting the journey, has made me work harder to get my life together. Knowing that they are watching me, seeing what's going on with my psyche, my inner well-being, has changed many of my priorities. I am less self-indul-gent.

GW. I hear that. What about your new work?

bh. The two works I'm most eager to do is the *Sisters of the Yam* and a short polemic work on decolonization. Sometimes, it seems that the work of Fanon, C.L.R. James, Memmi, Walter Rodney, answered lots of questions that I hear folks still raising. Often they are not even familiar with the work of these thinkers. Just talking with black folks in every-day life and at lectures really started me thinking that there was a need for a contemporary "take" on the concerns that their work raises, so I want to move forward in the spirit of that work. Of course, it's acutely obvious to me that most of the work that attempts to approach ques-tions of black liberation struggle within a framework that recognizes the importance of African diasporic community, that looks at issues of colonization and imperialism, has been done by black men. Certainly contemporary thinkers and writers like Stuart Hall, Paul Gilroy, Cornel West come to mind. I want to know what black women globally are thinking on these issues. I'm yearning to hear our voices speak to these concerns. In that spirit, I am challenged to speak, to bring my all to that altar of continued black liberation struggle.

SELECTED
BIBLIOGRAPHY

Alcoff, Linda. "Cultural Feminism versus Poststructuralism: The Identity Crisis in Feminist Theory," *Signs,* Vol. 13 No.3. University of Chicago. Spring 1988.

Baldwin, James. *Notes from a Native Son.* Boston: Beacon Press, 1955.

Bambara, Toni Cade. *The Black Woman.* New York: Random House, 1980.

——*The Salt Eaters.* New York: New American Library, 1970.

——*Are Seabirds Still Alive.* New York: Random House, 1977.

Benjamin, Jessica. *The Bonds of Love.* New York: Pantheon, 1988.

Berger, John. *Art and Revolution; Ernst Neizvestny and the Role of the Artist in the USSR.* New York: Pantheon Books, 1969.

——*Ways of Seeing.* Middlesex: Penguin, 1972.

Boas, Franz. *Shaping of American Anthropology.* New York: Basic Books, 1974.

Boone, Sylvia. *Radiance from the Waters.* New Haven: Yale University Press, 1986.

Bourdieu, Pierre. *Reproduction in Education, Society and Culture.* Beverly Hills: Sage Publications, 1977.

Cady, Linell. "A Feminist Christian Vision," *Embodied Love,* ed. Paula Cooley, Sharon Farmer, Mary Ellen Ross. New York: Harper Row 1987.

Carby, Hazel. *Reconstructing Womanhood.* New York: Oxford University Press, 1987.

Clark, Septima. *Ready from Within.* Navarro, CA: Wild Trees Press, 1986.

Cleaver, Eldridge. *Soul on Ice.* New York: McGraw-Hill, 1967.

Clement, Catherine. *Opera, the Undoing of Women.* Minneapolis: University of Minnesota Press, 1988.

Clifford, James. *The Predicament of Culture.* Cambridge, MA: Harvard University Press, 1988.

Crouch, Stanley. *Notes from a Hanging Judge: Essays and Reviews, 1979-1989.* New York: Oxford University Press, 1990.

de Lauretis, Teresa. *Alice Doesn't: Feminism, Semeiotics, Cinema.* Bloomington: Indiana University Press, 1984.

——*Feminist Studies, Critical Studies.* Bloomington: Indiana University Press, 1986.

Derrida, Jacques. *Writing and Difference.* Chicago: University of Chicago Press, 1978.

Desnoes, Edmundo. *Inconsolable Memories.* New York: New American Library, 1967.

Douglass, Frederick. *Narrative of the Life of Frederick Douglass.* Cambridge, MA: Belknap Press, 1960.

Duberman, Martin Bauml; Vicinus, Martha; Chauncey, George Jr., eds. *Hidden from History: Reclaiming the Gay and Lesbian Past.* New York: New American Library, 1989.

Dumas, Henry. *Goodbye Sweetwater.* New York: Thunder's Mouth Press, 1987.

Duras, Marguerite. *Whole Days in the Trees.* New York: Riverrun Press, 1984.

——*Hiroshima, mon amour: scenario et dialogue.* Paris: Gallimard, 1982, c. 1960.

——*The Malady of Death.* New York: Grove Press, 1986.

——*Outside: Selected Writings.* Boston: Beacon Press, 1986.

Dyson, Michael. "The Plight of Black Men," *Z Magazine,* February, 1989.

Ellis, Trey. *Platitudes.* New York: Vintage, 1988.

Estrich, Susan. *Real Rape.* Cambridge, MA: Harvard University Press, 1987.

Fanon, Franz. *Black Skin, White Masks.* New York: Grove Press, 1967.

——*The Wretched of the Earth.* New York: Grove Press, 1966.

Foucault, Michel. *History of Sexuality.* New York: Pantheon, 1978.

Freire, Paulo. *Pedagogy of the Oppressed.* New York: Seabury, 1970.

Friday, Nancy. *My Secret Garden.* New York: Trident, 1973.

Fugard, Athol. "Boesman and Lena, a play in two acts." New York: Oxford University Press, 1978.

Fusco, Coco. "Fantasies of Oppositionality," *Afterimage magazine.* December, 1988.

Genovese, Elizabeth Fox. *Within the Plantation Household: Black and White Women of the Old South.* Chapel Hill: University of North Carolina Press, 1988.

George, Nelson. *The Death of Rhythm and Blues.* New York: Pantheon, 1988.

Giddings, Paula. *When and Where We Enter: The Impact of Black Women on Race and Sex in America.* New York: Morrow, 1984.

Gordon, Deborah. "Writing Culture, Writing Feminism: The Poetics and Politics of Experimental Ethnography," *Inscriptions,* No. 3/4. Santa Cruz: University of Santa Cruz, 1988.

Grossberg, Lawrence. "Putting the Pop Back in Postmodernism," *Universal Abandon,* ed. Andrew Ross. University of Minnesota Press, 1988.

Hahn, Thich Nhat. *The Raft Is Not the Shore.* Boston: Beacon Press, 1975.

Hall, Stuart. *The Popular Arts.* Boston: Beacon Press, 1964.

Hallin, Daniel. "We Keep America on Top of the World," *Watching Television.* ed. Todd Gitlin. New York: Pantheon, 1986.

Hansberry, Lorraine. *A Raisin in the Sun.* New York: Random House, 1959.

——*To Be Young, Gifted, and Black.* Bergenfield, NJ: New American Library, 1970.

Head, Bessie. *Maru.* New York: McCall Publisher, 1971.

Hemenway, Robert. *Zora Neal Hurston: A Literary Biography.* Urbana: University of Illinois Press, 1979.

Hughes, Langston. *Good Morning Revolution.* New York: Lawrence Hill, 1973.

Hurston, Zora Neale. *Dustracks on the Road.* Philadelphia: Lippincott, 1971.

——*Their Eyes Were Watching God.* New York: Negro University Press, 1969.

——*Of Mules and Men.* New York: Negro University Press, 1969 (reprint of 1935 edition).

James, C.L.R. *The Black Jacobins.* New York: Vintage, 1963.

Jameson, Frederic. *Prison House of Language: The Political Unconscious.* Ithaca, NY: Cornell University Press, 1981.

Jones, Lois Mailou. "In a special section: interview and portfolio." *Callaloo,* Vol. 12, No. 2. University of Virginia, 1989.

Kureishi, Hanif. *The Rainbow Sign and My Beautiful Laundrette.* Boston: Faber and Faber, 1986.

Lee, Spike. *Do the Right Thing.* New York: Fireside, 1989.

Lorde, Audre. *Sister Outsider.* Trumansburg, NY: Crossing Press, 1984.

——*A Burst of Light.* Ithaca, NY: Firebrand Books, 1988.

Mackey, Nathaniel. *Bedouin Horn Book.* Callaloo fiction series. University of Kentucky, 1986.

Majors, Richard. "Cool Pose: the Proud Signature of Survival," *Changing Men,* No. 17, Winter, 1986.

Marshall, Paule. *Praisesong for the Widow.* New York: Putnam, 1983.

Memmi, Albert. *Colonizer and the Colonized.* New York: Orion Press, 1968.

Merton, Thomas. *New Seeds of Contemplation.* Norfolk, CT: New Directions, 1962.

Miller, Alice. *Drama of the Gifted Child.* New York: Basic Books, 1981.

——*For Your Own Good.* New York: Basic Books, 1983.

——*Thou Shall Not Be Aware.* New York: Farrar, Straus, Giroux, 1984.

Miller, Mark. "Deride and Conquer," *Watching Television,* ed. Todd Gitlin. New York: Pantheon Press, 1986.

Miller, Mark Crispin. *Boxed In.* Evanston, IL: Northwestern University Press, 1988.

Mishima, Yukio. *Hagakure.* New York: Penguin, 1979.

Morgan, Robin. *The Demon Lover: On the Sexuality of Terrorism.* New York: Norton, 1988.

Morrison, Toni. *Sula.* New York: Knopf, 1974.

——*Beloved.* Thorndike, ME: Thorndike, 1988.

——*The Bluest Eye.* New York: Washington Square, Pocket Books, 1972.

——*Tar Baby.* Boston: G.K. Hall, 1981.

——*Song of Solomon.* New York: New American Library, 1987.

Mulvey, Laura. "Frida Kahlo and Tina Modottit," *Visual and Other Pleasures.* Indiana University Press, 1989.

Myerson, Michael. *Memories of Underdevelopment.* New York: Grossman Publishers, 1973.

Naylor, Gloria. *Mama Day.* New York: Vintage, 1989.

——*The Women of Brewster Place.* New York: Viking, 1982.

——*Linden Hills.* New York: Ticknor and Fields, 1985.

Neal, Larry. *Black Fire.* New York: Morrow, 1968.

Ntozake, Shange. *Sassafras, Cypress, and Indigo.* New York: St. Martin's Press, 1982.

Rabinow, Paul, ed. *The Foucault Reader.* New York: Pantheon, 1984.

Radford-Hill, Sheila. "Considering Feminism as a Model for Social change," *Feminist Studies, Critical Studies.* ed. Teresa de Lauretis. University of Indiana, 1986.

Reed, Ishmael. *Writin' Is Fightin'.* New York: Atheneum, 1988.

Rich, Adrienne. *Blood, Bread and Poetry.* New York: Norton, 1986.

——*On Lies, Secrets and Silence.* New York: Norton, 1979.

——*Your Native Land, Your Life*. New York: Norton, 1986.

Richard, Pablo. Interview with Paulo Freire, *Dialogo Social*, March 1985.

Ritz, David. *Divided Soul: The Life of Marvin Gaye*. New York: McGraw-Hill, 1985.

Rodney, Walter. *How Europe Underdeveloped Africa*. Washington: Howard University Press, 1974.

Ross, Andrew. *No Respect: Intellectuals and Popular Culture*. New York: Routledge, 1989.

Said, Edward. *Orientalism*. New York: Pantheon, 1978.

Schatzman, Morton. *Soul Murder: Persecution in the Family*. New York: Random House, 1973.

Sessums, Kevin. "Yoko, Life After Lennon," *Interview Magazine*, February, 1989.

Smith, Valerie. *Self-discovery and Authority in Afro-American Narrative*. Cambridge: Harvard University Press, 1987.

Spelman, Elizabeth. *Inessential Woman*. Boston: Beacon Press, 1988.

Spivak, Guyatri. *Other Worlds*. New York: Methuen, 1987.

Storr, Robert. *Art in America*. New York: Abbeville Press, 1986.

Tanizaki, Jun'Ichiro. *In Praise of Shadows*. New Haven: Leete's Island Books, 1977.

Taylor, Clyde. "We Don't Need another Hero: Antithesis on Aesthetics," *Blackframes*, ed. Mbye Chom, Clair Andrade-Watkins. Cambridge: MIT Press, 1988.

Terborg-Penn, Rosalyn. *Afro-American Women: Struggles and Images*. Port Washington, NY: Naticus University Publishers, 1978.

Trungpa, Chogyam. *Cutting Through Spiritual Materialism*. Berkeley: Shambala, 1973.

Uhry, Alfred. *Driving Miss Daisy*. Lexington, NY: Theater Communications Group, 1988.

Walker, Alice. *The Color Purple*. New York: Pocket Books, 1985.

——*Living by the Word*. San Diego: Harcourt, Brace, Jovanovich, 1988.

——*Temple of My Familiar*. Thorndike, ME: Thorndike, 1989.

Wallace, Michele. *Black Macho and the Myth of the Superwoman*. New York: Dial Press, 1979.

West, Cornel. *Post Analytic Philosophy*. New York: Columbia University Press, 1985.

——*Prophetic Fragments*. Trenton: Africa World Press, 1988.

Whitman, Walt. *Leaves of Grass*. New York: Book League of America, 1942.

Williams, Sherley Anne. *Dessa Rose.* Thorndike, ME: Thorndike, 1987.

Wilson, August. "Joe Turner's Come and Gone." New York: New American Library, 1986.

—— *"Ma Rainey's Black Bottom."* New York: New American Library, 1986.

X, Malcolm. *The Autobiography of Malcolm X.* New York: Grove Press, 1965.

About South End Press

South End Press is a nonprofit, collectively run book publisher with over 150 titles in print. Since our founding in 1977, we have tried to meet the needs of readers who are exploring, or are already committed to, the politics of radical social change.

Our goal is to publish books that encourage critical thinking and constructive action on the key political, cultural, social, economic, and ecological issues shaping life in the United States and in the world. In this way, we hope to give expression to a wide diversity of democratic social movements and to provide an alternative to the products of corporate publishing.

If you would like a free catalog of South End Press books or information about our membership program—which offers two free books and a 40% discount on all titles—please write us at South End Press, 116 Saint Botolph Street, Boston, MA 02115.

Other titles of interest from South End Press:

Talking Back:
Thinking Feminist, Thinking Black
bell hooks

Feminist Theory:
from margin to center
bell hooks

Ain't I a Woman:
black women and feminism
bell hooks